Foreign Language Learning,
Today and Tomorrow

Related Titles

*F*oreign Language Learning, Today and Tomorrow

Essays in Honor of Emma M. Birkmaier

Edited by
Jermaine D. Arendt
Dale L. Lange
Pamela J. Myers

Pergamon Press
New York □ Oxford □ Toronto □ Sydney □ Frankfurt □ Paris

Pergamon Press Offices:

U.S.A.   Pergamon Press Inc., Maxwell House, Fairview Park, Elmsford, New York 10523, U.S.A.

U.K.   Pergamon Press Ltd., Headington Hill Hall, Oxford OX3 0BW, England

CANADA   Pergamon of Canada, Ltd., 150 Consumers Road, Willowdale, Ontario M2J, 1P9, Canada

AUSTRALIA   Pergamon Press (Aust) Pty. Ltd., P O Box 544, Potts Point, NSW 2011, Australia

FRANCE   Pergamon Press SARL, 24 rue des Ecoles, 75240 Paris, Cedex 05, France

FEDERAL REPUBLIC   Pergamon Press GmbH, 6242 Kronberg/Taunus,
OF GERMANY   Pferdstrasse 1, Federal Republic of Germany

Library of Congress Cataloging in Publication Data
Main entry under title:

Foreign language learning, today and tomorrow.

   Includes index.
   CONTENTS: Grittner, F.M. and Fearing, P.B.
Futurism in foreign language learning.—Lieberman, S. L.
Humanism in learning foreign languages.—Jorstad, H. L.
Objectives for new programs. [etc.]
   1. Language and languages—Study and teaching—United
States—Addresses, essays, lectures. 2. Birkmaier,
Emma Marie, 1908-   I. Birkmaier, Emma Marie,
1908-   II. Arendt, Jermaine D. III. Lange, Dale L.
IV. Myers, Pamela J.
P57.U7F65   407   79-972
ISBN 0-08-024628-1

Printed in the United States of America

It is appropriate that this volume on the future of second language education be dedicated to Emma Marie Birkmaier, currently Professor Emeritus, University of Minnesota. Dr. Birkmaier has been, and will always be, an inspiration to teachers at all levels in second language education. Her unparalleled professionalism has been evidenced in her role as the first President of the American Council on the Teaching of Foreign Languages, and through her work with professional organizations such as the American Association of Teachers of German and the Central States Modern Language Teachers Association. She has made presentations at conferences too numerous to mention, and has done much behind-the-scenes organizational work for which she has never taken credit.

Professor Birkmaier has always been on the leading edge of her field. Her sound scholarship and nimble mind have enabled her to think about new directions while others were still trying to digest the past. She has instilled in her students the balance between the necessity to challenge ideas in second language teaching and the quest to excel in the classroom. If this volume points to the future as its editors and writers intend, then once more the inspiration of Emma Marie Birkmaier will serve the profession.

Contents

Introduction

Alvin Toffler did not discover the future. Nor did Marshall MacLuhan. Nor were they the first to discover that the future can represent hope or threat. What Toffler has described is a rapidly changing world for which mankind is poorly prepared. His book, *Future Shock*, has spawned a host of futurists who are in great demand at conventions, conferences, and workshops. The schools, reacting to criticism that they are not preparing students for the future, have introduced future-oriented courses as electives. However, neither the schools nor society have changed much by these recent visions of the future.

This volume represents an attempt by some foreign language educators to deal with the challenge of the future. Past experiences in foreign language learning in schools are noted and suggestions are made so that language learning can meet the current needs and interests of students while preparing them for life in the world of tomorrow.

Grittner, whose chapter begins this book, discusses the ideas of Toffler and others who attempt to face the future and its new demands on individuals and on society as a whole. Grittner discusses what futurism is and is not in education. He shows how foreign language learning can contribute to building a system of skills in three areas—learning how to learn, relating to other people, and making intelligent choices.

Are humanistic ideals outmoded? Not according to Lieberman, author of "Humanism in Learning Foreign Languages." Teachers of the classical world offer norms for civilized living and see man as endowed with reason and in control of his emotions. Despite countercurrents, Lieberman sees a continuing humanistic tradition in America and points out its value for helping students to understand themselves and their world.

In "Objectives for New Programs," Jorstad suggests that much of the recent emphasis on objective writing has had only limited benefits for language learning; individual needs, interests, and styles of learning have been largely ignored. She proposes a different classroom content and activities that will result in greater interest and learning in the foreign language classroom of the future.

In "Individualization of Foreign Language Learning," Hunter defines the critical attributes which must be dealt with in individualized instruction. The content of the learning task, individual factors in each learner, and the teacher's use of the principles of learning are examined. An important goal of learning activities is to develop self-direction and self-propulsion; this and other properties of individualized programs are discussed and evaluated.

Andersson moves from the HEW Right-to-Read Program to an examination of the double problem of bilingual children who often read poorly, if at all, not only in one language but in two. "The 'Right to Read' in Two Languages" cites research which indicates that children can learn to read far earlier than is generally supposed; and it concludes that children born into a non-English-speaking family would particularly benefit from early reading instruction in their home language.

The rising tide of insistence upon accountability in education is noted by Reynolds in her paper, "From Accountability to Program Evaluation." She describes a system for evaluation of a foreign language program using the Program Evaluation Review Technique (PERT). This system helps a foreign language staff to determine "what is." Afterwards, the staff can determine "what ought to be."

How should students learn in the future? Wattenmaker and Wilson believe they have found the key to winning and keeping students interested. In "Communication that is Relevant, Enjoyable, and Live," they explain that foreign language can be a tool for meaningful communication when students can deal with questions about themselves. This chapter describes a sequence of learning activities that work well in the classroom.

In "Windmills and Dragons," Arendt and Hallock describe an attempt to use a consumer survey to gather information from students who did, and who did not, enroll in second language classes. Student replies in many cases contradicted the authors' hypotheses about why students enroll or do not enroll. The results suggest future directions in language learning that may enable it to thrive as an elective in American schools.

Seelye's concern is with those students and persons who go abroad and must interface with another culture. Pre-entry, the first twenty-four hours, the initial month, the second through fourth months, and the fifth month and beyond are the five phases set forth in "Individualizing and Sequencing Training for Inter-Cultural Communication." The model is suggested as a means of overcoming the hurdles to an effective cultural adjustment.

Alternative schools have found a way to bring about change in education, according to Jennings. "Alternatives in Education" points out that parents are divided regarding the kind of education they want for their children. Some parents clamor for one type of school, while others are steadfastly in favor of another. The alternative movement shortcuts lengthy argumentation by giving parents a voice and a choice. One alternative, the open school, has made use of learning activities that are difficult to carry out in the traditional school. Jennings describes how foreign language learning can be a part of the alternative school curriculum.

In the final chapter, Lange reviews seven principles related to teacher education in second languages. These principles, emphasizing the necessity for continued development of teacher education programs, are applied to both pre- and in-service teacher education. In a sense, the chapter provides a capstone to the book; many of the basic ideas in the other chapters fit in with the seven principles, and they all share Lange's concern with the quality of second language education.

All chapters in this book look toward the future. Ideas have been offered here which suggest that direction. We hope readers will use and discuss these ideas with colleagues. From those discussions, other ideas will be generated. Constant attention to language teaching and learning will assure them an important place in the future of education.

Foreign Language Learning, Today and Tomorrow

Chapter One
Futurism in Foreign Language Learning
Frank M. Grittner
Percy B. Fearing

Nietzsche once said that it is the future that lays down the law of today. As this quotation indicates, it has long been recognized that the collective futuristic perceptions of the people within a culture have tended to shape the direction of education for the young people of that culture. When ultra-conservatives or reactionaries gain control of curricular decisions, their perception of the future is directed backward in time toward the "good old days"; they see the future as a replication of the past, and the school program is structured accordingly.

The need for universal literacy is taken for granted in most developed nations today. As evidence, in the United States we have a federally supported "Right to Read" program. However, if we push back the centuries far enough we find that the European forebears of today's literacy advocates had a vastly different image of future educational needs. Literacy was seen as irrelevant for all but a few scribes, upper echelon priests, and certain selected members of the nobility. To the rulers of that era, it was clear that the vast majority of young people needed only to learn farming and the other menial duties of serfdom. Millers, carpenters, armorers, tinkers, tailors, and harness makers were also needed to sustain the military, the priesthood, and the ruling nobility. For many generations the past served as a good predictor of the future. There were, of course, periods of cataclysmic change, but these were generally followed by a new stability and a new period in which the past was again a guide to the future.

To a considerable degree, the past is still used in education to develop curricula and instructional procedures. However, according to the futurists, we have long since passed the point where extrapolations from past practices are sufficient bases for building educational programs. We are now said to be in the "super-industrial" era. According to Toffler (*28*), the future is rushing upon us like "a roaring current of change, a current so powerful today that it overturns institutions, shifts our values and shrivels our roots" (p. 1).

THE NEED FOR FUTURISM IN EDUCATION

In the face of a rapidly changing contemporary world, increasing numbers of people tend to fall into a state of "future shock." Like the traveler in a foreign country who cannot cope with the language and the customs, many young people today are disoriented when thrust into situations for which their background and schooling have left them unprepared. As Strudler (25) expressed it, our backward-oriented systems of education are producing "a generation of future-retarded children" (p. 178). Toffler (28) claims that education has not responded to the real needs of the future because educators are too busy building budgets, establishing pay scales, and protecting the status of their members. Also, rigid entrance requirements in higher education have tended to fossilize the curricula of colleges and secondary schools; they are said to have become locked into an inflexible pattern of studies reflecting the vocational and social requirements of a vanishing society (p. 410). Because of this, the argument continues, we end up with a "very narrow data base" which is essentially the same for all students, and which does not pertain to most of them. What is worse, the data base is said to be largely outmoded, incorrect, or irrelevant at the time the teacher or professor is attempting to impose it upon his students. "The instinctive recognition of this fact by young people," says Toffler (30), "has been one of the key factors behind the collapse of teacher authority" (p. 13).

Another factor which has to do with the alienation of students is the problem of "overchoice." As McDanield (12) expressed it, "There is so much that *could* be taught that it is almost impossible to decide what *should* be taught" (p. 105). Once again, the student is aware that the curriculum is nothing more than an arbitrary set of choices from an illimitable pool of information; it is based upon the teacher's preferences and inclinations rather than upon the student's needs or desires. In some instances, both change and "overchoice" combine to produce a set of confusing prospects. Some of us in the field of foreign languages, for example, have over a period of years been confronted with choices relating to historical grammar, traditional grammar, structural linguistics, generative grammar, and, more recently, the emerging school of "generative semantics." To the uninitiated student of foreign language education and the teacher who must cope with large numbers of students daily, the rapid emergence of these new approaches to linguistic analysis is disconcerting, to say the least. In this one small area of scholarship, the study of human language, there are vast and conflicting bodies of highly esoteric data. Furthermore, each linguistic approach is regularly declared either valid or invalid by "authorities" of seemingly comparable status in one camp or the other. The only thing that appears certain is that yet another conflicting school of linguistics or semantics will soon emerge, and its proponents will claim to have developed an improved way of looking at language. The same situation exists in other relevant fields, such as the study of culture, language pedagogy, and learning psychology. Each of these areas presents the student and the practitioner with rapidly changing theories and "overchoice" in curricular content.

THE NATURE OF FUTURISM

The purpose of the futurist movement in education is to find a new basis for organizing the curriculum and the instructional process. However, it is not easy to describe what futurism is. Many of those who profess to being futurists are quite emphatic regarding what futurism is *not*. In the introduction to an anthology on the role of the future in education, Toffler (*29*) disassociates futurism from a Buck Rogerish preoccupation with technological advances; at the outset, he notes that the volume contains "virtually no reference to computers in the classroom, to programmed instruction, to audio-visual delights or to other technological aids" (p. 1). Similarly, Buchen (*5*) states that "futurism is neither supergadgetry nor salvationist ideology. It does not traffic in hysterics or lullabys" (p. 140). He also notes that it cannot have a fixed body of content that exists apart from what it seeks to comprehend. In the futurists' view, to establish such a curriculum would be to commit the same deadly sin that the traditional academic subjects have committed: they have fossilized their curricula into allegedly respectable, but functionally irrelevant, bodies of knowledge. However, Buchen is quick to add that futurism is not an enemy of existing humanistic disciplines; on the contrary, the purpose of the futurist movement is to delimit traditional disciplines and give them meaning.

Futurists are most sensitive in the area of prophecy; they emphasize that futurism does not predict what will happen. Its intent is not to supply a final projection, but to present an array of possibilities. "Futurists are not so much interested in predicting as in creating desirable futures; the stress is not on what *will* be but what *can* or should be" (pp. 142-43). As for the question of specific predictions for the future, Strudler (*25*) is quite emphatic in stating that "the last thing we need is a new priesthood wrapped in the cloak of prophecy" (p. 174).

We have learned what the futurist movement is *not*. Clearly, advocates of futurism do not see a pre-determined course which needs to be charted in advance so that educators can adjust students to the inevitable. Thus, they have not made the mistake committed by educational empiricists who have tended to confuse what *was* with what *ought to be*. For many decades certain educators have followed the practice of conducting empirical "needs" assessment in the belief that they could, through that process, make valid value judgments about future curricular decisions. Bode (*4*), one of the progressive educators of the 1930s, considered this a futile approach. To illustrate his point, he once noted that we could, in all probability, determine the number of burglaries committed in the United States each year; but from that data it would be impossible to know whether we should introduce burglary into the curriculum as a bona fide career-oriented course, or whether we should set up a program to train more policemen. According to Bode and other progressivists, education was based upon a value judgment; hence, one of the premises of progressive education was that the student must learn the process of making decisions and value judgments for himself. The progressivists emphasized learning by doing, rather than for the sake of doing, in order to help the student develop his own perspectives for coping with real life situations which might arise in the future. Thus, in many respects, the progressivists anticipated the futurists. A basic aim of progressive education was to help students cope with a changing industrial society. Futurists claim is that "industrial man" has been superseded by "superindustrial man"; it is no longer enough for the student to learn to cope with past or present-oriented situations based upon the values and ideas of the industrial era (Toffler, *28*, p. 414).

Using inferential statistical procedures, the systems approach, and computer technology, some futurists draw upon a number of present trends to suggest what might happen if one or the other of these trends continues on into the future; this aspect of futurism is perhaps as close as we come to having a "science of futurism." Other futurists contend that such data will be useful only insofar as it helps educators to make value judgments about what ought to be. Humanistically-oriented futurists tend to supplement, or even supplant, the "outputs" of the data gatherers with products of creative genius, such as the utopian and dystopian novels of Bellamy (*Looking Backward, 2000-1887*), Huxley (*Brave New World*), and Orwell (*Nineteen Eighty-Four*).

At the other end of the value spectrum from the humanistic futurists are the advocates of "human engineering," who believe that a technology of human manipulations will be the salvation of mankind in the future. Perhaps the most outspoken proponent of this view is B.F. Skinner (*22*), who favors deliberate manipulation of people so that they will fit the behavioral specifications and social patterns determined by the human engineers. The humanists' concept of autonomous man and their commitment to freedom and dignity are said to have produced such calamities as unchecked breeding, exhaustion of natural resources, pollution of the environment, and the imminence of nuclear war. As Skinner sees it, these and other human ills can be alleviated through behavioral technology. In a statement which he perceives as hopeful, and which humanists might view as threatening, Skinner notes: "In the analysis of human behavior . . . we are beginning to make technological applications. There are wonderful possibilities—and all the more wonderful because traditional approaches have been so ineffective" (p. 204). In his utopian novel, *Walden Two*, Skinner (*23*) writes off traditional education as hopelessly enmeshed in the past and, therefore, unequal to the demands of the future. In the future, education will have to "abandon the technical limitations which it has imposed upon itself and step forth into a broader sphere of human engineering. Nothing short of the complete revision of a culture would suffice" (p. 312).

Like Skinner, Orwell (*14*) projects a future in which humans are manipulated by means of technological control of the mind. However, unlike Skinner, he sees the negative utopia, dystopia, which is likely to result from this. *Nineteen Eighty-Four* describes how behavior can be dehumanized by an amoral, power-hungry group of bureaucrats. As one of the controllers states, "Power is in tearing human minds to pieces and putting them together again in new shapes of your own choosing" (p. 270). Even the emotions are totally manipulated. One's love and loyalty is to be directed to Big Brother, and all behavior is specified and strictly enforced by an all-powerful central Party. As the controller expresses it, "If you want a picture of the future, imagine a boot stamping on a human face—forever" (p. 271). However, in *Nineteen Eighty-Four*, the boot is language, not force. "Newspeak" is the official process whereby words mean only what the Party wishes them to mean at any given time.

Anthony Sampson (*18*), a British journalist writing in the *London Observer* in October 1973, viewed the language of the Watergate hearings as being a giant step in the direction of Orwellian Newspeak. He coined the word "Waterspeak" to refer to the way in which Watergate "team members" were willing to depersonalize themselves and their actions and to accept government as "essentially a machine, a complex piece of engineering, rather than a collection of people." Watergate rhetoric abounded with mechanical metaphors such as "input," "output," and "zero defect system"; and staff members frequently referred to themselves as "conduits." Also, unethical, immoral, or criminal behavior was converted to euphemistic rhetoric: A bribe became "a payment with increments in the form of currency"; burglary was described as "surreptitious entry"; an outright lie came out as, "My statement is inoperative." Sampson concluded his article by suggesting that "Waterspeak seems to indicate how men in power can become conditioned by language to regard themselves as part of a machine in which individualism is, to borrow a word, inoperative."

The various projections of possible future human societies offer a number of implications for education in general, and a few for foreign language education in particular. In the latter instance, the most obvious value might well be the resistance to linguistic manipulation that could result from the study of a symbolic system which refers to a culture other than one's own. That is, the student of foreign languages might be better attuned to understanding the relationship between symbol and meaning, and thus be able to recognize attempts to use language deceptively. This proposition carries with it a number of assumptions and value judgments: One is the belief that verbal deception is bad, a belief that might be contested by some people, those in the advertising business, for example; another is the belief that personal freedom is in some way related to the ability of the electorate to make accurate judgments of that which is spoken and written and this, in turn, implies a belief in freedom itself and in some form of democratic government. However, the most tenuous assumption here is perhaps the belief that the study of a second language tends to improve one's ability to analyze language. It is not the kind of assertion that is easily subject to proof; like the other beliefs mentioned, it must be accepted as "an article of faith" not susceptible to empirical examination.

A further problem with the futurist movement in foreign languages is that it will probably be difficult to convince others that the discipline has any real function in the futurist movement. As a matter of fact, the literature of futurism makes little reference to foreign language study except to use it as an example of what has been wrong with the old curriculum. For the most part, the futurist movement is in the hands of educators with social science backgrounds who appear to believe that the world is to become monolingual, or that a multilingual world can be adequately studied in English translation. For example, Bell, whose field is sociology, states that the comparative study of cultures has helped us to "avoid being trapped into one way of thinking and to look at knowledge as in need of constant revision"; he further suggests that the study of other societies helps to counteract "false prejudices, uncritical ethnocentrism, and ignorant parochialism" (2, p. 84). Bell's futurist must resemble the cultural anthropologist to the extent that he transcends the "cultural envelope" of the present in order to function in the future. Even when he goes on to discuss the need for worldwide study of universal human aspirations, the question of language does not arise, despite the fact that seven-eighths of the world's people do not speak English natively.

FUTURISM AND THE STUDENT

To this point, futurism has been discussed primarily as a science, an art, or a pseudo-discipline. However, another thrust of the movement has promising pedagogical applications: the concept of the future is closely tied to the motivation of the learner. It is a recurrent theme among futurists that students' perceptions of their personal futures relate directly to their academic performance and to their ability to cope with life in a rapidly changing society (15).

This generalization is neither new nor original. Goethe is purported to have stated: "If you treat an individual as he is, he will stay as he is, but if you treat him as if he were what he ought to be and could be, he will become what he ought to be and could be" (27, p. 32). Even Freud suggested, albeit with considerable skepticism, that an entire civilization might be educated to engage spontaneously in civilized behavior if only its members had experienced the benefits of civilization at an early enough age. To accomplish this, the small child would need models for future behavior in the form of "superior, unswerving and disinterested leaders ... who are to act as educators of the future generations" (6, p. 7). Not surprisingly, the modern educational world has approached the question not with aphorisms or psychological theorizing, but with empirical studies.

Perhaps the most widely known of these is Rosenthal's *Pygmalion in the Classroom* (*17*), a modern validation of Goethe's statement. Rosenthal randomly assigned high achievement test scores to a selected number of deprived youngsters. The teachers of these children believed that the test scores were valid predictors of high academic achievement; and the result was higher achievement on the part of those youngsters who had been identified as "promising" on the basis of the fictitious test scores. Apparently the teachers' belief in the abilities of the children carried over to them, so that each child began to become "what he ought to be and could be" rather than what, through accidents of fate, he happened to be.

According to the futurists, the Freudian movement is too heavily focused upon the past. They claim that a young person's view of what he can be in the future is more important than the models of human behavior to which he has been exposed in the past. Poussaint (*15*), for example, has noted the relationship between the lack of a strong positive future self-image and academic failure. There is a direct positive correlation between academic and personal failure and the inability to project what one will be doing at some future date. This lack of a future role for one's self is particularly strong among black adolescents and other minority group young people.

In the area of sexism, Pauline Bart contends that the schooling of girls progressively restricts a female's self-image, and thereby cripples her chances of assuming anything but a passive, culturally acceptable role. For example, one study of elementary textbooks showed that 75 percent of the stories centered around male characters; accounts of female adults were found to be almost non-existent. According to Bart, the central message that comes from the elementary and secondary program is that girls should look forward to a life of submission, housework, and child-bearing; "boys, by contrast, are strongly urged to achieve, advance and create" (*1*, p. 37). The school, of course, is not solely to blame; it merely reflects a situation which exists throughout society. However, the school does tend to reinforce society so that women, minorities, and a growing number of white male and female children from affluent middle class families are unable to form positive self-images of future active roles in the world of reality.

PEDAGOGICAL IMPLICATIONS OF FUTURISM

If it is true, as Singer (*21*) has suggested, that personal success is closely tied to a strong image of the "anticipated self," then the focus of the profession upon new administrative arrangements, instructional techniques, and technological gadgetry will not begin to solve the problems to be faced in the near future.

Success in foreign language studies, as well as in other academic subjects, appears to be closely related to the ability of the student to work for delayed gratifications. That is, the student must be able to picture vividly and positively a number of possible future situations in which the subject will function as a part of his or her mental and emotional equipment. A majority of American young people do not project themselves into future situations where the knowledge of a second language will be relevant. The language laboratory, pattern drills, and even personalized unipacs do not seem to have changed that state of affairs. The agonizingly slow incremental learning of "new key" methodologies does not tend to give the student the feeling of progressive control of language in any meaningful way. Too often, students get the message that they must memorize an enormous quantity of basically trivial utterances, while accepting on faith that it will eventually enable them to communicate with real human beings in a genuine social situation. With the emergence of the "now" generation, the degree to which such methods require delay of gratification in the form of questionable, ill-defined future rewards may insure the loss of all but a few students. It simply is not worth the trouble; more visible short-term rewards are available elsewhere in the curriculum. The implications, then, are that any drill work performed in the foreign language must lead rather quickly to an emotional "payoff" of some kind. Also needed are activities which tend to build, rather than destroy, a positive future self-image for the student. Many foreign language teachers are using simulation games, role playing, field trips to foreign environments, and other activities that make the foreign language learning process more real, immediate, and emotionally genuine (16).

The futurists, like the progressivists in the first half of this century, seek to cut through the formalism, compartmentalization, and rigidity of the existing modes of schooling without destroying the important elements contained in them. The futurists agree with the progressivists that there is not much value in looking at contemporary realities: As Bode said in 1938, "Conditions in industry are changing so rapidly that the problem of enabling the individual to readjust himself as circumstances may require becomes a matter of primary importance. The demand is for 'free intelligence' rather than for skills in connection with established patterns" (4, p. 92). Thus, in a sense, futurism is a return to some of the basic ideas of the progressivists. However, with a third of a century of added change and accumulated knowledge, the futurists' case is even more urgent (8, p. 197). Not only are occupations coming, going, and changing with increased rapidity, but human beings are more mobile than ever, and the whole structure of society undergoes massive shifts in short periods of time. This requires a "system of skills" involving 1) learning how to learn, 2) relating to other people, and 3) making intelligent choices (28).

If we were to apply the first category, learning how to learn, to the study of a foreign language, we would have to accept the idea that the specific "data" of learning a language are not nearly so important as the generalizations relating to the future acquisition of any language which might eventually be needed. If one accepts this line of reasoning, then he accepts with it the belief that the process of learning languages *per se* is more important that the ability to converse in Spanish, or to read German, or to write French. Presumably it is preferable to acquire some minimal acceptable level of competence in one language, and to view this acquisition principally as a vehicle for learning how to approach any language that might be encountered in a rapidly changing, highly mobile world. This line of reasoning implies a problem solving mode, one in which the student acquires a manageable set of principles and concepts that can be applied to the learning of Russian, Italian, Dutch, Chinese, German, or any other language that might be needed in the future.

Learning to relate to other people is important because of the growing instability of family, neighborhood, and community relationships. The futurists find it indefensible for 30 foreign language students to sit in a classroom "isolated together" by the fragmented nature of the subject matter and by the competitive nature of a grading system which precludes helping a fellow student. Such divisive arrangements are antithetical to the purposes of the futurist world From their standpoint, it is absurd to subject young people—most of whom are having difficulty communicating with parents and peers in English—to the bogus communication situations of dialogues and drills in a second language devoid of emotional meaning. Any subject, including foreign languages, that does not help young people make some personal, emotional contact with their fellow human beings is viewed as involving nothing more than idle incantations. Personal contact implies the need for such procedures as group dynamics, group process, or small group instruction. By using a foreign language to provide a satisfying socializing experience, foreign language educators could, conceivably, help their students learn to relate to other people. However, some of the more mechanistic schemes of individualized instruction could run contrary to this purpose: programmed instruction and teaching machines, for example, tend to separate the students not only from their classmates but from the teacher as well.

Nevertheless, learning how to learn and learning how to relate to other people will not suffice in the modern world. Perhaps more important than either is the cultivation of a "moral gyroscope" to help the student make choices and form a value system which will stabilize his progress through a chaotic and changing world (*10*). In this regard, both the advocates of progressive education and traditional academicians have failed. Perhaps as a reaction against the moralizing tone of early American textbooks, such as the *McGuffey Readers*, American educators have tended to restrict their activities to teaching facts, thereby letting students make up their own minds about values. This has led to a form of moral relativism that requires all phenomena in the curriculum to be treated with an appearance of scientific neutrality. The non-human, computer-like rhetoric of Watergate is a logical outcome of this neutral stance.

If this new focus on the curriculum is to be accomplished, many changes will have to be made in the psychoemotional and social climate for learning. The teacher can no longer be an authoritarian, knowledge-dispensing figure. Below is a summary of the kinds of changes suggested by Shane (20) and Warriner (31), who propose, among other things, that we need new, open-ended procedures.

FROM	TO
The teacher doing the teaching	Teachers and students learning from each other
Passive answer absorbing	Active answer seeking
Rigid daily programs for students and teachers	Flexible movement of students and teachers
Teacher-dominated curriculum planning	Student initiative and group planning of the curriculum
Isolated and compartmentalized subject matter	Interrelated and interdisciplinary content
Evaluation based upon memorized answers	Evaluation based upon student ability to solve problems and to apply what he has learned to unanticipated situations
Emphasis upon a given textbook or text series	Use of many media and real and simulated life experiences to supplement the textbook
View of the student as an object to be processed by the teacher	View of the student as one who learns with the teacher
A situation where the teacher makes the choices which he or she enforces upon students who are expected to comply	A situation where the students make meaningful choices for which they are then accountable

Educators at the Estes Park Conference in 1973 arrived at similar conclusions (11). In their opinion, efforts to solve the problems caused by the "knowledge explosion" have been misguided. A cultural pattern has been established which coerces ever-greater numbers of adolescents and young adults into school-based, formal education, and this broad extension of formal education has had several "unfortunate and unanticipated effects": one has been the substitution of "learning by reading, by watching, and by listening" for learning by doing; another has been "a shift from education as a preparation for coping with problems presented by the culture" to education as "a process of acquiring a prescribed body of knowledge for its own sake or because an accreditation agency deems that knowledge valuable." Thus, education has expanded quantitatively by adding additional years of information gathering, but has actually shrunk qualitatively by destroying the appreciation "of the value and power of learning." This effect has led to intense dissatisfaction among large numbers of students.

The future curriculum, as the Estes Park conferees see it, must re-establish the connections between school and society, between student concerns and the curriculum, and between students and the larger community. Further, the curriculum should not consist of facts and bodies of knowledge "set out in advance to be mastered." Instead, it should provide experiences "in which the real and dynamic quality of the world is represented in the classroom." Further, knowledge should not be looked upon as something to be stored up for possible future use. Instead, it should be viewed as "a means to identify, clarify, and seek solutions to problems that develop from real situations experienced by adolescents. . . . Learning does not begin in books, it begins when the student perceives inadequacies around him and feels dissatisfactions about them" (*11*, pp. 5-6).

BIBLIOGRAPHY

(1) Bart, Pauline B. "Why Women See the Future Differently from Men." In *Learning for Tomorrow: The Role of the Future in Education*, edited by Alvin Toffler, pp. 33-56. New York: Vintage Books, 1974.

(2) Bell, Wendell. "Social Science: The Future as a Missing Variable." In *Learning for Tomorrow: The Role of the Future in Education*, edited by Alvin Toffler, pp. 75-102. New York: Vintage Books, 1974.

(3) Bellamy, Edward. *Looking Backward, 2000-1887*. Cleveland: World Publishing Company, 1946. [Copyright 1888 by Houghton, Mifflin.]

(4) Bode, Boyd H. *Progressive Education at the Crossroads*. New York: Newson, 1938.

(5) Buchen, Irving H. "Humanism and Futurism: Enemies or Allies?" In *Learning for Tomorrow: The Role of the Future in Education*, edited by Alvin Toffler, pp. 132-43. New York: Vintage Books, 1974.

(6) Freud, Sigmund. *The Future of an Illusion*. Garden City, NY: Doubleday, 1964.

(7) Fulmer, Robert M. *Managing Associations for the 1980's*. Washington, D.C.: American Society of Association Executives, 1972.

(8) Griffith, Priscilla P. "Teaching the Twenty-First Century in a Twentieth-Century High School." In *Learning for Tomorrow: The Role of the Future in Education*, edited by Alvin Toffler, pp. 197-216. New York: Vintage Books, 1974.

(9) Huxley, Aldous. *Brave New World*. New York: Harper & Row, 1932.

(10) Kirschenbaum, Howard, and Sidney B. Simon. "Values and the Futures Movement in Education." In *Learning for Tomorrow: The Role of the Future in Education*, edited by Alvin Toffler, pp. 257-70. New York: Vintage Books, 1974.

(11) Lomon, Earl, ed. *Abridged Report of the Estes Park Conference on Learning Through Investigation and Action on Real Problems in Secondary Schools*. Newton, MA: Education Development Center, 1973.

(12) McDanield, Michael A. "Tomorrow's Curriculum Today." In *Learning for Tomorrow: The Role of the Future in Education*, edited by Alvin Toffler, pp. 103-31. New York: Vintage Books, 1974.

(13) *Members Appraise Their Associations*. Washington, DC: American Society of Association Executives, 1972.

(14) Orwell, George. *Nineteen Eighty-Four*. New York: Harcourt, Brace, 1949.

(15) Poussaint, Alvin F. "The Black Child's Image of the Future." In *Learning for Tomorrow: The Role of the Future in Education*, edited by Alvin Toffler, pp. 56-71. New York: Vintage Books, 1974.

(16) Rojas, Billy. "Futuristics, Games, and Educational Change." In *Learning for Tomorrow: The Role of the Future in Education*, edited by Alvin Toffler, pp. 217-33. New York: Vintage Books, 1974.

(17) Rosenthal, Robert, and Jacobson, Lenore. *Pygmalion in the Classroom: Teacher Expectation and Pupils' Intellectual Development*. New York: Holt, Rinehart, and Winston, 1968.

(18) Sampson, Anthony. "Waterspeak." From the *London Observer* as reprinted in the Madison, WI *The Capital Times* (October 29, 1973).

(19) Scebold, C. Edward. "The Future of Professional Associations." In *Responding to New Realities*, edited by Gilbert A. Jarvis, pp. 375-91. ACTFL Review of Foreign Language Education, vol. 5. Skokie, IL: National Textbook, 1974.

(20) Shane, Harold G., and Grant, June. "Educating the Youngest for Tomorrow." In *Learning for Tomorrow: The Role of the Future in Education*, edited by Alvin Toffler, pp. 181-96. New York: Vintage Books, 1974.

(21) Singer, Benjamin D. "The Future-Focused Role-Image." In *Learning for Tomorrow: The Role of the Future in Education*, edited by Alvin Toffler, pp. 19-32. New York: Vintage Books, 1974.

(22) Skinner, B.F. *Beyond Freedom and Dignity*. New York: Vintage, 1971.

(23) _____. *Walden Two*. New York: Macmillan, 1948.

(24) Strasheim, Lorraine A. "Rationale for the Individualization and Personalization of Foreign Language Instruction." In *Britannica Review of Foreign Language Education, Volume 2*, edited by Dale L. Lange, pp. 15-34. Chicago: Encyclopedia Britannica, 1970. [Reissued as *Individualization of Instruction*. Review of ACTFL Foreign Language Education, Volume 2. Skokie, IL: National Textbook.]

(25) Strudler, Harold L. "Educational Futurism: Perspective or Discipline?" In *Learning for Tomorrow: The Role of the Future in Education*, edited by Alvin Toffler, pp. 173-78. New York: Vintage Books, 1974.

(26) Sullivan, Brian. "AMA to Tackle Three Major Problems," [Associated Press Article.] *Greeley (CO) Tribune* (June 16, 1975).

(27) *Today's Education* 58, i (1969): 32.

(28) Toffler, Alvin. *Future Shock*. New York: Bantam, 1971.

(29) _____, ed. *Learning for Tomorrow: The Role of the Future in Education*. New York: Vintage Books, 1974.

(30) _____. "The Psychology of the Future." In *Learning for Tomorrow: The Role of the Future in Education*, edited by Alvin Toffler, pp. 3-18. New York: Vintage Books, 1974.

(31) Warriner, Helen P. "The Teacher as Quality Control: Program Options." In *Student Motivation and the Foreign Language Teacher*, edited by Frank M. Grittner, pp. 30-44. Report of the Central States Conference on Foreign Language Teaching. Skokie, IL: National Textbook, 1974.

(32) Werdell, Philip. "Futurism and the Reform of Higher Education." In *Learning for Tomorrow: The Role of the Future in Education*, edited by Alvin Toffler, pp. 272-311. New York: Vintage Books, 1974.

Chapter Two
Humanism in Learning
Foreign Languages
Samuel L. Lieberman

The more I think about humanism and foreign language learning, the more it bothers me. A generation or two ago, when Americans seemed sure of their values direction, the term "humanism" was so obviously part of our civilized heritage that no educated person needed to have it defined. Its place in the aims or environment of education, and especially in foreign language study, was not to be questioned. However, two World Wars and many destructive smaller ones, a tremendous explosion of technology and population, student revolts and "children's crusades," and an educational system in such disarray that the value of foreign language study is questioned by both young and old have made one wonder whether humanism is meaningful any longer except as a watered-down form of "good will to all." Not even such terms as "civilized heritage" or "educated person," once confident concepts, have wide currency except in rather old-fashioned commencement addresses. In the temper of today's times, humanism may seem inhuman. A pinch of mysticism appears more likely to spice up foreign language teaching than a peck of humanism. After reviewing what humanism actually means, how it was acquired, and how it stands in the world today, the question of its current relevance to foreign language learning and teaching in the United States can be more realistically addressed.

Greek and Roman thinkers discovered the human being and established a set of axioms and principles—humanism—for his behavior as an individual and in a group. Although these principles were frequently violated by individuals and states, they at least offered reasoned norms for civilized living. Therefore, humanism is a basic and inescapable element in the teaching of Latin and ancient Greek, so much so that a teacher of classical languages who neglects humanism will nullify the reason for his subject being in the curriculum (6).

To what extent does this apply to the teaching of all foreign languages, and especially modern foreign languages? To what extent is humanism basic and essential to their study? Because humanism is a value-laden word that every educated person has been trained to associate with the aforementioned "good will to all," such questions may seem presumptuous and self-answerable; and they may seem all the more so because many of the languages of Western Europe and America are descendants of Latin. Even in non-Latin areas, European and American cultures have a strong classical base, especially in their literatures and philosophical ideas. Then what is the humanistic content of some of the languages and cultures entering the curriculum, such as Chinese, Japanese, Arabic, and Swahili? In the present era which values feeling more than thinking, students and their elders may not be attracted to a rigorous, rational approach to foreign language, or any other field of study. Basic axioms may seem outmoded, and the terms "reason" and "nature" may strike some as more suitable to Greeks and Romans in flowing robes fixed in marble, or to eighteenth-century *philosphes* in knee breeches and periwigs.

Not everything human is subsumed in the term "humanism," despite the famous *homo sum* aphorism. First, humanism emphasizes reason. Both nature and the human being are seen as rational; the former issues physical and moral laws to which the latter, as a creature of nature and endowed with reason, can respond. A human being has reason and can express himself uniquely in speech; these two activities were so closely associated by the ancients that both could be expressed by a single Greek word, *logos*. From the ancient Greek point of view, it would seem that the teacher of speech or language could not help but be at the same time a teacher of reason. As seen by the ancient Greeks, a human is most natural when responding to reason and exercising self-control. The real or essential human being controlled his emotions and self-centeredness; he was co-operative rather than combative; he was responsible; he could plan; he could hope. As a result of nineteenth-century romanticism, today the word "natural" usually means the direct opposite of what it does to the humanist.

Second, humanism emphasizes this world as the only one we have. Morality, good-neighborliness, and other virtues are desirable not because of rewards and punishments by a Divinity in this or another world, but because they are intrinsically good and in accordance with the laws of nature. The ancients insisted that these moral principles were universal and that customs and practices, including man-made laws, contravening them were the result of humans and nature not heeding the voice of reason (2).

Out of this concept of *humanitas* or *human-being-ness*, whose distinguishing and unique feature was reason, came social and political concepts and ideals which have played an important role in the ideals of Western civilization: democracy was born of humanism. The basic tenets of humanism submerged with the decline of Roman civilization. They were revived and elaborated on in the Renaissance as part of an intellectual revolt against medievalism, and they reached a climax in the eighteenth-century revolutions which proclaimed confidence in reason and the rights of man. Ever since then, with varying degrees of success, the United States has striven to implement the inalienable rights guaranteed by the Declaration of Independence and the Constitution.

In recent years, although faith in the democratic corollaries of humanism is still strong, the basic humanistic ideals and assumptions which underlie them have come under severe attack. Nineteenth-century romantics started the attack with their emphasis on the emotions as the source of truth and their support of nationalism rather than the one world (*oecumene*) of Greek and Roman thinkers. Although the revolutionary leaders of the period and their romantic ideological supporters strove to establish some form of democratic government in their drive for national independence, the net result of their thinking was to challenge that which was basic to humanism. In the romantic's view, the human being was most natural and human when he responded to his emotions, his instincts, and his "blood" rather than to reason. This was a new view of human nature, and a complete reversal of the long-accepted meaning of the word and concept "natural."

Toward the end of the nineteenth century, the reality of the concept of reason and of the human being as a basically rational being was challenged on scientific grounds by Freudian psychologists. By pointing out the importance of emotional and instinctual drives as the basic causes of behavior, the psychologists seemed to dissolve the reality of reason and its function as a natural check on self-destructive and anti-social behavior. Rather, many of the troubles of the human psyche were attributable to "repressions," the control of instincts and emotions by that force which the humanists called reason. An offshoot of this has been prompted by studies in animal behavior. The currently popular human-as-animal school of thought, epitomized by Desmond Morris' *The Naked Ape*, questions whether humans are really civilizable and whether the humanists' reason is really a myth.

Humanism is directly and indirectly under attack. It has been accused of being corrupted by "materialism" and "instant satisfaction"; and this has led to a new search for God, especially among the young who have been attracted to exotic forms of religion, such as Buddhism, Hinduism, and Sufism, in their search for new forms of worship. The revival of mysticism and the "drug culture" are symptoms of a lack of confidence in the humanists' world of natural moral principles. All this is reflected by writers who present a world bereft of meaning, and painters whose almost blank canvases seem to be saying, "Emptiness is all."

Even scholars of Greek civilization have been calling attention to the many evidences of non-humanism, indicating that Greek culture cannot be fully understood otherwise. Consider the mystery cults, Dionysus worship, Pericles' "School of Hellas," the condemnation of Socrates for "introducing new gods"; and consider how Apollo, the patron and symbol of Greek rationality, communicated with his worshippers at Delphi through a priestess in a god-possessed ecstatic trance, a medium whose eyes rolled as her lips uttered the eerie sounds of the god which the priests converted into man's language, Greek (*3*).

Humanism is at bay today; the world is awash in anti-humanism, and young people seem to enjoy immersing themselves in it. Do the already-embattled teachers of foreign languages wish to risk adding to their problems by pledging themselves anew to humanism which has always been the implied underlying aim of teachers in all fields? I suppose we do, but if so, we have to understand that its key concept is the assumption of innate human rationality. Confidence in the possibility of harmonious relations among people is based on a respect for shared rationality, not on the currently popular "love" which in its social context is a Christian rather than a humanistic concept. Humanism implies a distrust of feelings and a wariness about emotions; thus it flies in the face of current life styles and a good many of the modern theories of human relations. To advocate humanism in its full meaning in the United States today is to risk being considered "square." Yet the study of any foreign language is a humanistic activity, even if a good part of the culture represented in it is not humanistic. One aspect of humanism *is* expressed by Terence's *homo sum: humani nil a me alienum puto*; "I am a human being: nothing human is alien to me." This insists on concern and responsibility for other humans and has implications that have long held out hope for mankind. It is a noble creed that is also shared by several religions, but, as I have tried to show, it is not all of humanism.

If we examine the history of the study of foreign languages and its relationship to humanism, we find that from the beginning of modern times the concepts of humanism were an intended outcome of the curriculum, centered as it was on the languages and literatures of the ancient Romans and Greeks. Education, especially secondary and higher, was originally class-based. In the years since modern education began, and particularly in the United States, the original narrow class base has broadened tremendously. As the school population increased, the original goal of education, and the confidence in that goal, has changed. Furthermore, the development of the natural and social sciences gradually caused the removal of classical languages from their central position in the curriculum; and then, with the growing emphasis on modernity and usefulness, these languages began to be replaced by the modern languages, especially in the United States. Now the educational role of modern languages is being questioned, even as tools for graduate study. In our defense of foreign language study, we in the profession may be both victims and agents of a "cultural lag," of an educational system and philosophy devised for conditions which are no longer suitable.

From the beginning of the modern period, the purpose of secondary and higher education was the training of an elite. It was deemed meaningful and necessary to sharpen their nature-given reason through training in language and ideology because they would someday lead their numerous inferiors and keep the world in balance. The intent of secondary education was either to produce "gentlemen" fit to take their rightful leading place in society, or to prepare students for entry into the university, a course pursued by only a very small percent of the young until this century was well advanced. The university provided professional training in theology, law, medicine, and in new professions as they developed. In Europe, the liberal arts aim of humanism was, and still is, confined to the secondary level; but in the United States, it continued as an aim in college, at least for the first two years. However, humanism has been threatened by the pressure for the need of professional training, and it is in serious danger now.

Until the beginning of the twentieth century, classical languages and literatures were studied in the original as part of the required curriculum, and humanism was the assumed outcome both here and abroad. The growing stress on the democratic ideal and the faith placed in education as an equalizer, social elevator, and as a training for democracy modified the curricula in the United States, enabling a greater percentage of the population to get an education on all levels. The political and social corollaries of humanism, rather than humanism itself, became both the reason for education and its widely proclaimed ideology. Foreign languages continued vigorously in secondary and college curricula, and the numbers of students studying them grew; modern languages far outstripped classical languages, which were pronounced useless for modern needs and were in danger of dying out altogether. The term "humanism" was no longer widely current in educational circles; its place was taken by "liberal arts" and "humanities." These centered on modern languages and literatures, art, music, philosophy, history, and, surprisingly, Latin and Greek literature in translation. The latter was usually taught as a separate course by a member of the English department.

Teachers in the United States today are engaged in two educational tasks, mass and elite education; and the problems of the differing needs, expectations, and approaches in educating the two groups of students involved have not been adequately faced or resolved. It may be that events have moved too fast for a proper resolution. Do both groups need humanism or liberal arts? Do both need foreign languages? Do both, or does either, need to have humanism presented through foreign languages? Can one ask such questions without being drummed out of the profession?

Having gone this far, let me ask another touchy question: If teachers are satisfied that Latin and Greek literature in translation introduces students to "the best that was thought and said" by those who planted the seeds of Western civilization, why not teach the literature of the modern foreign languages in translation in the foreign language classroom, as is of course already being done in Comparative Literature courses? Language study and literature in the original could be left to majors and those wishing to become specialists. I know I am playing into the hands of our opponents, but they have a right to this question and we owe them an answer.

Since the 1920s, education in the United States has receded from the humanistic ideal to a pragmatic or practical approach that has been considered more suitable to the needs of a growing and increasingly industrialized society.

This started with the decline of classical languages, continued with the growth of modern languages and other studies considered more relevant to modern needs, and has now reached a logical result in the decline of required courses in the colleges (*1*). Required courses were originally intended to supply the liberal arts or humanistic basis for professional specialization in the junior and senior year and in graduate school; their decline means that many colleges will stress professional aims throughout the four years. In the last few years, the most severe blow to foreign language study has come from some of the most serious students in the colleges. They have attacked foreign languages as useless, ineffectually taught, and unhumanistic. By placing a new stress on how human beings speaking the languages actually think and behave, can we get an additional measure of salvation from humanism?

Paradoxically, the profession faces challenge from a phenomenon which could have been expected to supply our strongest allies—the new ethnic emphasis in the United States. The ideal of "the melting pot," so frequently proclaimed during those earlier more confident years when humanism still commanded respect, is no longer welcomed by the new or newly vocal minorities, their leaders, and their supporters. It is seen as an instrument for producing second-class citizens by denying the rights of ethnic minorities. Although the insistence on rights is based on the ideals of humanism, ethnic emphasis may be basically anti-humanistic. Ethnic consciousness-raising stresses ethnic and racial pride rather than pride as a human being in the universalist humanistic sense. The ethnic leaders say: let us first establish ethnic pride and ethnic rights; our human pride will continue to be denied without them. This is a cogent argument, but the danger is that the means may take over the ends and the humanistic end may never get a chance for consideration.

Having been accustomed to teaching the "standard" form of a foreign language to students who did not speak it at home and for whom its study was intended to be a broadening experience, teachers now have to consider how to handle the language in such a way as not to lower the self-esteem of those students who speak a non-standard form at home. Yet there have been gains in second language education. However, some of them begin to cut into the dominant position of the long established standbys, French, Spanish, and German. There has been growth in Spanish in the centers of the new immigration, with the attendant problems mentioned above; there has been a growing interest in the study of French among speakers of its dialects in Louisiana; and there has been an increase in introducing languages that were seldom studied a generation ago—Italian, Hebrew, Chinese, Russian, the Scandinavian languages, Japanese, and other "less commonly taught languages" (*1*). In some of these cultures, the Western humanist element plays little or no part. Like Greek and Latin teachers before them, modern language teachers have had to adjust their methods, content, and philosophy to maintain their subjects in the curriculum. They have had to remind themselves that they were not just teaching language but were educating young people, and they have had to become involved in bilingual teaching, cultural differences, and the relevance of humanism. After all, this is humanism in action. Even classicists have responded to the new challenges. The successful growth of the Latin programs in the strongly ethnocentric inner-city schools of Washington, D.C. and Philadelphia may point to new directions for a harmonious merger of humanistic and ethnic values (5; 7). Perhaps these linear heirs of the original humanists will show the way.

Nevertheless, there is a bothersome reality which may cause us to re-examine our usually stated reasons for foreign language study and may make any concern with humanism irrelevant or incidental. If one examines the history of foreign language study from its beginnings in Western civilization, one may come to the conclusion that such study was most successful among that limited portion of the population for whom it had practical value in political, economic, social, or religious life. Although humanistic values may have been conveyed through the concepts in some of the literature, foreign languages were put into the curriculum as a practical measure.

The Romans, the first in Western civilization to study a foreign language in school, needed a knowledge of Greek in order to rule and administer their Greek-speaking eastern empire and maintain their status as a world power; they also needed Greek literature as a source of models and skills for the orator-administrator (8). As a result, Rome, like many of the Mediterranean states she took over, became part of the Hellenistic civilization.

In the medieval period, the foreign language of the relatively few lettered people, mostly clergy, was Latin. It was the language of the Western church, of leading ideas, of teaching and scholarship, and of international diplomacy through which learned clergymen served their less educated royal masters.

In the independent states of Renaissance Italy, where humanism revived to become the powerful "wave of the future," Latin and Greek literatures were the source of ideology and political theory, as well as models for the new literature. Polybius and Tacitus, among others, supported Italian statecraft; and Dante, a pioneer in making the "vulgar" Italian tongue into a superb literary medium, used Vergil as his guide. Soon the rest of Western Europe followed the Italians; renascent Greek was added to Latin, and the two became key studies in the schools. Italian was also studied in Western Europe in order to maintain communication with an international source of power and to keep abreast of new fashions in culture and the arts, and all other aspects of Italian life.

From the eighteenth through the nineteenth century, although the classical languages continued to flourish, French became the important language for those who sought power, or contact with the powerful; French was used for international trade, technology, and economic and political innovations, as well as for new ideas and new fashions. French was the favored language in upper-class Prussia when Frederick the Great was laying the foundations of empire; later, upper-class Russians adopted it as they sought to Europeanize and modernize their country; and Turkey, "the sick man of Europe," thought French might help it to recover.

Power languages were as important as gunboats. When a newly unified Germany became a leader in science, thought, and industry, its language began to enter the curricula. The popularity of Spanish in the United States predates the intensive post-World War II immigration. America's recognition of the importance of "our good neighbors to the south" spurred an interest in their language, perhaps for the same reason that Greek was of interest to the Romans.

The pattern continues in the late twentieth century, accompanied in this country by the prospect that the "big three" of the language field will face challenges from the languages of new world powers. English has replaced French as the preferred foreign language in the schools of Europe and Asia. Russian, Chinese, and, to a lesser extent, Japanese have come into the secondary and undergraduate curriculum of the United States, where there are also signs of a growing interest in Arabic. Foreign language study in the next generation may favor the languages of these newly emerged peoples. The older, more traditional languages that have dominated the classroom may follow the way of Latin and Greek, finding only a modicum of justification in their being the vehicles of Western culture and expressers of humanistic concepts. This is the situation we begin to see today. Today's young people, unconsciously echoing the attitudes of political leaders, seem to be saying that what is thought, spoken, and done in Spanish-speaking countries, France, and Germany is not very important. What is seen as important is happening in Mao's China, in the new Russian imperium, in the oil-rich Middle East, and in Japan, where cherry blossoms and kimonos are being replaced by transistors, oil tankers, and industrial smog. Whether large numbers of students will be inclined to undergo the discipline of learning these languages remains to be seen.

Can these foreign cultures that are now attracting attention in the classroom teach us humanistic values? Not in the sense that has been discussed. However, each of the four has a rich and unique culture. Studying their values, experiences, life-styles, and viewpoints can be richly rewarding. Of course, some students are motivated by the humanistic impulse to see all peoples as members of "the family of man," although little interest was evinced in this area until the countries began to assert their power politically and economically. One may argue that the study of these languages, as has been said about others, may aid international understanding and world peace; but this is not why they are being studied, any more than this is why foreigners all over the world are studying English. By now it is quite clear that speaking one another's language does not necessarily lead to peace.

Where does that leave the foreign language teacher and humanistic values? Shall we give up? Or shall we concentrate on training specialists and forget the others? Is the humanistic ideal and the hope of understanding other cultures in the classroom an illusion? We prefer not to think so. Like Galileo in his reported demurrer, *eppur' si muove*, we feel we would be betraying our own deeply felt convictions if we denied the importance of humanism in foreign language or any other teaching. After all, to repeat, in the plural this time, *homines sumus!*

Because humanism means more than trying to get to know other humans by studying their languages and cultures, can students appreciate humanistic values after two or three years of studying a foreign language the usual limit nowadays? The new emphasis on culture will not be sufficient for this purpose, for the everyday habits, institutions, practices, and assumptions of a society are not usually expressions of humanism (*4, 9*). In the case of the original Greco-Roman formulation of this doctrine, the ideas emerged in the surviving literature, ideas that were frequently contradicted by everyday practices, habits, and institutions. In the case of modern foreign languages, there is the opportunity to study living cultures more or less directly; but, here too, it is in the literature that these values, if present, are best expressed. Therefore, if we are sincere about humanism as an aspect of foreign language study, literature will have to play a much greater role at an earlier level of a student's linguistic competency than it has in the past. Just as it is shortsighted to keep Latin students from the riches of Vergil, Horace, Ovid, and other Roman masters until they have mastered the language, it is equally so to keep students from Spanish, French, German, and other foreign masterpieces until they are sufficiently adept at these tongues. If students are encouraged to read a country's classics in a foreign language class, they can begin to grapple with ideas such as humanism in their foreign language study; and if they have satisfactory experiences with pieces of literature in translation in their classes, some students may be stimulated to read further on their own in the original, or to elect courses in which they will do so. In addition, the foreign language teacher can bring out insights and nuances because he is familiar with a particular literature in the original. In a comparative literature course, an instructor deals with several different foreign literatures, not all of which he can read in the original.

To avoid distorting the realities of a culture and its literature, those aspects which are not humanistic will also have to be brought out for balance and truth, as is being done more and more with Greek culture. The humanist, moreover, does not reject the study of cultures not in his tradition which are attracting growing interest because of the realities of international power. It would be parochial and unhumanistic to do so; the world is too interrelated. I call again on the quotation from the Greek-influenced, African-born Roman playwright Terence: These societies like ours are made up of human beings with whom we share hopes, desires, needs, and, if it is not a myth, reason.

It is now time to sum up and see what we are left with as language teachers and humanists. I feel myself in the role of a bearer of unwelcome tidings who sometimes is blamed for the news he brings. However, it is necessary to be realistic; facing our problems and their implications will enable us to improve the present and plan for the future. We must have clear definitions of our goals, realistic assessments of them, and sensible approaches to them. In that way, if we succeed, we will know why and can continue; and if we fail, we will know why and can try to correct our errors. This is one of the most difficult times in the history of the profession. Facing the problems discussed in this paper, together with the other efforts already being exerted, may help solve these difficulties. Perhaps some of the points I have presented can be successfully refuted; although the monsters may turn out to be "paper tigers," they must be grappled with.

Despite the current unpopularity of humanism in America, there is some reason for optimism. Throughout all the political and social turmoil of the past several years, there has been a strong, sometimes unspoken humanist tradition that has surfaced when actions have not lived up to professed ideals. The orderly, rational, and natural transfer of political power to a new administration after the Watergate scandals showed the strength of that humanistically based document, the United States Constitution, at the very time when many were questioning the tenets of humanism. The existence of reason in the human being can be challenged on scientific grounds as not provable; although this brings into question the reality of the assumptions of humanism, it does not invalidate the reality of humanism as a set of *values*. The facts and achievements of science and other fields of learning are not ends in themselves. They are to be used together with all other available data and resources to realize the values of society. We must reassert these humanistic values; by doing so through foreign language teaching, we will be doing what we can to guide the young to a decent world.

If our goal was to provide varying levels of competency in performance, as in commercial language schools, and if our students came highly motivated because foreign language proficiency was essential for a job, our task would be easy; there would be no *crises de conscience*. However, we are educators, not trainers. Although we wish to give students as much foreign language proficiency as possible in the time available, we have other equally important purposes. Like our colleagues in other fields, we try to get students to understand, to think, to relate what they have learned to their own culture and society. When they have a better understanding of themselves and their world, they can face and act on their responsibilities as individuals, citizens, and human beings. This is a humanistic aim and involves a humanistic approach. We must accept and understand the whole humanistic package and impart the ideals and attitudes contained in it by our methods, by what we have our students study, and by our own example. The ideals of humanism are essential to an enlightened and democratic society.

BIBLIOGRAPHY

(1) Brod, Richard I. "Foreign Language Enrollments in U.S. Colleges: Fall 1972." *Foreign Language Annals* 7, ii (1973): 209-13. [Originally published under the same title in the *ADFL Bulletin* 5, i (1973): 54-60. For the latest figures in public secondary schools, see the table entitled "Summary Comparisons, by Region, of Public Secondary School (PSS) Enrollment and Foreign Language Enrollments, Grades 7-12: Fall 1965, 1968, and 1970" in the same issue of *FLA* (p. 214), whose data, however, go no further than 1970. (See also Brod's report, "Foreign Language Enrollments in U.S. Colleges: Fall 1974" in the *ADFL Bulletin* 7, ii (1975): 37-42.) Table 2 (p. 210) indicates the following declines in colleges between 1970 and 1972: French, 18.4%; German, 12.6%; Spanish, 6.3%; Italian, 2.7%; Latin, 11.6%. In the same period, ancient Greek grew by 23.3%, from 16,697 to 20,585. The "less commonly taught languages" as a whole registered a 30.1% gain in this period. Between 1960 and 1972 (p. 211, Table 4) they grew as follows: Arabic, 541 to 1,669; Chinese, 1,844 to 10,044; Hebrew, 3,834 to 21,901; Japanese 1,746 to 8,273 with comparable substantial increases in Norwegian, Polish, Portuguese, Swahili, Swedish, and Yiddish. Comparable data for secondary schools are not available at this writing.]

(2) Cicero, Marcus Tullius. *De Legibus Libri*. Edited by J. Vahlen. Berlin, 1883. [On the Laws. Written in 52 B.C. Cicero, the Roman orator and statesman, is even more important to Western civilization as the chief interpreter and spreader of Greek philosophical ideas to his people and to us. His works in this field were for a long time their chief source for the West, even after the revival of Greek learning. He apparently coined the term *humanitas* from which the word "humanism" was ultimately derived. His *De Legibus* discusses the concepts of nature, natural law and morality, human reason as a natural faculty, etc. In Book I, 10, 29 regarding the universality of moral principles and their apparent diversity in practice, he writes: "For there is nothing more similar, more like to another than we humans to one another. And if the corruption of customs, the falseness of opinions did not twist and turn our minds from the course they started with (i.e., the course laid out by nature), no one would resemble himself as much as all of us (humans) resemble one another." In I, 10, 30 he writes of reason, which among living beings is peculiar to humans, and of speech, "the interpreter of the mind," which "agrees in the ideas it conveys though it may differ in the syllables (i.e., sounds of different languages) that express them."]

(3) Dodds, E.R. *The Greeks and the Irrational*. Berkeley and Los Angeles: University of California Press, 1968. [Originally published in 1951. Dodds, an important scholar in this field, indicates (p. 68) that Plato and the Greek tradition in general make Apollo the patron of "prophetic madness." His Chapter V (pp. 135-75) deals with what Dodds calls "The Greek Shamans," a term not previously applied to such leaders of Greek thought as Pythagoras, Empedocles, and others. The very title of his book signalizes the new approach to Greek culture.]

(4) Dodge, James W., ed. *Other Words, Other Worlds: Language-in-Culture*. Reports of the Working Committees of the Northeast Conference on the Teaching of Foreign Languages. Montpelier, VT: The Northeast Conference on the Teaching of Foreign Languages, 1972. [This issue is devoted entirely to about a dozen articles summarizing the main features of the cultures (in the sociological sense) of the main languages taught in American schools and colleges. In none of the cultures described (except ancient Greek and Roman) does humanism play a significant role. In fact, in one of the articles in which the term is used, that on German

culture, the author, Harry F. Young (9), makes this statement (p. 67): "The acceptance of a formal culture and the support of it with one's presence do not necessarily mean more literary understanding or a more tolerant humanistic view of the world." The same may be taken to apply to the other modern cultures described.]

(5)   LeBovit, Judith. *The Teaching of Latin in Elementary Schools*. McLean, VA: Latin for the Modern School Associates, n.d. [8542 Georgetown Pike, 22101.]

(6)   Lieberman, Samuel. "The Humanities as Human Studies." *Classical World* 64 (1971): 262-63. [This article is based on more extended remarks delivered at a panel discussion on "The Classical Humanities and Education" at the ACL Classical Institute, Oxford, Ohio, June 19, 1970. The writer states that one reason for the decline in Classical Studies in the last 50 to 60 years is "that in much of the teaching of Classical Humanities and Languages, the human qualities, the human aims and ideals, have been lost sight of." He also stressed that "the teachers of these subjects must return to their original function as humanists with an emphasis on the human," as some have with considerable success.]

(7)   Masciantonio, Rudolph. "The Implications of Innovative Classical Programs in the Public Schools of Philadelphia." *Classical World* 64 (1971): 263-65.

(8)   Quintilianus, Marcus Fabius. *Institutionis Oratoriae*. Edited by F.H. Colson. Cambridge: Cambridge University Press, 1924. [Education of an Orator. Written in 92 A.D. Quintilian, the leading and influential Roman educator of the first century A.D., is known especially for this book which deals with the education of an upper class Roman from the elementary stage to its culmination in the ancient form of higher education to produce the *vir bonus dicendi peritus*, "the good man expert at speaking." In that highly oral culture oratory was the chief civilian vehicle for the leader in the law courts or administration. In his Book X Quintilian presents a survey of Greek and Roman literature including oratory and specifically states that his purpose is not a course in what we would call appreciation of literature but to supply the budding orator and leader with models for his own compositions and with the source of suitable and effective ideas, examples, and vocabulary.]

(9)   Young, Harry F. "An Approach to Courses in German Culture," 64-70 in James W. Dodge, ed., *Other Words, Other Worlds: Language-in-Culture*. Reports of the Working Committees of the Northeast Conference on the Teaching of Foreign Languages. Montpelier, VT: The Northeast Conference on the Teaching of Foreign Languages, 1972.

Chapter Three
Objectives for New Programs:
A Thematic Approach in
Second Language Learning
Helen L. Jorstad

Millions of words have probably been written about objectives, whether behavioral, performance, or instructional. Journals have published pro and con articles (*8, 9, 19, 31*); taxonomies have been suggested (*4, 15, 20, 32*); and several ways of writing objectives have been advocated (*14, 18, 24*).

At the elementary and secondary school levels, second language teachers either have already written or are in the process of writing objectives for their programs. Some efforts have been successful and some have not. The purpose of this paper is not to join the debate for or against writing objectives for language programs. Its purpose is to examine the movement and suggest applications for language programs which stress general curriculum-planning concerns.

OBJECTIVES AND LANGUAGE PROGRAMS

The literature dealing with objectives specifically intended for language teachers has focused on the specification of clearly formulated behavioral outcomes in each of the language skills and in culture. When textbook series included specification of objectives, they have tended to focus on the same areas. Valette and Disick include a section on "attitudes, feelings, and values," and suggest ways to measure them formally and informally through checklists, attitude scales, and observation of student behavior. They stress the admonition that affective objectives should be determined in connection with cognitive outcomes throughout the language instruction process. They also warn against limiting objectives to the lower stages of the taxonomy, against "overly specific objectives," and against objectives overly narrow in scope (*32*, p. 66). The handbook appeared at a time when more and more teachers were becoming aware, through dropping enrollments, that their language programs were in trouble. Here, through specification of objectives, was a way to individualize instruction and meet the needs of more students. Because the literature was replete with articles and books about individualizing instruction in languages (*1,*

13, 22), and because a number of successful programs was being described in the literature (*23, 22*) and at conventions, teachers believed that they could really do something about enrollments if they followed along.

The movement toward individualizing instruction coincided with a growing stress on accountability in the schools, and the concomitant demand by parents and administrators for specification of objectives for all subjects, including languages. State departments of education organized groups of teachers to prepare statements for language programs. Similar efforts went on throughout the nation in school districts, groups of schools, and within separate schools. The resulting objectives tend to stress discrete points of language, grammatical rules, and productive skills. Most of the objectives are easy to test, and procedures for record-keeping and testing are easy enough to follow so that even the neophyte teacher can institute and carry out an individualized language program.

It is not the purpose of this paper to criticize individualization of instruction. On the other hand, since the movement was reborn, in a sense, with the behavioral objectives movement, it is in order perhaps to comment briefly on what happened to objectives in the process. In the first place, most of what passed for individualization did not really take into account either the divergent interests of different students or their various modes of learning; individualized programs were principally self-paced. They were "individualized" only in so far as they allowed for differing rates of learning. Every student still went through the same body of material, passed the same tests, worked on the same activities. The classrooms looked different because students proceeded through their packets or contracts at different rates. However, the objectives for all students were stated by the teacher or by the materials, and they were the same for every student. The objectives were also tested in the same way for each student, usually in writing, and the student either passed ahead or worked through the same material again until the criterion behaviors could be met. Only rarely was a student "branched" in the process of working through materials. The technology which would permit a student to choose his own objective, receive training in the mode most suitable to meet that objective, and be tested on whether the objective had been attained did not exist, and does not exist today.

An "individualized" program is not necessarily a "personalized" program. Because too much was expected from them, there was no way these programs could deliver on all their promises. True, there are some programs which function well. Some teachers have found that their energies are more profitably used with self-paced instruction because they can spend more time with smaller groups of students. In some cases, students are motivated to continue language study longer. General disillusionment with such programs, however, has led teachers to blame the specification of objectives for the failures instead of the fact that the broad promises were impossible to keep.

Meanwhile, colleges of education have kept the promises going. A little slow to move, they now train prospective teachers who can individualize; for teachers in-service, regular workshops help to spread the movement. Still, individualized instruction has not reached universal acceptance. Carroll's model for school learning involved consideration of a wide range of factors which may be as important as the rate of learning (6). The quality of instruction is also a factor; if a student is bored by the impersonality of the "individualized" program which he is following, learning does not result.

Meanwhile, book publishers, a few steps behind the profession, have realized that the movement is more than transitory; they are now publishing materials which pre-specify learner objectives and give the teacher pre-prepared learning contracts, lists of objectives, and progress tests. The individual student is once again the victim, this time of a super-glossy set of individualized materials instead of a teacher-made thermofaxed and dittoed set. And, because there is another set of unkeepable promises, the teacher is also a victim. A truly "individualized" program "means that each student has learning experiences suited to his unique characteristics as a learner" (25, p. 14). McAshen points out that such a program is possible only with "adequate and flexible learning materials." A program should take a child's educational goals and objectives into account, and his "talents, needs, interests, and abilities" should be uppermost in the planning (25, p. 15). The objectives for each student will differ; it is clear that there is no way that the new modularized materials offered by publishers can meet such criteria.

Objectives are a permanent part of the educational scene in other ways as well. The long catalogs of objectives prepared in states and schools throughout the country are unmistakable evidence that the movement has affected language teaching permanently, though possibly not as intended. Even where groups of teachers have spent months or years preparing their lists of objectives for every aspect of the language-learning process, evidence of the use of those objectives in the language classroom is not easy to find. As a result, the effect of objectives is more evident in teachers than it is in students. Teachers may have spent considerable time and effort writing objectives to please an administration, a school board, the public, or a professor at a nearby university, and only secondarily to please themselves or their students. Once the objectives have been written, they can go on teaching as usual. Many of the lists of objectives are simply lists of items presented in the usual text lesson, with an objective for each grammatical point treated; each such item matches a discrete-point test item from the textbook test. Neither the teachers, nor the students, nor the content of the courses have been affected deeply or lastingly. Is it any wonder that teachers, administrators, and students can say that they have "tried objectives" and found them ineffective?

Empirically, there is little evidence that objectives have much effect on learning. The many studies which have been carried out have yielded contradictory data which is far from conclusive (*18*, p. 7). One reason for the inconclusive findings, according to Kibler, is the fact that the methods used to carry out the studies are inconsistent. There is often no definition of treatment, no training in using objectives, and no specification about the differentiation of treatments in the studies; thus, the results are suspect. However, Popham effectively contradicts arguments against using behavioral objectives (*26*).

Although some aspects of the movement are an unwarranted waste of time, it is also clear that a number of benefits could be claimed for specification of objectives. It might be wise to examine some of them briefly before discussing future classroom applications.

The chief benefit attendant upon clearly specified, even trivial, statements of objectives is that attention is focused, often for the first time, on what is expected of the student at the end of a specified lesson or unit of study. In classrooms where there is no specification of objectives, it is not uncommon to find the teacher concerned about what he or she is going to teach on a particular day, rather than about what the student will learn from the lesson and how he will be able to use it. Or, just as commonly, the teacher is concerned primarily with how much of the text lesson can be covered in the class period. Such a teacher "covers" the book with little regard for what students have learned. However, specified objectives which closely parallel the text's units have little effect on the direction of the classroom activities; the major concern is still with what is presented in the book, and not with what the student brings to and takes from the lesson.

Second, objectives focus attention on the kinds of evaluation which are used in the classroom. In classrooms which lack specified objectives, evaluation often takes the form of publisher-prepared tests to accompany a text which may be totally unrelated to the learning stressed by a particular teacher. In such classrooms, quizzes are frequently intended as a means of checking student completion of homework assignments rather than as criterion-based instruments which can help students evaluate their learning. The specification of objectives usually brings with it items for quizzes and tests which are directed to the objectives. Students may grow accustomed to having quiz and test items reflect objectives that have been stated in advance, and more purposeful learning may result. In a few classrooms which have adopted a mastery model and in self-paced programs the benefits of objectives in terms of "letting students in on what they are learning" have sometimes been startling.

Third, specification of objectives has led to closer scrutiny of language programs. While there are still too many courses of study which "teach the textbook," some programs now attend to the development of all areas of language learning and cultural understanding. Even when these programs are not successful, attention is being given to the evaluation of all areas of language learning and cultural understanding.

Fourth, more cooperation among schools is possible when there is agreement on districtwide objectives. Articulation from level to level and school to school can be less of a problem when language teachers have made the objectives of their programs clear to each other.

Fifth, it is easier to communicate with administrators and parents when there is a clearly visible statement of objectives for a language program. The results of instruction can be reported to parents in terms of the objectives, facilitating communication about what is happening in the classroom.

On the other hand, there are many shortcomings in objectives as they now exist, whether written by teachers or others. Yet one can still accept the basic premise that more learning will result when students know what they will be asked to learn, when teachers are aware of the directions in which courses should move, and when evaluation reflects the domains identified for mastery. Such responses may answer some of the most specific and articulate critics (*31*).

Excellent descriptions of precisely how to prepare instructional objectives exist in a number of publications, each differing in basic focus. Attention is particularly directed to Valette and Disick (*32*), Banathy and Lange (*3*), Gronlund (*14*), and Kibler, et al. (*18*) for extremely useful discussions.

The remainder of this paper focuses on the ways in which objectives can form part of a process of curriculum planning in languages. In the discussion, an "objective" is understood to be a motivating statement directed to the student, and formulated by means of the following process: 1) the end product desired by the student is identified in a needs analysis; 2) intermediate steps are examined that will contribute the competencies needed for the student to attain the end product and 3) the tasks needed for attainment of the end product are ordered, building from known to unknown in careful steps.

A RATIONAL BASIS FOR INSTRUCTIONAL PLANNING

Determine Culminating Performance Goals

Now is the time for courage. Ignore the textbook's sequencing or choice of topics; or even ignore the textbook totally. The advice may sound drastic, but general textbooks cannot completely meet the needs of specific students; the needs of high school sophomores, college freshmen, and middle school students are bound to differ. Teachers tend to believe that the content of textbooks is sacrosanct, and that the sequencing of vocabulary and structures is based on a logical rationale. However, materials developers ignore many significant aspects of language, select for instruction what they wish to select, and use tradition rather than clear criteria for inclusion and sequencing of vocabulary and structures. Carroll suggests that teachers "not worry about the exact sequence in which instructional material is selected and presented, as long as there is careful account taken of what the student is presumed to know at any given point," (*7*,

p. 144). He also suggests parallel streams of controlled and uncontrolled structures and vocabulary. As you think about your students and their special needs, try to be unconventional. Through long conditioning, teachers are most likely to identify reading and writing as the most obvious needs of their students. If this is the case, you may not be being honest with yourself. You would be on safer grounds if you were to distribute a simple questionnaire to your present first-year class to find out what they really would have liked to study in their French course. If you can make the students stop trying to please you by saying what they think you want them to say, the result would probably be a list of basic cultural topics, such as "making food," "how French kids act on dates," or "how one should act in a visit to a family." If they are being completely honest, rarely will students tell you that they wish to study the *imparfait-passé composé* contrast more fully. They may say that they wish they could talk more or learn to read better, but most students are unlikely to request French literature of the seventeenth or any other century.

Now, armed with some basic information about the interests of the students, you can begin to build a curriculum. Choose three or four basic topics suggested by the students. Think carefully about the suggestions they made as you try to think about some culminating goals for work with the topics. Do students want to be able to "talk more" about life on French farms? During first-year work, what is a reasonable, reachable goal for such "talk"? Can you expect perfect pronunciation? Can you expect complete control of the conditional? Or can you simply expect the student to be understood as he or she talks about certain aspects of farm life? At this point, your goal should not be accuracy of pronunciation or correctness of speech; instead, it should identify the content about which students should be able to talk.

Along the way you will find yourself needing more information. A "cluster" of related nouns and verbs should be identified if the student is to perform adequately at the end of a unit of study about farm occupations in France. Because learning theory (7) and research (16) have determined that students are more able to learn vocabulary that is grouped than vocabulary presented in isolation, you establish a basic list of necessary vocabulary, a list of related vocabulary, and a list vocabulary which certain students might be able to use. You are unlikely to find reference materials already organized in topical units to help you. Your lists will be arbitrary, but just as logical as other, equally arbitrary lists of vocabulary and structures suggested by experts. *You* are the expert in this case. Keep in mind the vocabulary and structures your students already know, but which should be re-introduced.

Depending on the topic dictated by your students' interests, your goals may or may not resemble the overall goals you have worked with in the past. Continued examination of the goals will lead you to the fact that you have not planned the vocabulary and structures in a "normal sequence." Be comforted by the fact that no one has established that there is a "normal sequence" of vocabulary or structures for language-learning, despite the fact that we have been conditioned to believe that there is something easier about "er" verbs than "ir" verbs, something simpler about the present tense than about the past tenses. There is no proof that this is the case; there is no empirical evidence that some structures should be mastered before certain others are introduced. Meanwhile, there is evidence that students learn what they need and want to learn faster than what they have no motivation to learn (7, 30), and that they learn more in context than they learn in isolation (30, 2).

Intermediate Competencies

So far you have a set of statements about what your students should be able to do with a certain body of language, as well as some topical lists of related vocabulary and structures. Examine these culminating goals carefully: they probably center around the active use of a body of material. Consider next how your students can achieve real use of the language you have decided to present. You are now considering contributing competencies, which serve to clarify and specify more precisely the content of the unit of instruction which you are planning. To be considered are the tasks the students need to perform in order to meet the culminating goals.

Rivers (28) presents a useful framework for leading a student from initial acquaintance with new material to mastery and use of such material: the student is first given a chance to try on the new material and model his utterance after a pattern; he is then given the opportunity to try it in many contexts, varying it by establishing some links with previously known material, thus transferring "old" knowledge about well-known material to the new structure; and, finally, he is given the opportunity to use the new utterance in many new contexts. The new material thus becomes a permanent part of the student's repertory of language, usable in any context. The teacher has effectively established a body of learning contexts which helps the student to bridge the gap between initial acquaintance and total mastery. Intermediate goals elaborate on the classroom activities that help the student to make the appropriate connections and master the material so that he is using it in the context in which he wants to use it as quickly as possible.

Getting a student to this point obviously means that the new material will be heard and tried out in a number of contexts. Because each student will be choosing his objectives according to his interests and best modes of learning, you are obviously not going to be able to be the model for all the new language each student will be learning. In most cases, you can call upon previously prepared materials which you have edited for these new objectives. Some materials can be presented by a cassette recorder, a language lab, or a Language-Master. Some students will choose to learn new materials through reading, so you will need to provide quantities of reading material at several levels of difficulty. The entire community can be considered as source material. Of course, you should examine the hardware and programs you already have and determine how they might be adapted to your new purposes. Often the students can help you prepare materials.

To this point, you have asked the students to participate in the planning a number of times, and in a number of ways. They have helped you envision the culminating goals for the unit. They have assisted you in planning the culminating activity for the unit and in identifying the means for carrying it out, indicating contributing competencies and even specific objectives along the way. You have worked with the class so that it recognizes the activities needed to prepare for the culminating activity. You have consulted the students as you selected resource materials; these can range from parents and other community resource persons to the talents of the students themselves, from artwork to magazines, newspapers, library books, and even to textbooks. As you and your class designed the culminating goals and activities, and the contributing competencies, it was decided how the class could be best organized for the work: some activities might be accomplished as a large group; some could best be effected by each student working alone; others could be carried out in small groups or with partners; and some could best be teacher-directed or planned, while others could be student-directed or planned. Time constraints should also have been considered.

The classroom you have now arranged looks quite different from the one you may have been used to; certainly it is different from the usual secondary school classroom. You and the students have transformed it with materials of all descriptions that focus on a topic. Such a room would not seem out of place in an elementary school, where for generations students have been working and learning topically rather than sequentially, and in many curriculum areas simultaneously. Some years ago, I taught an ungraded primary class in which almost all class activities from reading through social studies, math, and science centered about Afghanistan for many weeks. Children who normally read at primer level struggled through very difficult materials because they wanted to find out specific information at that particular moment. There was no real sequence to a large portion of their learning; their interests ranged from what people eat in Afghanistan to how they are housed, from the games children play to how they dress. Culminating goals included information the students could find and use, and contributing competencies included processes they could use for obtaining the information; and there were many kinds of activities which could provide learning experiences.

Specific Objectives

What do you expect of your students? Of course, there are behavioral objectives with which you are already familiar; but there are other behaviors which have not usually been specified as objectives. For example, students may be able to carry out a specific conversational exchange, with appropriate gestures and body language. Jakobovits and Gordon call these "transactions," interactions of student with student (17). However, in many classrooms today, teacher-talk still dominates, with very little real student-to-student interaction; students are expected to sit still and absorb what the teacher says. On the other hand, completely individualized programs which are self-paced seem lackluster because everyone in the class is expected to do the same things, albeit at different times. Although for the most part students work alone or in small groups, the *nature* of the work reflects minimal correlation between what students want to learn and what they have to go through to learn it. The specific objectives are inappropriate, not because it is inappropriate to specify objectives, but because the students did not help in the selection of the objectives. Therefore, they have little meaning for the class. There is usually little real interchange between students in a foreign language; the structure of the materials is such that each student is learning structures or vocabulary in isolation. Language is communication, but it is not often taught in our schools as communication activity; part of the blame rests with the specific objectives which we have been using in our teaching.

If we were to reverse the procedure normally used for constructing curriculum materials, we could begin by specifying those "transactions" that we wish to result from a particular unit of work. Banathy and Lange (3, pp. 56-57, 60) and Jakobovits and Gordon (17) The objectives would specify a level of acceptable performance, but that level would not be in terms of precision of pronunciation, vocabulary, or structures; rather, it would specify the kind of information which should be understood and/or transmitted in the interchange. If we are prepared to accept the premise that language is not naturally sequenced, that it is not more "normal" to start speaking in the present tense and using "I," then we can be guided and directed by the needs and interests of the students. Not all students would have to meet the same objectives, which is a sine qua non of the proposed procedures. Students could choose their own objectives, thereby personalizing their programs. It should be possible for Nancy to learn to read a weather report or grain exchange information if she wishes to do so; and Jim could plan crop rotation with his neighbors, if he so wishes. Specification of the objectives would call into play all modes of instruction, all available media, all manner of materials. The objectives specified would be limited only by the unit being studied, the materials available, and the needs of the students. The teacher should meet with the students as they select their personal objectives and help them to choose activities which suit their best modes of learning; then interactions among students and other personnel should be arranged. At times, the work would be performed by the group as a whole; at times, by a number of smaller groups, or by pairs of students; and sometimes the student would work with materials on his own. Drill, which can be drudgery, can be easier if a student knows it will be rewarded, if, for example, he knows he has to master it before he can find out some needed information. At the same time, because all students are working with materials which revolve around a topical unit, there is much common ground to be explored. It is also possible to incorporate input from several curriculum areas so that by carrying out a French project a student might also be meeting science objectives.

Consider the following portion of a possible set of objectives for individual students in a first-year class which is working on a unit on French agriculture. The example focuses on a single culminating goal, a portion of the possible intermediate competencies, and a few specific instructional outcomes. It is assumed that the complete topical unit would include several culminating goals with subcategories. Included in parentheses are some of the learning tasks and classroom activities which individuals or groups of students could use to help them achieve the objectives. At the senior high level, the entire unit of work may take from four to six weeks of class time, meeting about fifty minutes daily.

I. GOAL: To understand the role of the weather in the conduct of farming.

    A. *Intermediate Competencies*: To determine the tasks the French farmer needs to perform in each of the four seasons, taking into account the weather.

        Objective 1: You are a farmer who meets a friend in town on a rainy day. You discuss the effect of the rain on your crops. (Students need skill in responding to statements, restating ideas and questions, commenting, and interacting. Language should be introduced with tapes or other media. Students may work individually or in pairs in the beginning.)

            Sub-objective a: To know how rain affects the various crops you raise. (Reading seed catalogs, and other resource materials can be used.)

            Sub-objective b: To decide on a region of France in which to farm and determine its weather, how much it rains, what crops are raised there.

        Objective 2: You are a farmer in Brittany. You need to plan your planting for next spring so that you can order seeds and fertilizer. You will have to find out the weather conditions in your area, and what crops will be most suitable for the length of your growing season and your soil. You have ten hectares and you work the farm with your grown daughter. (Students should have access to weather reports from a newspaper for a year in order to adapt their crops. Use *Quid** for help. Students can work alone or with a classmate.)

   Sub-objective a: Go to a seed store in Rennes to order your seed.
   Sub-objective b: Talk to an agriculture specialist about average rainfall in your area.
B. *Intermediate Competencies*: To determine the role of regional weather conditions on the conduct of farming in a number of regions of France.

   Objective 1: You have a farm in southern France and have been having severe difficulties with wind damage. You talk to a neighbor about the problem, and together you consider possible solutions.

   Objective 2: You own land on a mountainside in the Alps. You must determine the crops you could raise, identify your main problems, and indicate possible solutions for them.

It is clear that not all students will choose the same objectives, and that within objectives they may not all choose the same sub-objectives. It is equally clear that there will be a good deal of student learning going on. Some of the work could profitably be done as a full-class group; in fact, some work daily in the full-class group is logical, as students need audiences, helpers, and colleagues with whom to work.

Problems: 1) Materials

Supplies that are different from those normally found in language classrooms will be needed. Seed catalogs, mail order catalogs, magazines, newspapers, tapes, cassettes, pictures, filmstrips, almanacs, even flannel boards and children's books on the subject should be assembled. Many of the materials will serve several units of work, and students at various levels may be working with the same materials for different purposes. Moreover, a unit of this kind can be economically beneficial; textbooks and the accompanying materials are very expensive, and they would eventually not need to be purchased in the quantity normally used. Sometimes assorted sample texts and readers will be useful for introducing material; they can be cut apart and the resulting readings, exercises, and supplementary activities can be used within the topical units. Also the objectives of some students may include collecting or organizing topical materials for you. Certainly students can prepare bulletin boards and displays.

Collecting materials will of necessity be gradual; you can start a file for whichever topic you are treating and ask friends and students to help gather materials. Through the years, a good collection on a variety of topics can be developed.

Quid? tout pour tous. Paris: Editions Robert Laffont, published annually.

Problems: 2) Dealing with Language Errors

Teachers imbued with well-learned convictions that students should not be allowed to "say things wrong" in the classroom will initially feel frustrated in this classroom. Students will try out and discard language because objectives center on successful exchanges of information instead of perfection in pronunciation or structure. The students may make errors in language, but they will keep going, and they will be able to circumlocute to make themselves understood, something students in "normal" classes find difficult. They can also use the language they have learned well in a number of contexts, something "normal" students find almost impossible at this level. "Errors" are considered important in helping students to formulate how the language works; their "errors" are really an important stage in language learning, and it is important that the teacher be willing to help students learn to feel comfortable in expressing themselves, no matter the stage of their language control.

Students may have stressed speaking and neglected reading, or vice-versa, at any given point in time. Using the process outlined above, they will eventually catch up. As a result, they are more likely to stay with the language and have a wide variety of experiences with it, rather than dropping out at the first opportunity.

Problems: 3) Evaluation

In such a program, traditional, norm-referenced testing and grading are clearly inappropriate. It is necessary to consider an evaluation system which permits measurement at appropriate checkpoints against criteria related to the task and objectives, instead of measurement against other students. Students need to know that they are learning and when they are ready to move ahead, instead of finding out how they perform on a specific test which is often designed to discover what they do *not* know. Because the program is performance-based, however, it seems logical that the evaluation be based on the student's ability to perform. Much of the evaluation should take place in private conferences between student and teacher, and should guide the student into other materials to help him build on what he knows.

Problems: 4) Organization of the Classroom

Assuming that students are scheduled into a class for one period each day, the most common practice in most schools, the following organization has been borrowed rather liberally from an elementary school classroom situation in which each group has some time alone with the teacher. It assumes a fifty-minute period. Students work in groups based on objectives and sub-objectives; and these groups may change from day to day. The first ten minutes of the period are spent in large group planning, deciding who will be doing what and who will be working with what materials. Fill in the following chart with student names; do it on the board and leave it there through the period. The

	Group 1 (list student names)	Group 2	Group 3	Group 4
	___ ___ ___ ___	___ ___ ___ ___	___ ___ ___ ___	___ ___ ___ ___
9:00	Planning	Planning	Planning	Planning
9:10	With teacher, activity	Film	Small group, task with newspapers	Individual work
9:30	Pairs, acting	With teacher, activity based on film	Group, slides	Group, practice performance
9:45	Watch Group 4 performance	Watch Group 4 performance	Watch Group 4 performance	Performs
9:50	Evaluation of period quickly; then dismiss class.			

FIG. 3.1. Classroom Organization.

chart lines might be semi-permanent so that they would always be convenient for hourly planning sessions. The meetings with the teacher during the smaller sessions are intended to give the teacher and students opportunities for self-checking and reporting progress. Each individual works directly with the teacher as needed, and at other times performs alone or with a group working on the same objective.

The proposed program has the following features:

1. Students work in a variety of ways—alone, in pairs, in small groups, in large groups directed either by the teacher or by other students.
2. Students use a variety of materials—texts, magazines, newspapers, community sources, parental, and other volunteer help.
3. Work is directed toward a culminating activity.
4. The focus of the work is student-to-student interaction, which has been stressed in the objectives.
5. The stress on sequencing structures and vocabulary is subordinated to sequencing material so that students move from known to unknown.

6. Errors are de-emphasized in favor of effective transmission of meaning.
7. Students are involved in planning units to be studied, planning culminating activities, planning classroom activity times and their own activities, talking with other students in the language and developing their skills in giving and receiving information for a purpose.
8. Evaluation of a student's performance is based on his ability to carry out interactions according to the objectives he has selected.

Problems: 5) Getting Started
Because of the scope of the change, the transition from a traditional secondary school classroom should be gradual.

A single two to four-week unit could be tested in one class. Discuss the change you wish to make with the students and determine a logical starting date. Enlist student help in planning a daily schedule and finding and organizing materials. Students should be encouraged to think about their own objectives for a special, topical unit of work. Allow several weeks for initial planning. The more exciting the culminating activity, a festival, a program, a field trip, the more eager the students will be to cooperate in planning and working.

During the planning time, occasionally allow for a flexible class period which will permit students to perform single communication exchanges. Allow as much freedom as possible during those times, but make it clear to students that the goal is to speak in the language as much as possible; the atmosphere should become one of helping each other, and learning from their own attempts to speak the language. Then, when the topical unit begins, the students will know what is expected of them.

Have students help set up special areas of the classroom for specific purposes. A screen can divide a conversation corner from the rest of the room: cushions and a rug made of salesmen's samples pieced together can take the place of furniture. An activity corner for art, games, or music can be set apart from the rest of the room. Display areas can be discovered in places that are not normally used such as dividers, hallways, and cloak or storage rooms. An area should also be set aside for collecting materials and organizing them as they become available.

If you know someone in the country where the language you teach is spoken, perhaps he or she might send you free or inexpensive materials such as advertisements, brochures, seed catalogs, mail-order catalogs, and magazines. If you have enough time for planning, these materials can be sent by regular mail, using low book rates.

The administrative and teaching staffs should be informed as far as possible in advance of the unit so that they will be prepared for your new classroom organization. Involving the principal and other teachers in your planning, and possibly working with another teacher to make the topical unit interdisciplinary, can pay good dividends to your students.

SUMMARY

Careful thought must accompany the planning of unit teaching: goals and objectives must be determined; interests and needs of students must be assessed; culminating goals and intermediate competencies must be set; and shorter-term objectives must be based on interactions. Together, the teacher and the class can prepare culminating activities, collect relevant materials, plan classroom organization, and appraise student progress.

Teachers should pre-assess where each student is so that progression of individual learning can go from known to unknown. We need to produce materials for topical use that are highly motivating, and to collect materials from the culture that provide students with the information they need. We need to involve students more in planning instruction and materials preparation and use. We need teachers who can understand and use criterion-referenced procedures instead of norm-referenced testing and grading. We need teachers with counseling and guidance skills to direct individual learning. And we need to explore ways to use existing technology to meet individual student needs.

The problems and changes involved in such an approach are multiple, but careful use of objectives for restructuring second language learning should be well worth the time and effort.

BIBLIOGRAPHY

(1) Altman, Howard B., and Robert L. Politzer. *Individualized Foreign Language Instruction*. Rowley, MA: Newbury House, 1971.

(2) Ausubel, David P. *Educational Psychology: A Cognitive View*. New York: Holt, Rinehart, and Winston, 1968.

(3) Banathy, Bela H., and Dale L. Lange. *A Design for Foreign Language Curriculum*. Lexington, MA: D.C. Heath, 1972.

(4) Bloom, Benjamin S., ed. *Taxonomy of Educational Objectives: The Classification of Educational Goals: Handbook I: Cognitive Domain*. New York: David McKay, 1956.

(5) Born, Warren C., ed. *Goals Clarification: Curriculum, Teaching, Evaluation*. Middlebury, VT: Northeast Conference on the Teaching of Foreign Languages, 1975.

(6) Carroll, John B. "A Model of School Learning," *Teachers College Record* 64 (1963): 723-33.

(7) _____. "Learning Theory for the Classroom Teacher." In *The Challenge of Communication*, edited by Gilbert A. Jarvis, pp. 113-49. ACTFL Review of Foreign Language Education, vol. 6. Skokie, IL: National Textbook, 1974.

(8) Combs, Arthur W. "Educational Accountability from a Humanistic Perspective." *Review of Educational Research* 42, ix (1973): 19-21.

(9) Day, James F. "Behavioral Technology: A Negative Stand." *Intellect* (1974): 304-306.

(10) Duchastel, Philippe C., and Paul F. Merrill. "The Effects of Behavioral Objectives on Learning: A Review of Empirical Studies." *Review of Educational Research* 43, i (1973): 53-69.

(11) Gagné, Robert M. "Behavioral Objectives? Yes!" *Educational Leadership* (1973): 394-96.

(12) Grittner, Frank M. "Individualized Instruction: An Historical Perspective." *The Modern Language Journal* 59 (1975): 323-33.

(13) _____, and Fred LaLeike. *Individual Foreign Language Instruction.* Skokie, IL: National Textbook, 1973.

(14) Gronlund, Norman E. *Stating Behavioral Objectives for Classroom Instruction.* New York: Macmillan, 1970.

(15) Harrow, Anita J. *A Taxonomy of the Psychomotor Domain: A Guide for Developing Behavioral Objectives.* New York: David McKay, 1972.

(16) Hayhurst, Hazel. "Children's Use of Categorization in Remembering Verbal Material." In *Applications of Linguistics,* edited by G.E. Perrin and J.L.M. Trim, pp. 279-86. Cambridge: Cambridge University Press, 1971.

(17) Jakobovits, Leon A., and Barbara Gordon. *The Context of Foreign Language Teaching.* Rowley, MA: Newbury House, 1974.

(18) Kibler, Robert J.; Cegala, Donald J.; Barker, Larry L. and Miles, David T. *Objectives for Instruction and Evaluation.* Boston: Allyn and Bacon, 1974.

(19) Kneller, George F. "Behavioral Objectives? No!" *Educational Leadership* (1972): 397-400.

(20) Kratwohl, David R.; Bloom, Benjamin S.; and Masia, Bertram B. *Taxonomy of Educational Objectives: The Classification of Educational Goals: Handbook II: Affective Domain.* New York: David McKay, 1964.

(21) Logan, Gerald. "Curricula for Individualized Instruction." In *Britannica Review of Foreign Language Education,* Vol. 2, edited by Dale L. Lange, pp. 133-55. Chicago: Encyclopaedia Britannica, 1970.

(22) _____. *Individualized Foreign Language Learning: An Organic Process.* Rowley, MA: Newbury House, 1973.

(23) Love, F. William D., and Honig, Lucille J. *Options and Perspectives.* New York: Modern Language Association, 1973.

(24) Mager, Robert F. *Preparing Instructional Objectives.* Palo Alto: CA: Fearon, 1962.

(25) McAshen, H.H. *The Goals Approach to Performance Objectives.* Philadelphia: W.B. Saunders, 1974.

(26) Popham, W. James. "Probing the Validity of Arguments Against Behavioral Goals." In *Objectives for Instruction and Evaluation,* edited by Robert J. Kibler, Donald J. Cegala, Larry L. Barker, and David T. Miles, pp. 9-17. Boston: Allyn and Bacon, 1974.

(27) _____. *The Uses of Instructional Objectives: A Personal Perspective.* Belmont, CA: Fearon, 1973.

(28) Rivers, Wilga. *A Practical Guide to the Teaching of French.* New York: Oxford University Press, 1975.

(29) _____. *Speaking in Many Tongues: Essays in Language Teaching.* Rowley, MA: Newbury House, 1972.

(30) Stevick, Earl W. *Memory, Meaning, and Method: Some Psychological Perspectives on Language Learning.* Rowley, MA: Newbury House, 1976.

(31) Valdman, Albert. "On the Specification of Performance Objectives in Individualized Foreign Language Instruction." *The Modern Language Journal* 59 (1975): 323-33.

(32) Valette, Rebecca J., and Renée S. Disick. *Modern Language Performance Objectives and Individualization: A Handbook.* New York: Harcourt Brace Jovanovich, 1972.

Chapter Four
Individualization of
Foreign Language Learning
Madeline Hunter
Margaret Brown

INTRODUCTION

Individualized learning has become the "Holy Grail" sought by twentieth-century educational crusaders as they ride their white curriculum chargers in dedicated quest, carrying banners of one program after another. Among these crusaders, those whose background is foreign language should be best equipped to avoid the current battleground of "teaching vs. learning." Linguistic sophistication points up "teach" as a proactive verb meaning "to cause to know or be able to"; "learn" is a reactive verb meaning that the organism "has acquired knowledge or come to be able to." The teaching-learning process implies that something has happened which caused (teaching) the learner to know or be able to (learning). Although an event—a TV documentary, a book, a lecture, a teacher's presentation—can be absolutely identical for any number of learners, the skill or what has come to be known will be different for each learner. From this point of view, "individualized learning" is a redundancy because there is no way to avoid individualized learning even if it were desirable. Consequently, the focus of this chapter is on what is being done to increase the probability of learning. That can range from the same-for-all assembly line techniques to a highly individualized program that is custom tailored for each student in order to contribute to his maximum learning. Because "what is done" can come from teachers, media, or the student himself, the term "instruction" rather than "teaching" is used to denote anything that is deliberately used or done to promote learning. It is in this area of instruction that giant strides have been made in the last decade; the teaching profession now has the knowledge to escalate a student's learning substantially.

A second danger in the crusade against assembly line instruction lurks in the word "individualized," which has become the inseparable modifier of the word "instruction" in elite educational society; too frequently individualized *instruction* is confused with individual *activity*. This confusion is understandable given our current, and long overdue, focus on the worth and dignity of the individual and his right to have instruction tailored to his needs, his right to make decisions that will affect his learning environment instead of only being affected by it, and his right to develop his own instructional decisions, pursue his own interests, and work at his own pace. As a result of this focus on the individual, the major concept of instruction can be overlooked or even ignored; potentially effective programs are diverted into individualized activities, which can range from each student "doing his own thing" to an arsenal of hardware and software with each student dutifully plugged into his assigned socket. This is not to say that in an effective program students don't "do their own thing" or don't use media and materials, but these are not the hallmarks of individualized instruction.

Teachers of foreign languages with their linguistic sophistication should, more than others, be able to avoid the distractor of "individualized" implying "by one's self" or "one to one." It might help to use the somewhat startling analogy of individualized pleasure or punishment: The ultimate in pleasure for one person might be a large noisy social gathering, and some people prefer one situation at one time and the opposite situation at another; in like manner, individualized punishment, rather than implying solitary confinement, is based on the situation that is distasteful to that particular person at a certain moment in time.

It is important that this concept of "individualized," meaning custom tailored to a particular student rather than "by one's self" or "different from others," be applied to designing individualized instruction. Students who are working by themselves, or who are in a one-to-one tutorial situation with a teacher, or who are using media *may* or *may not* be involved in individualized instruction. Students working either with or without a teacher in small groups or large groups *may* or *may not* be involved in individualized instruction.

Environments in themselves cannot be classified as individualized or not-individualized instructional settings. There is no way one can take a picture of a class and determine how individualized it is by visual data. The critical discriminators of individualized instruction are that the learning environment and whatever is happening in it are custom tailored for each student; conscious and deliberate professional decisions have been made to increase the probability of efficient and effective student learning as well as the development of productive feelings about "self" as a learner.

Because of the lack of discrimination between individualized instruction and individual activity, many teachers believe that individualized instruction requires an arsenal of special machines and materials, a high ratio of adults to students so assistance and checking is immediately available, and independent learners who have the ability to take responsibility for their own learning contracts. Although good materials, fine teachers, and responsible learners are desirable in any instructional setting, individualized instruction can be realized with whatever materials are available, with the student teacher ratio that exists, and with responsible and irresponsible learners—provided the teacher has developed the professional competence to diagnose and prescribe in the three areas which can change assembly line teaching to individualized or custom-tailored instruction. Without that professional competence, no teacher—no matter how many materials are available or how many responsible students are in the class—can achieve a high degree of effective individualization.

THE CRITICAL ATTRIBUTES OF INDIVIDUALIZED INSTRUCTION

Individualized instruction is not the label for a discrete state of reality, but is best represented by a continuum with assembly line instruction at one extreme and custom-tailored instruction at the other. The degree of adjustment of three critical attributes in relation to each learner determines the point of individualization on this continuum for any student, classroom, or program. The critical attributes which must be taken into account and adjusted in individualized instruction can be put into the following questions: 1) What is the task to be learned? 2) What are the factors within each learner which interact with his environment to influence his learning behavior? And 3) How does the *teacher's* conscious and purposeful use of the principles of learning, in combination with "use of self as instrument," promote learning?

Most so-called individualized instruction is focused on the learning task, but pays far too little attention to the individualization of what the student is doing to achieve that learning in an environment tailored to increase the probability of that achievement. In addition, there often is painful—not blissful—unawareness of the criticality of the pedagogical decisions, and proactive—not reactive— behaviors of the teacher in relation to each student. These pedagogical decisions and the resultant teacher behaviors constitute the new frontier in effective individualization.

Although there is a complex interdigitation of these three critical attributes of task, learner behavior and teacher behavior in every learning situation, it is useful to examine each attribute separately. In this way, sensitivity can be developed to the extensive possibilities for individualizing so that these attributes can contribute to maximum learning and an increase of positive feelings about self-as-learner.

The Learning Task

The learning task, or what is to be learned, has two dimensions. One dimension extends from easy to difficult content, and proceeds in increments with each more difficult learning supported and being made possible by the achievement of simpler learnings. Learning occurs in two types of incremental sequences: One is in a dependent sequence where the accomplishment of each new learning is dependent on other supporting or component learnings having been mastered; the other is an independent sequence of learning where it matters not which of a cluster of several learnings is mastered first, and, while learnings are related, they do not support each other in a linear fashion, nor is one necessary to another's achievement.

There is no agreement as to whether a true dependent sequence exists in second language learning. Clearly in math, one cannot count with comprehension from 10 to 20 if one has not already learned to count from 1 to 10. In like manner, one cannot deal with the concept of multiplication without having mastered the concept of addition. Each more difficult skill is dependent on having achieved the easier one.

The dependent sequence of first language learning would imply that until a child could, with meaning, deal with words, he could not comprehend the decoding or encoding of a sentence; and the latter skill must be accomplished before he can productively decode or encode paragraphs.

In second language learning, it is assumed that some first language linguistic learning blocks are already in place to support whatever concept or linguistic element is being learned in the second language. Second language learning rests on clusters of organized learnings, including the different patterns of sound or structure, plus linguistic skills that were originally learned as a dependent sequence in the first language, but which now are transferable to the target language.

As an example, in first language learning, understanding of the future tense is possible only when the concept of the present has been achieved. In second language learning, the concepts of past, present and future have been mastered, and one tense should be no more difficult than the others. It may appear logical to begin second language learning with the present tense, mastering all forms for all persons, plus some of the irregular forms, before proceeding to the other tenses. However, the contrast between the present, past and future forms of one person could be presented just as well, beginning, for example, with first person. Or, because we tend to speak more of events in the past, why not start with those forms?

Even in reputedly difficult areas, the main clusters of supporting learnings have already been achieved in the first language. For example, one of the more difficult distinctions for Americans who are learning Spanish as a second language is the contrast between the two forms of the past tense, the preterit and the imperfect. It really doesn't matter which is presented first, the morphology of one or both forms or the discriminators in reality that cue the choice between the two. The critical factor is that the teacher must know which clusters of learnings support the target learning, draw them from the learner's first language repertoire, and, if necessary, teach any missing supporting learnings that are essential to achievement of the objective in the second language.

In Spanish, the ability to communicate orally about an incident or a series of incidents in the past presupposes clusters of learnings which include mastery of the sound system, an adequate vocabulary, the morphology of the various kinds of verbs in both forms of the past tense, and the critical discriminators for choosing between the two.

Because there is no single sequence inherent in the nature or structure of a language, or even a best sequence for pedagogical purposes, the way in which content is sequenced is one of the variables available to accommodate diverse learners in individualizing instruction.

The dimension of incremental learning, which incorporates dependent and independent sequences, is a vertical dimension where simpler content proceeds to more difficult.

There also is a horizontal, "in-depth" dimension which exists at any point of the vertical dimension. The horizontal dimension encompasses responses which increase in cognitive complexity, affective internalization, psychomotor automation, or the synthesis of all three into an action pattern. Although the horizontal dimensions of cognitive, affective, and psychomotor responses do not exist in isolation, it is helpful to consider them separately, as each makes a unique contribution to the potential for individualizing instruction.

The cognitive domain presents the possibility of tailoring the degree of cognitive complexity of the foreign language task from the simple, but essential, task of recall and comprehension—the morphemes of a given tense of verbs—to the more complex cognitive skills of application, analysis, synthesis, and evaluation (3). In individualized instruction, the teacher and/or learner cannot only tailor the vertical dimension of difficulty of the task, but also the horizontal dimension of degree of complexity of thinking can be made appropriate to a particular learner. This individualization can occur even though the learner is working with a group of other learners who are dealing with the same content; simpler or more complex cognitive responses may be required of them.

Given an assortment of poems, tasks in increasing cognitive complexity might include the following: recite from memory the poem of your choice; explain the meaning of the poem; write or give an oral translation; convert a poem to prose; indicate how two poems are alike; compose a poem on the same subject or in the same style or form; evaluate two or more poems as to their poetic quality.

The horizontal dimension of the learner's affective responses—his interests, attitudes and appreciations—can be the focus of individualization, sometimes as the central objective, and at other times as an important by-product of a content objective. As described by Krathwohl (10) the degree of internalization in the affective domain ranges from simple receiving and responding, acting out orally described situations, to valuing; and that value is internalized into an organized system of values, which becomes characteristic of a particular learner.

In foreign language instruction, a student's attitude towards the language and culture are important learning outcomes, for the success of a program often is measured by the participant's desire to enroll in additional foreign language classes. Consequently, the possibilities presented by individualizing instruction in the affective domain are extremely powerful.

In the horizontal dimension of the psychomotor domain, which extends on a continuum from labored responses to cognitively directed automatic action patterns (14), the roots of bilingualism can be identified; translation no longer is a mediating step. Thinking and encoding of messages occurs directly in the target language for the bilingual. In the psychomotor domain, the labored responses of producing the phonemes of the target language gradually become automated to effortless generation of near native speech in a series of learned responses. These begin with a conscious mental set and a guided response, then progress to high speed automatic responses. Individualization of instruction in the psychomotor domain requires that the teacher be aware of the degree of internalization that is appropriate for each learner at a particular point in time so the student can proceed efficiently and effectively toward increased facility, fluency, and automation.

In summary, individualization of instruction implies that the learning task be custom tailored to the correct level of difficulty for each learner. This does not mean his task is necessarily different from the tasks of others or that he is working by himself.

Individualization does require, however, that the learning task be determined by what the student already knows; the next more difficult learning will then be identified by him and the teacher with conscious knowledge as to whether he is proceeding through a dependent or an independent sequence. Individualized instruction also takes into consideration the degree of complexity of thinking that is appropriate for a student at a particular point in time; this is not based on IQ or native ability but on what has already been learned. In addition, new accomplishments will be individualized in terms of a student's internalization of feelings that relate to the learning tasks, as well as to the degree of automation he has achieved with his responses.

These dimensions of degree of content difficulty on a vertical coordinate and cognitive complexity, and internalization of feelings and automation of responses on a horizontal coordinate provide a "map of individualization"; each learner's "latitude and longitude" can be plotted to identify his most productive position as the recipient of his own or the teacher's instruction. Focusing instruction on this point constitutes the first critical attribute of individualized instruction. If the learning task is not determined on the basis of the individual's current position, what he now knows and what he will learn next, all other efforts to individualize are "love's labor lost."

Factors Within the Learner and His Interaction With His Environment That Influence His Learning Behavior

The Learner's Input Systems

The human learner has many input systems which he uses singly and in combination in a learning situation. He prefers some of these input systems over others as a result of either genetic predisposition or the functional agility and comfort which is produced by practice. Some students learn best when they hear something before they see it in writing; for others, seeing and hearing at the same time make learning easier; and some need to see a nonverbal model before the oral or written verbalization is presented. The important concept in individualization is not which input system is best for a learner, but that the many available systems all should be used, both singly and in combination.

The reason for using all input systems rather than only the one which is preferred by the learner is that each is developed through practice, and the preferred modality already has had a great deal of use. Using other less-preferred or seldom-used modalities, singly or in combination, develops them so the learner is equipped with several effective input systems. Therefore, he can use many at will rather than using only one by default.

Recent brain research has revealed that, along with his sensory modalities, the learner uses each of his two cerebral hemispheres to process different kinds of data. The left hemisphere accommodates temporal input, where relationships and meaning are established across time. For example, the sentence just heard or read must be understood not only for itself, but in terms of what came before it and what is to come after it. This temporal processing is done in the propositional, or "left brain." The right cerebral hemisphere accommodates visual-spacial input, where relationships are perceived in space, as in the configuration of a word or a diagram, picture, map, or time line. This processing is done in the apositional, or "right brain."

Hemisphere differentiation begins in the very young child, and one cerebral input system may come to be preferred to the other. How much of the preference is the result of generic predisposition, and how much the result of facility which comes from practice has not been determined. The learner who prefers "left brain" input will find meaning and sentence construction easier, while the "right brained" student will learn the necessary vocabulary more quickly and with less effort. Obviously the goal is to help a student develop facility in both hemispheric input systems in order to become an integrated thinker with each brain strengthening and complementing the other. When a teacher is aware of "left" and "right brained" input systems, the temptation is to test the learner and use his preferred hemisphere. Individualization of instruction would mandate that hemispheric input systems be used separately and in concert, so both are strengthened through practice. However, both teacher and student should be aware that, when the less preferred input system is being used, more time and effort may be required for learning.

The Learning Environment

Each learner functions with different degrees of comfort, efficiency, and effectiveness in different learning environments. It is important to point out that, while comfort and effective learning are compatible and desirable objectives, they do not always go hand in hand. Being overly comfortable with a situation can free all the learner's psychic energy for the learning task, or can result in a euphoric state of equilibrium where no effort is put forth. Consequently, the environment in individualized instruction should contribute to the stimulation and acceleration of learning and should provide sufficient comfort and success so more is learned than in a different environment.

A few learners learn best by themselves; many seem to learn better with the high visibility and stimulation which results from a small group; others need the invisibility and invulnerability of a large group. Some learn better when they are working with a friend, while others are so distracted by their friends that a less familiar group of peers is indicated. Some are stimulated by a busy environment and can regulate their neural switchboards to exclude distractors; many who do not have this skill find that their neural circuitry jams from overload and they cannot function amidst potential distractors. The forms and movement of stimulating visual environment is a productive background for some learners, while others find it impossible to focus on a task until the visual or auditory "busyness" is reduced.

Individualization does not require an elaborate diagnosis of each student; rather, it requires a sensitivity to the factors in the environment which aid or distract the learner, and those factors should be designed and/or adjusted to optimize the probability of his learning.

The Emotional Climate

The emotional climate of the learning situation is the result of intra-learner feelings and actions which act upon, and are acted upon, by factors in the environment. This interaction is both proactive and reactive, resulting in a complex matrix of environmental press.

How a learner feels in a situation obviously affects the rate and degree of his learning. Fatigue, malnutrition, and physiological or neural dysfunction are excluded from this discussion, not because they are unimportant determiners, but because they are usually dependent upon out-of-school factors over which the teacher has little control. Consequently, one important objective of individualized instruction is to route around such interferences, or to design ways to minimize their impact on the student.

The intra-learner factors, over which the teacher of foreign language has more influence than has been previously acknowledged, are the in-school inhibitors and accelerators of learning. They are related to the learner's feelings about himself, his relationship to others, and the learning situation. These feelings are subject to modification. For example, a learner who finds foreign language difficult can experience more ease and success in learning as a result of appropriate instructional decisions; emotional verbal and non-verbal support, small learning steps, and prompts can contribute to a "this-is-easier-than-I-thought" attitude. Conversely, the student with a natural aptitude for language can be moved from complacency to diligence by a provocative and demanding task. Success and/or the lack of it can be metered out in terms of the individual's emotional needs, thereby generating feelings through prescribed experiences rather than through happenstance or a repetition of what the student is accustomed to experiencing.

The Learner's Output Systems

Just as a learner has preferred modalities for input, he has more comfort and facility with some of his output systems than he has with others. Again, this preference may result from generic predetermination or the facility that comes with practice. An independent learner must exercise all output systems, rather than "majoring" in the preferred one. However, both teacher and learner should have a different expectation for performance when a facile output system is being used than when a dormant one is being developed.

In foreign language, the verbal, oral or written, output system is the most obvious one, but others are available. For example, it is possible to test knowledge with no verbalization whatsoever by having the learner identify the correct response by listening or indicating. At times, a simple written response may be appropriate for those learners for whom the reproduction of sound or complex linguistic structure is difficult. Each learner, however, must have the practice necessary to develop both oral and written responses to the degree appropriate for him.

In summary, the complex interdigitation of all of the intra-learner factors should be stressed. They operate in concert, proactively and reactively, on learning, and on the environment in which that learning is occurring. Conscious and deliberate decisions by teacher and/or learner about the input and output systems utilized, as well as the emotional climate and the learning environment, can maximize productive interaction, and minimize interfering or destructive reaction. To ignore these decisions by intention or default is to lose a critically powerful possibility for individualizing instruction.

The Teacher's Use of Principles of Learning

Principles of learning are to education what powerful drugs are to medicine. Even though everything else is held constant, a learning situation can be made successful or unsuccessful by a teacher's use or abuse, consciously or inadvertently, of those principles which research has demonstrated can affect a student's learning. As with drugs, the degree of their effect will vary depending on a student's sensitivity to them and his particular state of being at the time. Although lethal for one student, negative feedback could be therapeutic for another. It is this difference in student response to the conditions created by using principles of learning that gives foreign language teachers a third powerful possibility for individualization or custom tailoring of instruction. The teacher should make deliberate decisions regarding the selection and use of principles of learning, thereby creating a learning climate that will elicit learner responses and increase achievement.

For convenience, learning principles have been grouped in four categories: the first concerns those which affect the motivation to learn; the second, those which affect the rate and degree of learning; the third, those which influence the retention of what has been learned; and the fourth, those which are related to the transfer of previous learning to current or future situations. These principles have been described in detail elsewhere (6, 7, 8, 9); therefore, no attempt will be made to include all of them in this discussion. One example in each category is cited as an example of the wide range of possibilities for individualization.

Motivation

One of six motivational variables that the teacher must take into account in individualizing instruction is the student's current level of concern about a learning task. If he responds productively and with increased effort to a higher degree of stress, the teacher should deliberately raise the level of his concern by increasing the difficulty of the task or expectations for accuracy and/or speed. If, at that point in time, the teacher judges that the student's learning would increase with a reduction in his concern about the learning task or situation, the teacher should deliberately lower the level of difficulty of the task, possibly moving to an easier example, reviewing previously learned material, or assisting with enough prompts to ensure success. The teacher also may use reassurance to lower expectations for speed and/or accuracy of performance—"Don't worry if you don't get it; everybody has trouble with this."

Rate and Degree of Learning

Meaning is one of many factors that affects the rate and degree of learning. It is one of the most powerful propellents of learning, but content that holds high interest and relevance for one student may not be nearly so meaningful for another. When learning tasks are assigned and responses are elicited, the student's interests and background of experience should be taken into account. For example, even in a simple substitution drill designed to practice "I like_____ ," the teacher can give different cues to learners in a group: clothes may appeal to one girl; food, to another; sports, to one boy; cars, to another. A teacher's deliberate use of what is interesting and most relevant, not only to the group but to each individual in the group, should be a consciously made professional decision that becomes an effective element in the custom tailoring of instruction.

Retention

The amount and nature of practice is one of the five important factors under the control of the teacher that promote retention of learning. Although the principle of massing practice at initial stages of learning results in rapid learning for some students, distributing practice produces durable learning for all students. John may only need to hear a response once, have two opportunities to make that response, and be given a chance to review the response before the period is over to ensure his successful recall the next day. Bill, however, may need to hear a response many times after it is introduced because his only obligation is to participate in choral response. After hearing that response modeled several times, he will be required to repeat it. Only at the end of the week can he be expected to generate that response without a model; and he will still need several practice opportunities the following week before the learning becomes a durable element in his response repertoire.

Using the same principles to promote retention, the teacher consciously increases the practice intervals for one student, while tailoring the practice schedule for another so the ratio of elapsed time to review grows in smaller increments.

Transfer

Instruction in foreign language too often has resulted in an outstanding demonstration of learning in one situation failing to transfer to a new situation when it was appropriate. Although a contrastive analysis of the native and target language has gone a long way toward providing data that contributes to positive transfer and eliminates negative transfer, much can be accomplished by a teacher who is sophisticated in the use of principles that affect transfer. Individualizing instruction should result in maximizing positive transfer and minimizing, or eliminating, negative transfer.

"What does this particular student know, or what has he already experienced that incorporates the same critical element as the current learning situation?" Consideration of this question enables the teacher to anticipate accelerators or inhibitors to learning. The student can then be assisted in "bringing forward" or "cutting off" the old learning, thus productively affecting the present learning.

In summary, although certain principles of learning apply to all students, the deliberate, sophisticated, and differentiated use of principles in individualization can result in a substantial increase in motivation to learn, the rate and degree of learning, the retention of that learning, and the productive transfer of old learning to new learning or performance behaviors. In the past, teacher education programs did not equip teachers with the ability to use principles of learning because the principles themselves were stated in the foreign language of psychological jargon. Now that they have been translated into "classroom language," they can be understood and practiced by any teacher.

STUDENT CONTROL OF DECISIONS
IN INDIVIDUALIZED INSTRUCTION

All learning activities are directed toward developing self-direction and self-propulsion that can be transferred into all future learning endeavors. Although students should participate more fully in making decisions about their learning than they have been allowed to do in the past, it is equally important to focus on the fact that even champions take lessons. Increased learning dividends are realized as a result of expert teaching. Student control of learning decisions is a skill that needs to be developed, but that skill is not in itself the primary hallmark of a successful learning program.

The degree of a student's control over his learning is related to his current position on a continuum which stretches from complete dependence on outside forces to appropriate and productive independence. His degree of control is also based on whether or not he possesses the information which is relevant to the current learning decision. Information related to his degree of fatigue and information related to the next more difficult learning task come from very different sources, one of which is available to the student and one of which may not be.

Instructional decisions are interrelated. For clarity in examining them, however, the decisions over which a learner might exert control are grouped under content related to purpose, methodology related to input and output systems, learning environment, and criteria of achievement.

Content Related to Purpose

A learner's purpose in studying a foreign language should affect the content. Clearly, the purpose and commitment of the language major are different from the purpose and commitment of a missionary preparing to proselytize in a foreign country. A student might want to learn a foreign language to read or speak the language, to prepare for a trip to a country where the language is spoken, or to meet an academic requirement which is non-foreign-language related. However, a beginning pre-collegiate student of foreign language may not have established any purpose at all, he may simply want to "do it" because others have been satisfied with their experiences, or because his parents and society attribute value to speaking a foreign language. Even elementary school youngsters can be helped to be self-reflective and to clarify their motivations by completing the statement: Learning foreign language is important to me because _____ . The ideas expressed by one group ranged from the instrumental—"It gives me a head start on junior high." "I may want to be an interpreter in the United Nations." "Along with my other skills, it may help me get a better position." "It helps me understand English better."—to reasons related to self-concept—"It makes me a better person." "It broadens my knowledge."—to reasons involving the desire to identify with others—"I enjoy teaching what I know to someone else." "I can be more helpful to foreigners who visit here." "I can interpret for people who only speak one language." "I can know more people and what they are thinking and how they are thinking." "Knowing languages brings people of different cultures together and makes better understanding of each other possible."—to the most intrinsic motivation of all—"It is satisfying to learn it for its own sake."

In individualization, it is appropriate to discuss orally or solicit in written form the answers to such questions as: What would you like to be able to talk about? Which of these stories shall we dramatize? Would you like a dialogue about an incident at school or at the beach? Would you prefer learning about the foods of the _____ speaking world or the places where _____ is spoken? Shall we talk about events in the past, the present, or the future? Which of these poems do you prefer to learn? Similar questions also can be asked at any point in the instructional sequence. The resourceful teacher incorporates these suggestions in presenting the underlying concepts and dependent sequences of phonology, morphology, syntax, and culture.

Note, however, the difference between these questions and the question, "What would you like to learn?" Once the content which reflects his purpose has been determined, the student's decisions can direct only independent sequences of content. It can be appropriate for the learner to select the target learning, but it is a waste of time and energy when that target is not attainable because unidentified supporting learnings are lacking.

Consequently, knowing whether a sequence of learning is dependent or independent is critical to a learner's decision-making in individualized instruction. As decisions related to the learning task are considered, it is not possible for a learner to make the decision concerning "what next" in a dependent sequence. The basis of that decision rests in a task analysis that reveals which simpler learnings support more complex learnings; and, therefore, those supporting learnings must be accomplished first. The only task decision the learner can make in a dependent sequence is to decide when he has mastered a learning and is ready to proceed to the next more difficult learning. This "when-to-proceed" decision is one of the most important decisions to be made by learner and/or teacher in individualized instruction. It is based on a diametrically different question than that of "assembly line" instruction. The latter asks, "Has it been done?" Individualized instruction asks, "Has it been learned?"

In an independent sequence of learning, the tasks may be accomplished in any order in terms of the learner's interest, ability to focus, fatigue, or comfort with the new learning. Often the learner's data are infinitely more relevant than those of a teacher or text book writer.

Students should also have the opportunity to make decisions related to the degree of cognitive complexity for any given content. Using the same body of content, and with the guidance of the teacher, the learner can choose the level that is appropriate for him. Suppose the content is verb morphology. After initial presentation, the choices might be to remain with the teacher for further input, to match two sets of cards with subjects printed on one set and the various forms of a single verb on the other, to write the forms of the tense being studied using previously unknown verbs, to write sentences using any subject and any known verb, to rewrite a paragraph changing the tense to the one being studied, or to compose a brief original narrative.

Methodology Related to a Learner's Input and Output Systems

Students can learn the difference between what is to be practiced—content—and how it is to be practiced—method. In individualized instruction, it is critical that a learner identify, as early as possible, the input and output systems that work best for him. Whether he learns more rapidly if he hears a word before he sees it in writing, whether he should see and hear it simultaneously, or whether he needs to write it is a teacher-learner decision which should evoke maximum learner responsibility as soon as possible. Paralleling that input decision should be a decision regarding the output behavior of the learning which demonstrates his active participation in the learning process and his learning achievement. He and the teacher should focus on the quality of his covert participation to determine the degree of his motivation. A highly motivated student may only need to rehearse a lesson subvocally; others may be required to say it aloud, or to write it.

Any aural discrimination, so important in language learning, is a covert response; that is, it takes place within the learner and cannot be directly observed. However, students may be asked to exhibit an observable behavior to indicate that the covert response has occurred: While I read this paragraph, raise your hand each time you hear a ____ (insert the particular sound being studied). As I say each three syllable word, indicate which syllable is stressed by raising one, two, or three fingers. On the tape you will hear a question and three answers. Write a, b, or c to indicate the best answer.

At intervals diagnostic questions should be asked: What do you like best about ____ class? What do you like least? Are you called on too much, too little, or about often enough? Which activities are easy or hard for you? What do we do too much of, and what not enough? Do you learn best by hearing, seeing, touching, or acting, or by a combination of these? Such questions increase self-awareness on the part of the learner, in addition to giving important feedback to the teacher.

Students who are confident that their teacher values their contributions and suggestions will feel free to offer them. The teacher may prefer to receive such suggestions outside of class time so as not to have extemporaneous responses result in inefficient use of pre-planned time.

Language learning methodology, research, and experience equip the teacher with information not possessed by the learner. The learner's decision-making power should focus on knowing when he is "not getting it"; and he should alert himself and signal the teacher that remediation or review is necessary at that point, instead of proceeding until he founders.

Learning Environment

Knowledge of the environment that promotes his best effort and maximum learning is critical to a student's effective control of learning decisions. He should be aware of the degree of stimulation that distracts him or promotes his best effort. With this knowledge, he can begin to assume responsibility for designing or adjusting his environment to meet his learning needs. Language labs can usurp his decision rights when the assumption is made that "plugging in" is right, or wrong, for all students learning a foreign language. Students should be encouraged, and eventually required, to be accountable for the learning results of their environmental decisions.

Students can exert direct control over their participation and learning in the group situation when an activity is set up that allows voluntary participation. An able, confident learner can be the first, or among the first, to offer a contribution, thus providing a model for the less able, who may then feel confident enough to perform. At times, a group of identified performers may be set up; here, responding to the built-in pressure that all will participate, each member usually takes a turn when he feels ready.

Criteria of Achievement

When has a student learned? This is a question that must be answered by the teacher and the particular student, with increasing right and responsibility for the answer being accorded to the student. The orientation of language programs is rapidly changing from "doing it" to "learning it," but that discrimination is not always clear to the student and teacher who are accustomed to "finishing" being the criterion of learning accomplishment.

The teacher and the learner have to determine what level of performance behavior constitutes appropriate mastery of the learning task. It then becomes the responsibility of the student to sensitize himself to the allowable deviation in that performance behavior that determines the critical area of his possession and retention of that learning. For some students, getting it almost right, and understanding what was wrong is all that is necessary. Others find it necessary to repeat the material until a perfect performance is achieved, or even several perfect performances. If a student is to exert productive control over his learning decisions, he must know the appropriate requirement for himself.

Evidence of Student Decision Making

In many cases, an individualized learning environment may not look dramatically different from the traditional classroom because the critical attributes of individualization are not visual.

In the early stages of foreign language learning, the dimensions of individualization should be exploited fully in the group setting, using the stimulation, protection, and pressure of the group environment to foster learning. Beginning students are almost invariably ready to participate in whatever activities the teacher has planned. Given a teacher skilled in attending to individual differences, the honeymoon of "impetus," enthusiasm, feeling of accomplishment, and success will last quite a while.

At first glance, an individualized, teacher-directed, student-centered classroom does not necessarily look different from an "assembly line" classroom. There is one teacher and the students, who may be seated conventionally or informally. The students are responding to the teacher and to each other, in chorus and individually; and, as the class period progresses they are engaged in a lively succession of different activities using all modalities. Audio-visual materials probably are in evidence. A sophisticated observer soon realizes, however, that this is no "assembly line." The differences may be subtle, but they are very real. The teacher custom tailors the tasks for individual learners by raising and lowering the level of difficulty or complexity, by varying the amount of support, by changing the topic of conversation; in short, all of the variables that affect the probability of each student's learning are manipulated.

Ideally, each learning activity is planned so that differentiation will occur. The following is a detailed, specific example of a multi-level activity:

The teacher has prepared a list of words for dictation and has ordered them to increase in difficulty. The first words have a one to one sound-symbol correspondence; then come those for which a spelling rule must be applied; the list progresses to those that must have been seen to be spelled correctly; and, finally, those words that can be spelled only if the meaning is known are given. Another dimension of difficulty can be varied in the same activity. Some learners might write only the beginning letter of each word; others, only the vowels; others, only the consonants; others, the whole word; and others, the whole word plus an indication of which syllable is stressed. In rare cases, an extremely able student might have time to add a word that might modify or logically follow the word, or he might be able to write a simple sentence containing the dictated word. Thus the teacher says each word only once to the whole class, and each student selects or follows the teacher's suggestion on his own level.

If the dictation is a practice exercise, the teacher, or an able student, writes the correct responses on the chalkboard so that all can see the results immediately. Only when it is a testing exercise are papers collected and checked by the teacher. A student may stop at any point in the sequence. However, instead of idling his intellectual motor, he selects a neighbor to watch, and continues with observational learning.

How does a classroom situation look when students are making their own learning decisions? Certainly it is not chaotic. Decision making must be individualized for all students, teachers, and situations. An occasional "your own choice" day for a group that is basically teacher-directed because of its level or learning needs can afford much pleasure and profit to the participants, and additional insights to the observing teacher. On the. day, all resources of the foreign language classroom are available, and the students make all decisions about peer group composition, content, practice, and change of activity. On one such occasion, the students pursued the following activities: three engaged in a game of Scrabble; two read the script of a play; one listened to records and followed the printed words of the songs; four danced to records; five jumped rope to accompanying rhymes; one wrote a word ladder, using the final letter of a preceding word as the beginning letter of the next; three played Hangman; three played Twister, with four observers; one studied a book brought from home, and subsequently recited accurately the generalizations of stress and accentuation; two read proverbs to each other then repeated them from memory; two practiced numbers, months, days, and the alphabet, while tossing a fleece ball back and forth; three read rhymes and stories; one read magazine articles in English about the target culture; two engaged in a very active game that involves trying to see and name the color pinned to the other's back; one found 97 smaller words, including *calamares*, in *latinoamericanos*; two checked each other on the memorization of several poems; and two practiced verb morphology by taking turns giving a subject and completing a sentence. A teacher-directed group can certainly be learner-centered.

As students mature in decision-making and acquire language skills, there can be increasing diversification and student control of content, goals, methodology, and learning environment. The continuum that begins with teacher-directed group work has independent study at the other end.

Even in the earliest stages of foreign language learning, a youngster can engage in independent study. A simple project of special interest can be shared with the group, or just with the teacher.

In summary, a student's control over learning decisions is a goal to be achieved for his future learning effectiveness. He must learn to make some decisions; others he cannot make because he does not possess the critical information. Decision-making is incremental and must be learned in the areas of content related to each student's purpose, his most productive input and output systems as they relate to methodology, his learning environment, and his determination of appropriate criterion achievement.

In an individualized program, some decisions will be made by the student and some by the teacher, but most decisions will reflect the interaction which utilizes information from both.

FIXED AND VARIABLE ASPECTS OF INDIVIDUALIZED INSTRUCTION

In planning for instruction, there are always certain constant or fixed elements that cannot be changed. The teacher must take these constants into account and organize the variables to accommodate both types of elements, thereby making maximum learning gains more probable.

This chapter has described the variable elements of individualized instruction in detail. However, it is critical that the constants or fixed elements of the target language, as well as the invariant principles of human learning, not be overlooked in the pilgrimage to individualization.

Linguistics is one of many disciplines that contributes some constants to foreign language education. The prime function of the linguistic sciences is to provide accurate data about all features of a language, phonological, morphological, syntactical, and semantical, as well as dialect variations. The linguistic generalizations most useful to the teacher are those that are precise, concise, and as all-encompassing as possible. A generalization that admits many exceptions and counter-examples is not useful except in advanced study.

Unfortunately, inadequacies of language description tend to persist in textbooks and other instructional materials, as well as in the minds of teachers. Too often, teachers teach as they were trained rather than avail themselves of the results of more recent scholarship, a phenomenon described by Bull and Lamadrid (4).

Just as accurate linguistic information is needed, so are accurate cultural data that go beyond trivial superficiality to attitudes, value systems, perceptions of reality, modes of thinking, and other important aspects of a culture. Nostrand (11) has long been on the cutting edge of this area of inquiry. His extensive bibliography opens many avenues for thought and investigation.

Facts can be manipulated through interpretation, emphasis, or omission to support whatever view one takes of the interrelatedness of language and culture, or the importance of one over the other. They can be ordered and sequenced to modify a program of instruction. However, the facts themselves are not subject to acceptance, modification, or control by manipulation.

On the basis of the "facts" of language, realistic and appropriate objectives must be formulated for specific learners, and learning opportunities must be created that will lead to the achievement of these objectives. Quinn (*13*) reviews the history of the unrealistic expectations of theoretical linguistics as a basis for methodological decisions.

Any curriculum in foreign language should be based on the totality of a language. The linguistic sciences supply essential fixed data about the language; and such disciplines as anthropology, social psychology, and sociology supply the cultural data.

CHARACTERISTICS OF AN INDIVIDUALIZED PROGRAM

Although the three critical attributes relating to task, learner, and teacher are the primary criteria of individualization, extensiveness, flexibility of methodology and scheduling, content, materials, and planning are complementary properties of such a program.

Extensiveness

The total curriculum of an entire district might be individualized. Or individualization could be limited to a single school, foreign language department within that school, or to one language within that department. It can also be put into effect by a committed and sophisticated teacher working alone in one classroom.

Flexibility of Methodology and Scheduling

At any point in the sequence of learning, alternatives can be made available for student choice. The content of a basic course can be offered using different methodologies—direct, audio-lingual, multi-skill, or eclectic. Differing rates of presentation may be offered—regular, intensive, acclerated, slower, or self-paced. Skill emphasis may vary—reading, translation, conversation, language concepts. Choice of scheduling may be offered—regular, modular, demand, cycles, mini-courses, independent study. Content itself may be focused differentially—basic, career preparation, or interdisciplinary. Students might also choose among alternatives in class organization and media—teacher-directed, laboratory practice, computer assisted, cassette recordings, small and large groups, contracts, individual conferences, programmed material, or any combination of these. Availability of resources of space, equipment, and personnel only partially dictate the limits of the alternatives offered. The real limits lie in the teacher's ability to think imaginatively in response to students' individual needs and interests.

Content

A strong case can be made for the establishment of a national common core of content that would minimize the problems of placement and articulation in our mobile population. The notion is not incongruent with some of the tenets of individualized learning, individualized pacing and accommodating learner variables, for example. A common core would probably be best used as the basis of a curriculum for the really serious language student.

Materials

It is theoretically possible to create an individualized foreign language program without using a textbook or any pre-packaged instructional materials. The teacher of such a program must have superb professional capabilities, a thorough knowledge of the target language and culture, an adequate background in linguistics, expertise in using scientific principles that facilitate human learning, experience in successful educational decision-making, and endless resourcefulness, creativity, and energy. Obviously, paragons are in short supply, and may be non-existent. Consequently, in most situations, other solutions must be sought.

A wealth of materials already exists. A walk-through of the publishers' exhibits at a recent, modest-sized regional conference yielded five pounds of catalogs. The task is to discriminate among this tremendous stockpile of texts, readers, tapes, moving and static visuals, workbooks, programmed materials, and learning activity packets. How many are appropriate for the objectives the teacher and/or learner have determined?

Criteria for evaluation of instructional materials are available. The Curriculum Inquiry Center at the University of California in Los Angeles has no less than 13 sets that are intended as a guide to production, as well as selection, of materials. One set of criteria groups recommendations under seven headings: Rationale, Specifications, Appropriateness, Effectiveness, Conditions, Practicality, and Dissemination (15). A few of the 29 recommendations that are particularly pertinent to individualized instruction are:

The technical manual should state in detail the objectives.
The kind of student for whom the materials are designed should be specified.
Materials should be evaluated in relation to different types of students, e.g.,
    intellectual level, sex, age, and socioeconomic level.
Procedures and arrangements for utilizing the materials for defined samples of

students—including procedures for administering the evaluation devices—
must be specified.

One looks in vain through most of the catalogs and at most of the materials for
this kind of information.

Fortunate indeed is the teacher with expertise who finds everything that is
needed to facilitate the attainment of individualized goals in a single commercially produced, multicomponent "package." The various components of such a
package would provide for flexibility in the pacing, in the size of learning steps,
and in the practice schedules. All input and output modalities would be
exercised. Different cognitive styles would be accommodated, inductive versus
deductive, concrete to abstract or the reverse. Some components of the
"package" would be designed for independent study with feedback; others, for
learning guided more directly by the teacher. A variety of moving and static
visuals, plus tapes and discs, would be offered. Evaluation instruments to ensure
a degree of mastery before moving on would be included.

Planning

An important factor in an individualized program is that planning *starts* with the
end goals and objectives and *proceeds* to the means, rather than the reverse.

Benefits are reaped from individualization when an assessment of available or
procurable resources is included in the planning; included in this should be staff
characteristics, space, texts, and materials, as well as the characteristics of the
student population. On the basis of a realistic survey, plans can be formulated
that are feasible to render individualized instruction operational in gradual stages
or all at once. The feasibility of what one intends to do in individualization is a
critical criterion of the success of any program.

When embarking on a new venture, it is useful to know what others have
done. Phillips describes many different situations where individualization is in
full or partial implementation at various levels, some programs having evolved
through several stages (*12*). The publications of professional associations are a
rich source, especially *Foreign Language Annals*, including the *ACTFL Bibliography* and Volumes 2 through 5 of the *ACTFL Review of Foreign Language
Education*. Personal observation of existing programs is often possible and
desirable, providing the substance of the critical attributes of individualization—
not just the form of materials and procedures—is perceived. Handbooks have
been written (*1, 2, 5, 16*), and a great deal is available in ERIC. All of these
sources provide guidelines to help teachers think through their situation in
advance in order to identify possible constraints and to avoid some pitfalls.
Pre-conference, weekend, and summer workshops are available for those ready
to implement individualized instruction.

EVALUATION

The primary purpose of evaluation is to provide information that will guide decisions. Consequently, central to any evaluation activity is the identification of the decision to be made. Educational decisions can vary from en route instructional decisions, such as what the student should learn next or whether the pacing should be accelerated, to organizational decisions, such as questioning whether method A was more successful than method B or whether a class should be given again next year.

Summative Evaluation

To answer the organizational questions, the evaluative data brought to decisions must be summative: these data give the total result of all the things that have happened in a program; they certify that program so that, if it is repeated, the same basic results can be predicted. The data can be normative, compared with other students in a class or with a national average that has been previously established; or they can be criterion-referenced, described in terms of mastery of specific performance criteria. Summative evaluation data are essential to organizational questions because they are future-oriented, in that they supply the information as to *what will happen* when certain decisions are made or programs are repeated.

Summative evaluation instruments may be administered periodically to assess a learner's general achievement in respect to previously studied material. The information yielded is a general alert to how successfully the students are proceeding. The basic purpose of individualized instruction is to eliminate the lower performance represented in a normal distribution and skew the curve toward higher performance.

Formative Evaluation

To answer the questions relevant to individualized instruction, formative evaluation data are used; instructional decisions are constantly being formed and reformed as a result of continuous evaluative scrutiny by the teacher and/or learner. For example, the way a student makes a statement, plus the way he seems to feel about his performance, determine whether he should say it again; his decision is not made on the basis of how most students would say it after the same number of practice trials. Formative evaluation has a cybernetic function; it contributes "right now" data that are fed back into the instructional process to improve the prediction of learning, rather than to achieve the same prediction as that action evoked in the past.

Some aspects of foreign language learning are, of course, easier to evaluate than others. Discrete items of linguistic competence may be assessed quite precisely and objectively. Performance in communication is a far more complex matter. Activities such as role playing, conducting interviews, or being interviewed are devices that yield useful data. It is in this area of assessing complex performance skills that the imagination and creativity of the teacher are most needed.

A parallel in the problem of evaluation can be drawn with regard to the study of culture. Possession of information about the target culture is more easily assessed than interaction performance in a cultural milieu.

Criterion Referenced Tests

Criterion referenced data are the backbone of individualized instruction because they are diagnosis-oriented. They reveal strengths and weaknesses in the learner's performance that permit adjustments to be made in his program at a time when it will make the most difference. Those developmental or criterion-referenced data give precise information as to the level of mastery of the objective. Because these data perform a formative evaluation function, they are essential to the instructional decision of whether a learner should proceed to a new objective or refocus his energy and effort on one not yet attained.

Norm Referenced Tests

Norm referenced data occupy a subordinate place in individualized instruction.

Program Evaluation

When programs are being evaluated for their degree of individualization, certain questions must be asked: To what degree is the task required of each learner at the right level of difficulty and complexity? Is the behavior of each learner appropriate for accomplishing the task in an optimum educational environment? Do the teacher's decisions and behavior reflect use of principles of learning that facilitate the achievement of the objective for this particular learner?

Affective Evaluation

One way of measuring the affective success of a program is to inspect enrollment figures at the beginning and continuing levels of study. A program that entices

90 percent of the student population to enroll in a beginning foreign language course encompasses something that is absent in a program that enrolls only 25 percent. When the holding power of a program is such that 90 percent enroll for a succeeding level, one suspects that more individualization of instruction is occurring than in the too-familiar 50 percent re-enrollment.

Ultimately the final evaluation of a foreign language program lies with the learner, for it is he who makes the decision to continue or discontinue the study of foreign language. A student is more likely to pursue further goals in the target language if he has learned to participate productively in the educational decision-making process, and has experienced success and satisfaction in reaching goals he perceived as worthwhile.

SUMMARY

The concept of pluralism in education is widely accepted and increasingly implemented. In foreign language programs, efforts are being made to attract a wider-based clientele, and to encourage continuing involvement in language learning activities. The current trend of easing or eliminating both entrance and degree requirements has impelled foreign language educators to consider methods that would improve the quality of instruction, increase the efficiency and effectiveness of learning, and make course offerings more attractive and more closely related to their clients' diverse personal goals, needs, abilities, and interests. Bravo!

Individualized instruction is not a discrete entity. It involves a state of mind, a considered way of making decisions, a process, an attitude, a posture, a philosophy; however, individualized instruction is not a methodology, not a constellation of techniques, not an arsenal of equipment. An idealized program of individualized foreign language learning provides for the continuous progress of each member of a diverse student population, taking into account the particular goals and attributes of each learner. All other factors—use of space, availability of equipment, staffing patterns, scheduling, instructional materials, organizational patterns, grouping, tracking, and on and on and on—are *means* to the end of individualized instructions. Means must be related to the desired end, but too often those means have become the end. Chaos, even organized chaos with "all these things going on at once" and every student "doing his own thing," does not an individualized program make. Furthermore, when one looks at the literature in individualized instruction in foreign language or in any other area of study, it is clear that there is no one best way, or combination of ways, to achieve the idealized program. What is effective in one situation, or at one time, may be counter-productive in other circumstances. There is no magic formula. When all of the complexities of a given situation are considered, it becomes obvious that it is necessary to *individualize the individualization*! Allons!

BIBLIOGRAPHY

(1) Altman, Howard B., ed. *Individualizing the Foreign Language Classroom: Perspectives for Teachers*. Rowley, MA: Newbury House, 1972.

(2) _____ , and Robert L. Politzer, eds. *Individualizing Foreign Language Instruction*. Rowley, MA: Newbury House, 1971.

(3) Bloom, Benjamin S., ed. *Taxonomy of Educational Objectives, Handbook I: Cognitive Domain*. New York: Longmans, Green, 1956.

(4) Bull, William E., and Lamadrid, Enrique E. "Our Grammar Rules are Hurting Us." *Modern Language Journal* 55 (1971): 449-54.

(5) Gougher, Ronald L., ed. *Individualization of Instruction in Foreign Languages: A Practical Guide*. Philadelphia: Center for Curriculum Development, 1972.

(6) Hunter, Madeline. *Motivation Theory for Teachers*. El Segundo, CA: TIP Publications, 1967. [P.O. Box 514.]

(7) _____ . *Retention Theory for Teachers*. El Segundo, CA: TIP Publications, 1967. [P.O. Box 514.]

(8) _____ . *Teach for Transfer*. El Segundo, CA: TIP Publications, 1971. [P.O. Box 514.]

(9) _____ . *Teach More–Faster!* El Segundo, CA: TIP Publications, 1969. [P.O. Box 514.]

(10) Krathwohl, David R.; Bloom, Benjamin S.; and Masia, Betram B. *Taxonomy of Educational Objectives, Handbook II: Affective Domain*. New York: David McKay, 1964.

(11) Nostrand, Howard L. "Empathy for a Second Culture: Motivations and Techniques." In *Responding to New Realities*, edited by Gilbert A. Jarvis, pp. 263-327. ACTFL Review of Foreign Language Education, vol. 5. Skokie, IL: National Textbook, 1974.

(12) Phillips, June K. "Individualization and Personalization." In *Responding to New Realities*, edited by Gilbert A. Jarvis, pp. 219-61. ACTFL Review of Foreign Language Education, vol. 5. Skokie, IL: National Textbook, 1974.

(13) Quinn, Terence J. "Theoretical Foundations in Linguistics and Related Fields." In *Responding to New Realities*, edited by Gilbert A. Jarvis, pp. 329-53. ACTFL Review of Foreign Language Education, vol. 5. Skokie, IL: National Textbook, 1974.

(14) Simpson, Elizabeth Jane. *The Classification of Education Objectives: Psychomotor Domain*. Champaign-Urbana: University of Illinois, 1966.

(15) Tyler, Louise L.; Klein, M. Frances; and Michael, William B. *Recommendations for Curriculum and Instructional Materials*. Los Angeles: Tyl Press, 1971.

(16) Valette, Rebecca M., and Disick, Renée S. *Modern Language Performance Objectives and Individualization: A Handbook*. New York: Harcourt Brace Jovanovich, 1972.

Chapter Five
The "Right to Read" in Two Languages
Theodore Andersson

INTRODUCTION

Reading, the first of the three Rs, has always occupied a central place in education, but bold indeed is the educator who would proclaim complete satisfaction with the way we teach it. Controversy over reading—the Great Debate, as Chall (4) calls it—promises to continue for a long time. As critics point out our shortcomings, and we keep trying to overcome past inadequacies through research.

In an effort to intensify reading research and at the same time to enlist public and governmental support, the late U.S. Commissioner of Education, James E. Allen, launched his Right to Read Program in 1969. No one denies children's right to read, but this slogan was meant to focus attention on the fact that about "one out of four students nationwide has significant reading deficiencies" (1, p. 2). Whether out of ignorance or indifference, we fail to teach reading effectively.

We have lately become conscious of a double failure in the case of bilingual children, who rarely learn to read their home language well, and often learn to read English only poorly. Americans who acquire a non-English first language by virtue of birth have a natural right to learn to read their mother tongue, and a duty to learn to read English. Some of the problems involved in learning to read two languages are considered in this chapter, especially *when* and *how* reading may best begin and *what kind* of reading should be recommended.

THE QUESTION OF *WHEN* READING MAY BEGIN

View of Dolores Durkin

A most controversial question is when to initiate reading. In the 1968 volume that the National Society for the Study of Education devoted to reading,

Dolores Durkin explores the question "When Should Children Begin to Read?" As a good academic, she eschews extremes; on the one hand, there is the idea that a mental age of 6.5 years is a prerequisite for reading (14, 22); and, on the other, the belief that children are ready to read as soon as they have an oral command of the language. Some educators are even convinced that children as young as ten months are ready to read, provided their mothers are "very clever" teachers (7). Having conducted longitudinal studies of preschool reading (8, 9, 10), Durkin knows that reading need not be delayed until age six and a half; however, articles espousing the other extreme annoy her. With some effort she succeeds in striking a balance:

> While nobody would want to give even a hint of support to the idea that mothers ought to be working on reading with their ten-month-old children, nobody, either, should discourage future research efforts to see whether there are characteristics of children younger than six that might provide a match for the requirements of beginning reading. What must be pointedly emphasized is that these efforts will be helped neither by outlandish claims about infants nor by sentimental views of childhood (11, p. 67).

This point of view constitutes a challenge for me, for I read the evidence quite differently from Durkin, as will become apparent; but I do this while respecting her generally comprehensive and intelligent grasp of a complex field. We have much to learn from her.

View of Glenn Doman

Doman summarizes his position by saying that "Children can read words when they are one year old, sentences when they are two, and whole books when they are three years old—and they love it (6, p. 1)." According to Doman, "There is no need to ask the question, 'Can very small children learn to read?' They've already answered that, they *can*" (6, p. 9). He explains:

> Very young children can and do learn to read words, sentences and paragraphs in exactly the same way they learn to understand spoken words, sentences and paragraphs. . . .
>
> When the ear apprehends, or picks up, a spoken word or message, this auditory message is broken down into a series of electrochemical impulses and flashed to the unhearing brain, which then reassembles and *comprehends* in terms of the meaning the word was intended to convey.
>
> In precisely the same manner it happens that when the eye apprehends a printed word or message, this visual message is broken down into a series of electro-chemical impulses and flashed to the unseeing brain to be reassembled and comprehended as reading.

It is a magical instrument, the brain. . . .

To begin understanding the human brain we must consider the instant of conception rather than the moment of birth, because the superb and very little understood process of brain growth begins at conception.

From conception on, the human brain grows at an explosive rate which is continually on a descending scale.

Explosive and *descending*.

The whole process is essentially complete at the age of eight.

At conception the fertile egg is microscopic in size. Twelve days later the embryo is large enough so that the brain can be differentiated. This is long before Mother knows she is pregnant, so phenomenally fast is the rate of growth.

While the *rate* of growth is fantastic, this rate is always slower than the day before.

By birth the child weighs six or seven pounds, which is millions of times what the egg weighed nine months earlier at conception. It is obvious that if his *rate* of growth were the same in the next nine months as it was in the previous nine months, he would weigh thousands of tons when he was nine months old and many millions of tons when he was eighteen months old.

The process of brain growth matches the body growth but is on an even more descending rate. This can be seen clearly when one appreciates the fact that at birth the child's brain makes up 11 percent of the total body weight, while in adults it is only 2.5 percent.

When the child is five the growth of the brain is 80 percent complete.

When he is eight the process of brain growth is, as we have said, virtually complete.

During the years between eight and eighty we have less brain growth than we had in the single year (and the slowest of the first eight years) between the ages of seven and eight (*6*, pp. 31-34).

View of Omar Khayyam Moore

O.K. Moore conceived the "talking typewriter," which was then invented by Kobler, developed by the Edison Research Laboratory of McGraw Edison Company, and marketed by the Responsive Environments Corporation.

[Moore] believes that children between the ages of two and six have a tremendous untapped capacity for learning—and, if placed in a responsive environment can make amazing progress. . . . As a result of this theory, Dr. Moore's children can read, write, type and take dictation before they enter first grade (*12*, p. 111).

Dorothy Johnson has described how this machine was used in a Research and Test Center of the Freeport, New York, Public Schools (*16*).

Critical Analysis and Tentative Conclusions

From the profuse literature on reading, I have selected two texts directed primarily to the question of when children should begin to read. Durkin has made a comprehensive survey of the literature bearing on this question from the vantage-point of one who has conducted longitudinal studies of preschool readers. Her cautious, middle-of-the-road position does not espouse the opinion of those who would equate readiness to read with a mental age of six and a half, and it rejects out of hand Doman's conviction that age two is the best age for a child to learn to read.

Frost (*12*), another reading specialist, is less disturbed than Durkin by Doman's contention, but he carefully refrains from endorsing Doman's position. Instead, he presents a range of counterbalancing opinions that, in some cases, do not appear to be relevant and, in others, are not particularly convincing. I have put together the evidence which I consider pertinent, and it comes closest to what Durkin calls the "outlandish" position of Doman.

The position I take is a hypothetical one; there is so much that is unknown or not understood about language acquisition and other forms of learning by infants and young children that one can hardly do more than hypothesize. Personal observation and experience have been corroborated by much of the literature on early childhood: the young child has an extraordinary ability to learn and to create. Montessori asserted that "Only a child under three can construct the mechanism of language, and he can speak any number of languages if they are in his environment at birth" (*21*, p. 40). Susuki has successfully taught music to children of three. Children's eidetic imagery and extraordinary talent for imaginative expression in art and in poetry have led me to accept without much difficulty the contention that age one and a half or two is perhaps the most favorable for learning to read.

Interactional Synchrony

The latest research always seems to be the most astounding, especially in the field of science. For example, under the title "Listening Motion," *Newsweek* reported the following:

> Two years ago, [William S.] Condon [a psychiatrist at the Boston University Medical Center] and his colleague Louis W. Sander turned their attention to interactional synchrony in children, and last month [January 1974] they reported an astonishing finding: bodily responses to human speech are apparent in babies twelve hours old,

and may even exist in the womb. Such instinctive responses, the researchers suspect, represent vital steps in learning to talk.

The researchers' subjects were eleven American babies between the ages of twelve hours and two months. The infants were filmed as they heard a variety of sounds from different sources, including live speech from their mothers and other adults, tape recordings of English and Chinese speech and tapes of disconnected vowels and tapping sounds.

When Condon and Sander analyzed the films, they discovered that the babies' movements synchronized with the sounds they heard whenever they were exposed to real speech, whether English or Chinese. Movements of the infants' heads, hands, elbows, hips and legs corresponded exactly to the rhythm of speech. When the babies were exposed to disconnected speech or to plain tapping sounds, however, the rhythmic pattern was not observed. Condon concludes that babies motoristically lock into speech rhythm from the first day of life. . . . (18, p. 79).

Science (29) treats this same subject in more detail.

Trevarathen (Young, 40), a New Zealand-born biologist who began his experiments with infants at Harvard and is now continuing his research at the University of Edinburgh, "argues that babies are born far smarter than psychologists have given them credit for—that infants come into the world with a good deal of innate intelligence, including an embryonic form of speech" (40, p. 20). Trevarthen has taken hours and hours of movies of more than 200 infants. He places the baby in an infant seat in front of the mother and by means of a mirror catches both on the film.

At Harvard, Trevarthen, Martin Richards, and Berry Brazelton quickly found that at two months infants know the difference between people and objects and that they make deliberate attempts to converse with their mothers and other adults. . . .

Trevarthen has greatly expanded his studies of infant speech and gestures since joining the Edinburgh faculty in 1971. . . .

At two months, Trevarthen detects in infants what he calls "prespeech," a distinct pattern of elaborate lip and mouth movements that resemble the movements of adult speech. . . .

Mothers . . . apparently unconsciously, adjust the pace of their talk to allow the baby to join in. The mother speaks, pauses, listens to her baby, and speaks again after letting the infant have his say (40, p. 20).

Trevarthen concludes from his study that "man's language ability is present in innate form at birth. But language development, he agrees, definitely depends on each child's experiences. 'Environment has a tremendous voice,' Trevarthen says." He also finds the beginnings of hand communication in the first month of life. " 'The shape of a hand greeting—a wave—exists at three weeks and is fully distinct at eight weeks,' Trevarthen says." Trevarthen's team also found that

A distinct change in infant-mother communication begins toward the end of the baby's third month of life. . . . The baby becomes rude to its mother.

When the mother begins speaking, the baby turns away, often looking at some object or toy, and refuses to answer. At first the mother increases her conversation, then lapses into silence. Finally she picks up a toy, usually the one the baby is looking at, and tries to interest the child in it. Then the baby responds. . . .

What we believe happens is the baby introduces the mother to the idea their mutual communication can involve objects. . . . The baby says, "We've got to stop this chat and find something to chat about."

The mother is being trained by the baby. Having established a relationship, the baby transforms it and teaches the mother to be a teacher. And we take that as a general prototype for all education. I think children invented school (p. 20).

Young observes that "Trevarthen's research has provided major new insights into the linguistic and behavioral abilities of infants" (40, p. 20).

Corresponding roughly to the growth of the brain is the development of human intelligence. Bloom has come to the following conclusions:

. . . we may now begin to describe the development of general intelligence. Using either Bayley's correlation data (r^2) or the Thorndike absolute scale (both of which yield essentially the same results), it is possible to say, that in terms of intelligence measured at age 17, at least 20% is developed by age 1, 50% by about age 4, 80% by about age 8 and 92% by age 13. Put in terms of intelligence measured at age 17, from conception to age 4, the individual develops 50% of his mature intelligence, from ages 4 to 8 he develops another 30%, and from ages 8 to 17 the remaining 20%. This differentially accelerated growth is very similar to the phenomenon we have noted in Chapter 2 with regard to height growth.

With this in mind, we would question the notion of an absolutely constant I.Q. Intelligence is a developmental concept, just as is height, weight, or strength. There is increased stability in intelligence measurements with time. However, we should be quick to point out that by about age 4, 50% of the variation in intelligence at age 17 is accounted for. This would suggest the very rapid growth of intelligence in the early years and the possible great influence of the early environment on this development.

We would expect the variations in the environments to have relatively little effect on the I.Q. after age 8, but we would expect such variation to have marked effect on the I.Q. before that age, with the greatest effect likely to take place between the ages of about 1 to 5 (3, p. 68).

Similar evidence is being assembled by White and Walls, who emphasize the importance of the period from birth to three years: "If most of the qualities that distinguish outstanding six-year-olds can be achieved in large measure by age three, the focus of the project could be narrowed dramatically. We rather abruptly found ourselves concentrating on the zero-to-three age range" (39, p. 20).

White's continuing research has led him to the following conclusions:

ιy belief that the educational developments that take place in the year or so that begins when a child is about eight months old are *the most important and most in need of attention of any that occur in human life.* . . . Once more, my view is that not more than two-thirds of our children currently get adequate development in the areas dealt with here, and no more than ten percent of our children do as well as they could during the first years of their lives. This state of affairs may be a tragedy, but it is by no means a twentieth-century tragedy. *In the history of Western education there has never been a society that recognized the educational importance of the earliest years, or sponsored any systematic preparation and assistance to families or any other institution in guiding the early formation of children (38,* pp. 129-30).

Early reading depends, of course, on early language development. Take the matter of speech sounds. After studying the recorded vocalizations of an infant in the first year of life, Osgood asserts: "The first observation of note was that within the data for the first two months of life may be found all of the speech sounds that the human vocal system can produce" (*23*, p. 118).

Or consider the subject of vocabulary. Children's vocabulary acquisition is a source of amazement to grown-ups, whose learning of words has almost come to a halt. Using the Seashore-Eckerson English Recognition Vocabulary Test (*30*), Smith found that, "for grade one, the average number of basic words known was 16,900, with a range from 5,500 to 32,800. . . . For grade one the average number of words in the total vocabulary (basic plus derivative words) was 23,700, with a range from 6,000 to 48,000" (*31*, pp. 343-44). In a study of children's active vocabulary Rinsland used written sources supplemented by children's conversation to count 5,099 different words used by first graders out of 353,874 running words (*25*, p. 12).

As Montessori has observed, children in a plurilingual setting are apparently capable of learning the languages in their immediate environment with no greater difficulty than the monolingual child has learning his one language. A number of such cases have been recorded or described (*17, 24, 26, 28, 35, 37*).

One of the best known cases of early multilingualism is that cited by the British psychologist J.W. Tomb:

It is a common experience in the district in Bengal in which the writer resided to hear English children of three or four years old who have been born in the country conversing freely at different times with their parents in English, with their *ayahs* (nurses) in Bengali, with the garden coolies in Santali, and with the house servants in Hindustani, while their parents have learned with the aid of a *munshi* (teacher) and much laborious effort just sufficient Hindustani to comprehend what the house servants are saying (provided they do not speak too quickly) and to issue simple orders to them connected with domestic affairs. It is even not unusual to see English parents in India unable to understand what their servants are saying to them in Hindustani and being driven in consequence to bring along an English child of four or five years old, if available, to act as an interpreter (*36*, pp. 53-54).

Early Reading

Doman, Director of the Institutes for the Achievement of Human Potential in Philiadelpha, has worked with brain-damaged children over a period of some twenty-five years. In collaboration with other specialists, he has stated most clearly and most convincingly that "Tiny children *want* to learn to read. Tiny children *can* learn to read. Tiny children *are* learning to read. Tiny children *should* learn to read" (*6*, p. 9).

Doman recounts how he and his colleagues first discovered that reading could be used as a remedial treatment for retardation due to brain injury; they later became aware that normal children also want to, and can, learn to read once the obstacles usually put in their way are removed. Here are Doman's words:

> When you are confronted with a brain-injured two-year-old who is no further advanced than a newborn babe—who gives no evidence of being able to see or hear, let alone crawl or raise his head—teaching him to read isn't the first thing you think about, what you think about is how to get through to him, by any method, on any level.

> Young Tommy was such a child. His eyes wouldn't follow you, or follow a light, or work together. A loud noise wouldn't make him start. You could pinch him and get no reaction. In fact, the first time we ever got a reaction out of Tommy was when we stuck pins in him: he smiled. It was a great moment, for us and for him. We had established contact.

> That was when Tommy was two. By the time he was four he was reading, and thereby hangs a tale. Let me tell it to you just as it happened, because we didn't set out to teach him to read; it just happened along the way, as part of our overall problem of establishing communication (*6*, pp. 14-15).

"But," asks Doman rhetorically, "isn't it easier for a child to understand a spoken word rather than a written one? Not at all."

> The child's brain, which is the only organ that has learning capacity, "hears" the clear, loud television words through the ear and interprets them as only the brain can. Simultaneously the child's brain "sees" the big, clear television words through his eye and interprets them in exactly the same manner.

> It makes no difference to the brain whether it "sees" a sight or "hears" a sound. It can understand both equally well. All that is required is that the sounds be loud enough and clear enough for the ear to hear and the words big enough and clear enough for the eye to see so that the brain can interpret them—the former we have done but the latter we have failed to do (*6*, pp. 5-6).

According to this view, reading, like walking and talking, is a developmental skill. Apparently it has not been learned as well as it should have been because adults are insensitive to children's wants at a critical time. And when that time has passed, adults try to remedy the situation by overanalysis,

analysis better calculated to satisfy adult appetites than children's curiosity. Someone once remarked that the best way to produce a nervous breakdown in a centipede would be to try to *teach* him to walk. Likewise the best way to *prevent* a child from learning to walk would be to try to *teach* him. Let us ponder the implications for the learning-to-read process.

In 1965, Söderbergh, a professor of child language at the University of Stockholm, decided to teach her two-year-old daughter to read by the Doman method. Here is how she describes her experiment:

> The reading experiment was carried through with a purely linguistic aim. I wanted to find out how a small child that is shown cards with whole words written on them—one word on each card—and is told what is written on the cards, finally succeeds all by himself in learning to read. I wanted to find out about the process behind such an acquisition of reading ability. The experiment showed that the girl "stored" the words in her memory, and as soon as a new word was presented to her she compared this word with the earlier learnt ones. Through analyses of and comparisons between words the child gradually succeeded in breaking the words up into smaller and smaller units; first she recognized and was able to read morphemes, especially endings, later also graphemes (i.e., letters) and at last she arrived at a full knowledge of the correspondences between graphemes and phonemes ("letters and sounds"): She had broken the code and was able to read any new word presented to her. In the experiment this breaking of the code was achieved within 14 months (with a daily reading session of 5-20 minutes). . . . The overall experience from the different children that learnt to read between one and a half and three was that they did so with surprising ease, absorbing written language with great interest and as easily as they acquire spoken language, given that language deals with matters that mean something to them (*33*, pp. 14-15).

Tentative conclusions can be drawn from the foregoing and from other evidence (*27*):

1. Ages one and a half to three seem to be the most favorable for encouraging children to read.

2. If the word "teaching" is used for initiating a child into reading, it should be understood to have a special sense. The teacher serves as an important model for reading as well as for speaking, senses the interests of the child, and helps provide suitable learning materials to satisfy these interests.

3. The best teacher is in general the mother.

4. The best "school" is the home.

5. Reading, like walking and talking, is a developmental task; but, unlike walking and talking, it can more easily be inhibited, retarded, or shortcircuited if not encouraged at the proper time and in the proper way.

6. In reading, as in other forms of learning, most rapid progress is made when there is the best 'match' between a child's intellectual development and environmental stimulation.

THE QUESTION OF *HOW* READING MAY BEST BEGIN

The *how* of reading flows naturally from the *when*. If the best time to initiate a child into the wonderful world of reading is between the ages of one and a half and two, then the countless books and articles which debate the relative merits of such questions as meaning versus phonics, letter versus sound, whole word versus letter are focused on the wrong age. The reading readiness concept, associated as it is with the state of development at ages five and six, also becomes irrelevant.

When reading begins at age two or ages five or six, the grown-up responsible for initiating the child into reading has to bridge the gulf between childhood and maturity by using imagination. The adult who can imagine most vividly the desires and impulses of a child, his "needs," is likely to be best able to satisfy what John Ciardi (5) has called the child's "happy hunger" for learning. This is not to deny the importance of knowledge derived from observation and research; but this knowledge, like the observation and research producing it, needs to be guided by imagination. Grown-ups responsible for children need to be on their guard constantly against the disease of adultism, the enemy of imagination. The analytical games that adults play are not necessarily fun for children.

It is not my intention to try to provide a blueprint for initiating a child into reading. My purpose is rather to encourage predisposed individuals to experiment along the lines suggested by the educators already cited. These individual experiments are the first stage in a long period of experimentation and development. Realizing that educators are not yet "ready," Doman has addressed his book to mothers, the natural teachers of pre-school children.

By good luck, Doman's book attracted the attention of Söderbergh, who successfully used the Doman method to teach her daughter to read. The multiplication of such experiments, resulting in more and more reports, will constitute a second stage of development toward early reading.

A possible third stage may be the inclusion of reading in one or more of the many early childhood development projects that are springing up in many parts of the country.

A fourth stage might be sponsorship of broader experimentation in early reading by school systems authorized to begin schooling at age four or earlier.

And finally, once school systems are convinced that ages one and a half to three are indeed most favorable for a start in reading, a regular home-school collaboration can initiate young children into reading as well as other forms of early education.

Objectives

The objectives of such projects would be to take advantage of and to satisfy the child's interests and so help him grow, develop, and learn pleasurably. Such learning should, of course, include physical, sensory, cognitive, moral, and esthetic development.

Rationale

Parents and teachers are united in wanting the best possible education for their children. The primary responsibility for this education belongs to parents during a child's infancy and early childhood. However, if a school, or a teacher, were to have special knowledge concerning the education of pre-school children, parents might willingly accept help or advice. The preparatory stage would be the most important. Teachers should not only understand thoroughly the principles and procedures of early childhood reading, but also be able to explain these principles and procedures so clearly that parents would be willing to give them a try. In turn, parents should dispel their doubts that very young children can easily learn to read. The more they doubt, the more they inhibit their children's learning. They should expect success in their children's early reading (27); indeed, such success appears to be normal.

Given the opportunity, many children teach themselves to read signs, words on billboards, labels, and words on the TV screen. A Spanish-speaking student described to me how he learned to read Spanish long before he went to school: he would take a copy of *La Prensa*, a Spanish newspaper formerly published in San Antonio, point first to individual letters, then to words, and ask some member of his family to name them. In this way, he discovered the relationship between sound and letter, and between letter and word, and was able to break the code.

Who is the teacher and who is the learner when a small child and a parent interact? Trevarthen (40) suggests that it may be the child who is the teacher. To be sure, the parent supplies playthings in the form of words written or printed in large letters on pieces of cardboard. What words to select may be decided by watching the child and sensing his interests. At first, the child may well enjoy stories made up by the parent out of words already known, but he will soon get pleasure from dictating a story to the parent, who can write or print it in large letters on paper or cardboard. The underlying principle is that it must be fun for the child. Presumably, if it is fun for the child, it will also be fun for the parent. So basic is this principle that Doman devoted his final chapter, "On Joyousness," to it (6).

How to Teach Your Baby to Read

Doman lays out a detailed methodology which divides the mother's task into six steps. He suggests learning sessions of no more than five minutes. These should be held in a quiet place without distractions at a time when both mother and child are in a relaxed mood, and they may be repeated as many as five times a day with at least a half hour separation. All sessions should end *before* the child wants to stop.

According to Doman, it is possible for a child to begin to learn to read as early as ten months of age. "We have seen several children who can read many words they cannot say . . . It is almost always true that an adult can read a great deal more of a *new* language than he can understand of that language through his ear. Remember that a baby *is* learning a new language" (*6*, p. 121).

The materials used should contain the following components:

1. The words *mommy* and *daddy* on separate cards, 6" high by 24" long. The letters should be 5" by 4" with approximately ½" between letters; they should be red and printed in lower case. . . .

2. The twenty basic "self" words [parts of the body] (p. 118) on white cards 5" high, approximately 24" long, in red lower-case letters 4" high. . . .

3. The basic words of the child's immediate world (pp. 124-27) on white cards 3" high, in red lower-case letters 2" high. . . .

4. The sentence-structure vocabulary: single-word cards 3" high, with black lower-case words 2" high. . . .

5. The structured-phrase vocabulary: phrase cards with words printed in black lower-case letters 1" high. These cards are punched and assembled into a book by the use of 1" loose-leaf rings. The cards must therefore be large enough to accommodate the text of each page. . . .

6. A book using a limited vocabulary printed in black upper- and lower-case letters ¼" high.

7. The alphabet on 4" by 4" cards with black upper- and lower-case letters 3" high (*6*, pp. 107-10).

Here is a description of the initial procedure suggested under the first step:

Hold up the word *mommy*, just beyond his reach, and say to him clearly, "This says Mommy."

Give the child no more description and do not elaborate. Permit him to see for no more than ten seconds.

Now play with him, give him your undivided affection for a minute or two, then present the word again for a second time. Again allow him to see it for ten seconds, again tell him just once in a clear voice, "This says Mommy."

Do not ask him what it is.

The first session is now over and you have spent slightly less than five minutes (6, p. 111).

The procedures of the second day and the rest of the first week are described in equal detail, as are the succeeding steps. Gradually, the size of the letters is reduced and the red color yields to black; then single words lead to sentences, and whole pages of text to whole books; finally there is a list of thirty-nine books suitable for young children.

Doman warns against boring a child by proceeding too rapidly or too slowly or by testing him too much. A child should never be pressured, and should never be taught after he has been naughty—lessons should be associated with fun, not punishment. The alphabet should not be taught until a child has read his first book.

On the other hand, Doman encourages parents to be lavish in their praise of a child's success, and to answer all the child's questions. If a child asks about certain words, they should be added to his reading vocabulary, thereby giving him meaningful material to read.

Söderbergh's Reading Kit for Children
Who Have Just Begun to Talk

Following her 1965 success in teaching her daughter to read, Söderbergh (33) confirmed her findings by observation of five other children between the ages one and a half and three. After these children learned to read Swedish "with surprising ease," Söderbergh put together a reading kit consisting of 208 reading cards and a booklet of instructions. A different word is printed on each of 201 cards; the seven blank cards are intended for the name of the child being taught and for other words commonly used with the child. These cards are plastic covered and, by using washable ink which is easily erased, can be used many times.

The instruction book contains general information about child language and early reading, as well as detailed procedures for guiding the child's learning. The procedures are very similar to Doman's.

Summary

Doman and Söderbergh, having discovered and confirmed that ages one and a half to three are indeed the best time to initiate children into reading, have made a good start in elaborating initiation procedures. Like Ashton-Warner (2) and any sensitive teacher of young children, they start with words that are most meaningful to young children. Both guide their young learners through progressive stages to the independent reading of stories. Both stress the use of content words—first nouns, then verbs—in the early stages. However, Söderbergh is more conscious than Doman of syntax and orders her materials in such a way as to enable the child to master structures relatively early.

The differences in Doman's and Söderbergh's approaches are complementary, indicating the great variety of methods that can be expected as more and more educators discover the natural age for beginning reading. Doman believes that it is not difficult to teach a baby to read if one has a basic understanding of children and is sensitive to their drives.

It is hoped that educators will not feel the need to evolve any single reading methodology for young children. Because the teaching of reading to children between ages one and a half and three has been done on a one-to-one basis and, therefore, has not been institutionalized, there is at least a chance that the uniqueness of the individual child may be recognized. In this way, there is a greater likelihood that a fortuitous "match" between the child's individual personality and the stimulation of a sensitive parent-teacher will result in the early acquisition of one basic component of a good education, the joy of reading.

Doman cited a collective quote from "many, many mothers": "I don't think we really got to know each other until we played the learning-to-read game together" (6, p. 147).

THE QUESTION OF WHAT TO READ

Building a Child's Library

A child's library should consist of books that are *his*, books that he has read because they interested him. Even for a very small child, books are made of words as well as pictures. Words can be interesting if they are presented to a child in a fascinating way.

Ruth Weir Hirsch reports one interesting way to capture a child's language corpus. Over a two-month period when Anthony Hirsch was two and a half years old, his parents devised a system for recording his speech as he talked to himself just before falling asleep. Commenting on the approximately 680 different words so recorded, Hirsch reported that, "Compared with the child's repertoire during the day, the poverty of vocabulary and of topics in his monologues is striking" (*15*, p. 99). Of the content words that occurred most frequently, "Bobo," a favorite toy, or "Bobo's," was repeated 135 times; "blanket," 125; "Mommy," "Mommy's," or "Mama," 90; "Anthony" or "Anthony's," 89; "Daddy" or "Daddy's," 75; "please," 50; "Kitty" or "Kitty's," 48; "book" or "books," 44; "Alice," the name of the girl living with the family, 26; "Cobbers," the dog, 26; "bottle," 26; and "Fifi," the cat, 25.

Both Doman and Söderbergh provide the child with words that they know from experience will be interesting. These words form sentences and stories. As soon as the child has read his first book, whether it is a story made up by the parent or a story in a real book which the child has learned to read word by word and sentence by sentence, this book becomes the first in the child's library.

Although the baby's own vocabulary is a prime source of reading material, it should be supplemented by words and phrases used by adults closest to the child. Another source, and perhaps the most important of all, are books themselves. Doman recommends a list of 39 books suitable for a child who has learned to read independently. These have been selected according to four criteria: the print is large; the print is not intertwined with pictures; the vocabulary is limited; and the subject matter is interesting and suitable. However, a child should never be restricted to books which he can read himself; he should be read to by members of the family, and this should be done from the first weeks of his life. The research of Condon and Sander (*18*) stresses the fact that the human infant reacts physically to the sound of human speech from the first day of life. The infant may very well not understand "the story" to begin with, but who can doubt that he enjoys the sound of a loving voice and gets some meaning from the varied expressions in the reading? Although I can still remember the voluptuous pleasure I experienced as a four year old listening to the stories my aunt told or read me, I have long since forgotten the stories themselves.

It is often contended that reading material must not be over the heads of children. There is some truth to this with respect to children's independent reading, but almost none with respect to what is read to them, provided the subject matter is interesting and suitable. One mother who began reading to her children well before their first birthday remarked that, although she began by selecting books suitable for very young children, she found that she could quickly move on to much more mature children's literature. By reading "good" literature, she not only gave her children pleasure, but also cultivated in them an early appreciation of style. There is an art to reading aloud; it should be interesting, varied, full of expression, and always *natural*, as though spoken.

Summary

What should be read by the beginning reader? Essentially, ᵥ
and there are virtually no limits to the interests of a one-and-a-half- ₜₒ
three-year-old child. He is out to make the world his, and the handiest
instrument for this conquest is language, both spoken and written. Almost from
the beginning, he uses speech to manipulate those around him. Then he discovers
that speech also exists in notes, letters, newspapers, magazines, and books—to
say nothing of TV advertising, labels, billboards, signs, and names of stores. So
out he sets to crack the code, but most of the print is too small, and most of
those around him think it's an impossible task; so, more often than not, he gives
up before he starts.

When he finds that one or two grown-ups believe he can do it and think that
it is even normal and easy, he's off to a flying start. Big words that he hears are
explained to him and written in big letters, and suddenly he sees the connection
between objects and their names, both spoken and written. And every night, just
before bedtime, they play learning-to-read games with him or they read to him
or tell him stories, entrancing stories. They help him to make his own books out
of stories he has learned to read. There's no limit. If his parents can't answer his
questions, he can look for answers in the encyclopedia or dictionary, or he can
go to the library. Best of all are those fairy stories, legends, adventures, and
poetry, which are such fun to learn by heart.

THE "RIGHT TO READ" IN TWO LANGUAGES

So far we have been concerned with the child's natural "right to read" his native
language. In this "land of immigrants," the native language may very well not be
English. As we come to understand the value of our native multilanguage
resources, we will become increasingly united in conserving this aspect of our
intellectual ecology. Respect for other languages and cultures, the growing
realization of their value in our plurilingual international dialogues, and even a
little jealousy of those who can communicate and feel comfortable with
representatives of other nations are all healthy signs.

Nor is there any need for conflict here. The baby who is born into a
non-English-speaking family and acquires a non-English language in warm,
affectionate surroundings, can also learn to read his mother tongue. When this
initiation into reading occurs with love and enthusiasm and with the free play of
imagination, the child acquires not only the skill of getting meaning out of print,
but also a lively sense of curiosity and a taste for words and language. He has
been introduced to literature. After a child has learned to read in his native
language, there is still time for him to acquire the rudiments of understanding,
speaking, and reading English before entering nursery school at age four,
kindergarten at age five, or first grade at age six.

Art, music, numbers, and science can add interest and stimulation to the young child's expanding view of the world. No teacher could complain about such a child's lack of readiness for formal schooling. He can read; he can also write; and he has a running start in two languages, either of which is sufficiently developed to bear the full burden of instruction. What teachers will find difficult is how to teach in such a way as to insure the continued education of children who can already read and write in two languages.

Inevitably there will be a long, awkward, transitional period during which bilingual, biliterate children, their parents, and the home-visiting teachers who have collaborated in this "gentle revolution" may be regarded as nuisances. During this period more parents will learn how easy and how much fun it is to teach their babies to read. And as more teachers are trained to be home visitors, they will become adept at working with parents and will gradually develop guidelines for home-based pre-school education. Ultimately this education could include not only reading and writing in one or two languages, but also pleasurable learning in the areas of physical, ethical, esthetic, and cognitive development. Thanks to the pioneering research of Doman and Söderbergh, we are in a good position to perfect our technique in the area of reading and writing, but we should not neglect the other areas for long.

Does an infant born into a non-English-speaking family have a "right" to learn how to read and write in two languages? It seems obvious that he does indeed have such a right with respect to his first language, which, together with the total culture of which it is a part, is by definition his birthright. Does he also have a "right" to learn to read English; or does he have both a right and a duty to become fluent in this second language? It seems to me that the word "right" applies better to the first language and the word "duty" better to the second. The right to one's mother tongue and the cultural heritage it symbolizes is inherited at birth. It is part of a person's identity, tying him intimately to family, ancestors, community, and history. This may be accompanied by a sense of duty to preserve and cultivate a cultural heritage and language.

However, it is clearly the *duty* of native-born or naturalized Americans to learn to read English as well as possible. Anyone who asserts his right to preserve and cultivate his native language for his family and his children should be enthusiastically encouraged by his English-speaking fellow Americans. He will then gladly fulfill his duty to learn his second language, English. Furthermore, the more successfully he has learned to read and write his own language, the easier he will find it to become fluent and literate in English.

CONCLUSION

What a remarkable creature is the newborn babe! Between conception and birth there has taken place such growth and development as to elude our utmost efforts to understand. At birth the infant's brain accounts for eleven percent of his total weight, as compared with two-and-a-half percent for the adult. This clue to the infant's learning potential has been obscured by another observation; namely, the human infant is relatively helpless and requires a long period of protective care. This observation has led us to overlook the baby's instinctive urge to use his senses and his brain to understand and control the world around him. The newborn babe's main tool for dealing with his environment is his voice. From the very first day of life, the infant reacts physically to human speech; within the first two months of life, he is elaborating a form of prespeech and gestural system.

Another remarkable aspect of infancy is the fact that every single infant, even each of identical twins, is an absolutely unique product of genetic components. When he comes into the world, the infant, already genetically different from every other infant in the world, encounters an infinitely varied environment. It is idle to speculate whether heritage or environment is more important in determining the direction of the infant's development, for it is only the environment that can be manipulated by those responsible for the young child's education. Manipulating the child's environment can provide stimulation in all areas of development; we have discussed only how it can affect his potential for language acquisition, and especially for early reading and writing in one or two languages.

In truth, the young child generally belongs to an oppressed minority. Children in general are misunderstood by adults; and children in a non-English-speaking ethnic group are likely to be doubly misunderstood—by their own group and especially by the English-speaking majority.

It is the sheerest luck when an individual child is partially understood by those responsible for him. It is almost inevitable for a parent or teacher, limited by his own experience, to seek to form a child in his own image instead of rejoicing in the child's unique differences. One should observe a child closely, be sensitive to hints of special interest and curiosity, and learn to respond imaginatively to his initiatives. We teachers cannot serve as adequate models for the young child's imagination. In the field of art, it would require a Picasso; in music, a Bach; in literature, a Cervantes; in science, a Huxley; in philosophy, a Santayana. We should least try to pursue an ideal.

If we really believe in the popular "right to read" slogan, we had better learn to apply it at the child's most favorable learning age. Non-English-speaking children share with all children the "right" to learn to read their own native language between ages one and a half and three; in addition, they have a duty to learn to read English, an objective which can also best be achieved before age six.

BIBLIOGRAPHY

(1) Allen, James E., Jr. "The Right to Read: Target for the 70's." Paper presented at the Annual Convention of the National Association of State Boards of Education, Los Angeles, September, 23, 1969. [Text on microcard FS 5.8: A1 53/7, No. 15641, 1969.]

(2) Ashton-Warner, Sylvia. *Teacher*. New York: Simon and Schuster, 1963.

(3) Bloom, Benjamin S. *Stability and Change in Human Characteristics*. New York: John Wiley and Sons, 1964.

(4) Chall, Jeanne S. *Learning to Read: The Great Debate*. New York: McGraw-Hill, 1967.

(5) Ciardi, John. "When Do They Know Too Much?" *Saturday Review* 46(May 11, 1963): 16.

(6) Doman, Glenn. *How to Teach Your Baby to Read: The Gentle Revolution*. New York: Random House, 1964.

(7) _____ , G.N. Stevens, and Orem, R.C. "You can Teach Your Baby to Read." *Ladies Home Journal* 80 (1963): 62, 124-126.

(8) Durkin, Dolores. "A Study of Children Who Learned to Read Prior to First Grade." *California Journal of Educational Research* 10 (1959): 109-13.

(9) _____ . *Children Who Read Early*. New York: Teachers College Press, 1966.

(10) _____ . "Early Readers: Reflections After Six Years of Research." *Reading Teacher* 18, i (1964): 3-7.

(11) _____ . "When Should Children Begin to Read?" In *Innovation and Change in Reading Instruction*, edited by Helen M. Robinson, pp. 30-71. The Sixty-Seventh Yearbook of the National Society for the Study of Education, Part II. Chicago: University of Chicago Press, 1968.

(12) Frost, Joe L. *Issues and Innovations in the Teaching of Reading*. Glenview, IL: Scott, Foresman, 1967.

(13) Fuller, R. Buckminster. "Emergent Man: His Environment and Education," In George L. Stevens and R.C. Orem, *The Case for Early Reading*, pp. i-xxiv. St. Louis: Warren H. Green, 1968.

(14) Heffernan, Helen. "Significance of Kindergarten Education." *Childhood Education* 36 (1960): 313-19.

(15) Hirsch, Ruth Weir. *Language in the Crib*. The Hague: Mouton, 1962.

(16) Johnson, Dorothy K. "The O.K. Moore Typewriter Procedure." *Journal of the Reading Specialist* 5, iii (1966): 87-91.

(17) Leopold, Werner F. *Speech Development of a Bilingual Child*. 4 volumes. Evanston, IL: Northwestern University Press, 1939-1949.

(18) "Listening Motion." *Newsweek* (February 18, 1974): 79.

(19) Mackey, William F., and Andersson, Theodore, eds. *Bilingualism in Early Childhood: Proceedings of a Conference on Child Language*. Rowley, MA: Newbury House, 1977.

(20) Montessori, Maria. *Child in the Church: Essays on the Religious Education of Children and the Training of Character*. Edited by Mortimer Standing. London: Sands, 1929.

(21) _____ . *Education for a New World*. Third impression. Adyar, Madras, India: Kalakshetra Publications, 1959.

(22) Morphett, Mabel Vogel, and Washburne, Carleton. "When Should Children Begin to Read?" *Elementary School Journal* 31 (1931): 496-503.

(23) Osgood, Charles. *Method and Theory in Experimental Psychology*. New York: Oxford University Press, 1953.

(24) Pavlovitch, Milivoïe. *Le langage enfantin: Acquisition du serbe et du francais par un enfant serbe*. Paris: Librairie Ancienne Honoré Champion, 1920.

(25) Rinsland, Henry D. *A Basic Vocabulary of Elementary School Children*. New York: Macmillan, 1945.
(26) Ronjat, Jules. *Le développement du langage observé chez un enfant bilingue*. Paris: Librairie Ancienne Honoré Champion, 1913.
(27) Rosenthal, Robert, and Jacobson, Lenore. *Pygmalion in the Classroom: Teacher Expectation and Pupils' Intellectual Development*. New York: Holt, Rinehart, and Winston, 1968.
(28) Rüke-Dravina, V. *Mehrsprachigkeit im Vorschulalter*. Lund: Gleerup, 1967.
(29) *Science* (January 11, 1974): 99-101. [Gives a fuller account than reference (*18*).]
(30) Seashore, Robert N. "How Many Words Do Children Know?" *The Packet* (November 1947): 3-17. [Describes procedure for measuring size of children's vocabulary.]
(31) Smith, Mary Katherine. "Measurement of the Size of General English Vocabulary Through the Elementary Grades and High School." *Genetic Psychology Monographs* 24 (1941): 311-45.
(32) Söderbergh, Ragnhild. *Läspaket för Barn som nyss lärt att tala*. Stockholm: Scriptor, 1973.
(33) ———. *Project Early Reading: A Theoretical Investigation and Its Practical Applications*. Report No. 2. Stockholm: Stockholms Universitet, Institutionen för Nordiska Sprak, 1973.
(34) ———. *Reading in Early Childhood: A Linguistic Study of a Swedish Preschool Child's Gradual Acquisition of Reading Ability*. 2nd ed. Foreword by Theodore Andersson. Introduction by Robert Lado. Washington, DC: Georgetown University Press, 1977. [Originally published in Stockholm: Almquist and Wiksell, 1971.]
(35) Tits, Désiré. *Le mécanisme de l'acquisition d'une langue se substituant à la langue maternelle chez un enfant espagnole âgée de six ans*. Bruxelles: Imprimerie Veldeman, 1948.
(36) Tomb, J.W. "On the Intuitive Capacity of Children to Understand Spoken Language." *British Journal of Psychology* 16, Part 1 (1925): 53-55.
(37) Vildomec, V. *Multilingualism*. The Hague: A.W. Sijthoff-Leyden, 1963.
(38) White, Burton L. *The First Three Years of Life*. Englewood Cliffs, NJ: Prentice-Hall, 1975.
(39) ———, and Watts, Jean Carew. *Experience and Environment: Major Influences on the Development of the Young Child*. Englewood Cliffs, NJ: Prentice-Hall, 1973.
(40) Young, Patrick. " 'Babies Can Communicate at Birth.' " *The National Observer* 15, xxx (week ending July 24, 1976): 20.

Chapter Six
From Accountability to Program Evaluation
Meta Sue Reynolds

INTRODUCTION

A Gallup Poll (*17*) conducted in 1970 showed that approximately two out of every three people felt that teachers and administrators should be held more accountable. Responsible educators should take a first step toward a system of accountability by determining "what is"; they will then be able to make decisions about "what ought to be."

The term "accountability" did not appear in the *Education Index* until 1970 (*17*). Since then, its promiscuous use has filled many pages in professional journals and formed the subject of numerous papers and theses for advanced degrees. Although its roots go back to the early writings of Thorndike (*33*) in the first quarter of the century, Lessinger (*19*) coined the phrase "educational accountability" in 1970. At that time, the industrial model was used as his point of reference. However, since then the term has been applied to the statement of instructional objectives, performance contracting, voucher systems, economic input-output analysis, and accreditations.

Needs Assessment and Accountability

The Elementary and Secondary Education Act of 1965 required school systems to assess needs before beginning a program of improvement. One method of determining needs has four steps: 1) the goals or objectives of the system should be established or identified; 2) the level of achievement of students should be measured on each side of the goals; 3) the amount by which achievement falls short of each of these goals should be determined; and 4) the needs should be ranked in order of importance to point out those which are to receive major attention.

Accountability generally establishes performance objectives and publicly discloses these objectives, tests for meeting these objectives, and reteaches and remediates. Needs assessment may become a part of an accountability plan; certainly focusing more clearly on what we want to do and having feedback as to whether we have accomplished these goals and objectives should do nothing less than improve education—which is the thrust of needs assessment and accountability (23).

Accountability Means Responsibility

There is a close, often interfacing, relationship between needs assessment and accountability. Accountability means accepting responsibility for educational results. This responsibility and its consequences are given to teachers and school administrators (17), thus focusing attention on the results of the educational system.

How can we as educators be more responsible, more accountable? Can we improve programs currently in operation? Can we really have foresight and not hindsight? All these questions can be answered in the affirmative. The first step in moving toward accountability is program evaluation, an operation which will help us think more precisely about the things that really matter. Is that not what education is all about, thinking more precisely about things that matter?

PROGRAM EVALUATION

The focus of this chapter is evaluation in foreign language programs. For accountability to be effective and purposeful, program evaluation must be planned and implemented. Before it can be assumed that a change would be an improvement it is necessary to know what is currently being done (12).

It is the task of this chapter to present a definition of evaluation for foreign language programs, the critical aspects of such an evaluation, and a model for structuring and implementing such an evaluation.

A Definition of Program Evaluation

Educational evaluation is the process of delineating, obtaining, and providing useful information for judging decision alternatives (25, p. 40). Within this definition are eight key terms which require definition:

1) *Process* is a continuing activity which involves many techniques and methods. It is important to view evaluation of a foreign language program as a continuing and recycling process rather than as a terminal one.

2) *Delineating* means identifying what evaluative information on the foreign language program is required for the types of decisions for which one is obtaining information.

3) *Obtaining* is gaining information through such processes as collecting, organizing, and analyzing data. Measurement, data processing, and statistical analyses are also employed.

4) *Providing* involves fitting the information about the foreign language program together in systems and subsystems that best serve the decision-maker who must choose among decision alternatives.

5) *Useful* suggests information which is appropriate, practical, scientific, and meets established criteria.

6) *Information* involves descriptive and interpretative data about entities in the foreign language program and their relationships to evaluation.

7) *Judging* is the act of decision making, choosing among decision alternatives which have been presented.

8) *Decision alternatives* present two or more different actions which might be taken in response to some situations in a foreign language program which require change (*25*, pp. 40-43).

Evaluating a foreign language program is a process that furnishes useful information for decision-making. Evaluation always involves a decision in response to a question. Should foreign language teachers use language laboratories and mechanical aids? Should new textbooks be adopted? Is practice congruent with theory? Is new content needed in foreign language courses? Should teachers be required to study in a foreign country for a year before teaching its language? Although these are rhetorical questions at this point, the answers to such questions involve decisions.

The Decision-Making Process

Decision-making, the crux of any program evaluation, has four stages: one must be aware that a decision is needed; the decision situation must be designed; one must choose among alternatives; and the chosen alternative must be enacted (*25*, p. 50).

Awareness. As a common frame of reference to illustrate this process, consider a rarely used language laboratory. What are the possible considerations which generate the awareness stage? First of all, the language lab had sat unused in the school for a lengthy period of time. The principal asked the foreign language teachers why they did not use it. Their response was that it was old and inoperative. Thus, the principal became aware that a decision was needed. Should the lab be repaired? Would the lab be useful if repaired or was it obsolete? These questions lead into the second stage.

Information Gathering. The principal discussed space needs and allocations for the following year with his superior. An electrical technician skilled in repairing language laboratories assessed the condition of the laboratory and indicated that the lab, although old, could be repaired. When the foreign language teachers were asked how they wanted to use the lab, they expressed a preference for tape recorders in their classrooms.

Choosing Among Alternatives. Using all of this information to design the decision situation, five decision alternatives emerge: the lab could be left in the school to be used by other subject areas; it could be transferred to another school; it could be left intact for future foreign language teachers who might be more positively inclined toward using it; the current foreign language teaching staff could be retrained to use the lab appropriately; or the lab could be dismantled and its parts stored for use in repairing other labs in the school district. Faced with these alternatives, the knowledge that there would be insufficient classroom space in the future, and the lack of teacher interest in the language lab, the decision was made to dismantle the lab and store the usable parts.

Action. The fourth and final stage is enacting the chosen alternative, thus concluding the decision process. This involves placing responsibility for implementation of the chosen alternative, putting the selective alternative into action, reflecting on the efficacy of the operationalized alternative, and executing the alternative or recycling (25, p. 53).

Decision Types

Just as there are four stages to the decision making process, so there are four types of decisions. These are planning decisions, structuring decisions, implementing decisions, and recycling decisions.

Planning Decisions. Planning decisions identify and specify major changes that are needed in a program. For example: Should career education be brought into the curriculum? Should teachers utilize values clarification strategies? Should program goals be changed? What are the top priorities for foreign language programs now and in the future? What are the characteristics of the problems involved in meeting top priority needs? What behaviors should the students exhibit following their participation in a program (25, pp. 80-81)?

Structuring Decisions. Structuring decisions specify the means to achieve the ends established as a result of planning decisions. Such questions as these would characterize structuring decisions: Should audio-lingual, traditional, or communicative methods be used to attain the goals? Does the method match the approach? What facilities are needed? How much will it cost to implement this new approach in foreign language teaching (25, p. 81)?

Implementing Decisions. Pertinent to implementing decisions are the following questions: should a professional-growth course in teaching culture be offered? Should the role of technology in learning a foreign language be assessed? Should new procedures be instituted? Should additional resources be sought? Should responsibilities be reassigned among the foreign language teaching staff? How should the value of foreign language learning be presented to the public? Implementing decisions comprise much of the day-by-day duties of operating any program (*25*, p. 83).

Recycling Decisions. At any point in decision-making, decisions may need to be recycled. The following questions illustrate what is meant by recycling decisions: Are the students' needs being met? Is the current course in translating French needed? Are curricular offerings pertinent to our changing society? Are the problems being solved in the manner that was intended? Was the product worth the investment? Is the foreign language pilot project succeeding? Should more be invested in resourses? Has the project resulted in improved teacher competence? Have school-community relations been improved? Have students improved their self-concepts?

For the four stages in the decision making process to be operative, relevant decision questions must clarify and illuminate the problem (*25*, p. 84).

Composition and Function of Teams

To initiate an evaluation of a foreign language program, we suggest that a leadership team, an evaluator team, and a decision-making team be set up to assist and facilitate the evaluative process.

The leadership team of foreign language teachers is chaired by the foreign language coordinator. Representation is broad enough to cover the different levels of languages taught, all subject areas, and various approaches to the teaching of a foreign language. Prior to data collection, the leadership team should meet for a two-to-three week workshop, which could explore answers to some of the following questions: Why evaluate the foreign language program? What is our philosophy of foreign language learning? What are the goals of our foreign language program? How can we describe our approaches for teaching a foreign language? What data do we want to collect? How can we glean data for information? Who should comprise the evaluator team?

The leadership team forms a link between the decision-making team and the foreign language teaching staff. For an evaluation of a foreign language program to be effective, the teaching staff must be involved from the onset and aware of the purpose of evaluation. Otherwise, suspicion and skepticism might accompany the evaluation process. Although it may be utopian to hope that each person on a foreign language teaching staff will welcome a program evaluation, resistance can be minimized through system-wide in-service, newsletters, and special study sessions.

The evaluator team is composed of people who have skill in collecting and analyzing data and in presenting this data to the decision-makers. Their role must be clarified from the beginning. It is vital that members of this team understand their role and agree with the role description as defined by the project director. This team is chosen by the leadership team, and it is advisable to select foreign language consultants from outside the system who can be more objective in their evaluation. As plans are made by the leadership team, they can be directed to the evaluator team for comment, analysis, and approval.

As experts in the foreign language field, the evaluators provide feedback related to the soundness of each step in the planning and structuring of a program evaluation. Their overall purpose is to increase the rationality of decisions. Through delineating, obtaining, and providing information, the team seeks to reduce the effects of bias, limited perspective, inadequate understanding, and other sources of irrationality in the decision process (25).

The decision making team includes the supervisor as the project director, his or her immediate superior, and the Director of Research for the school system. Final decisions about recommended program changes and implementation of these changes rest with this team. The leadership and evaluating teams supply pertinent, precise information for formulating these decisions. A high degree of cooperation and professionalism must exist among these teams.

The different roles of the three teams who plan and implement an evaluation often overlap. The one person constant on each team is the foreign language supervisor who, as the project director, provides leadership and direction.

Modeling a Program Evaluation

There are many designs for modeling a program evaluation (25). PERT (Program Evaluation and Review Technique) (6) was utilized by the foreign language department of the Nashville Metropolitan Schools in the evaluation of their program in 1970-71 (28). An evaluation design requires specifically stated objectives, delineated major work units, and identified tasks to be accomplished. In Nashville's Evaluation Design the following components of PERT proved of value in constructing a model: 1) a work breakdown structure, and charts representing this structure, and 2) a network ordering and sequencing the activities.

Work Breakdown Structure. The first step in this process is to state the objectives of the evaluation. This structure reflects a top-to-bottom approach to planning, which then must be sub-divided into small, manageable units. Figure 6.1 shows the major work units in the project, and illustrates one way of

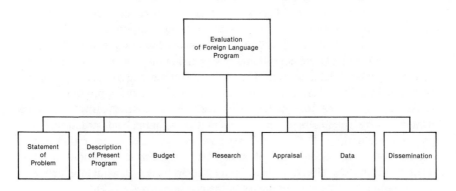

FIG. 6.1. Major Work Units of Program Evaluation

ordering priorities. These work breakdowns of activities stated the problem, described the program, and planned budgeting, research, appraisal, data collection, and dissemination. The next level is a sub-division of the previous level of work units. This process is continued until all components of each major division of work are identified. The level of detail shown in the work breakdown structure would vary according to the complexity of the project. Further sub-division is shown in Fig. 6.2, which identifies the components of each unit. A work breakdown structure may also be developed using the format shown in Fig. 6.3, which depicts the major units of work at Level 1, the components of each unit at Level 2, and the work packages at Level 3.

Network. A network, illustrated in Fig. 6.4, is the foundation of the PERT system. It shows the plan established to reach project objectives: some activities can go on simultaneously; some are interrelated and interdependent, and are "constrained" by other activities that have to proceed them; and some activities rank as priorities.

A network is composed of events and activities: events represent the start or completion of an activity; activities, which necessitate the use of personnel and resources over a period of time, are the tasks required to complete a project. These activities are represented in the circles of Fig. 6.4; for an alternate way,

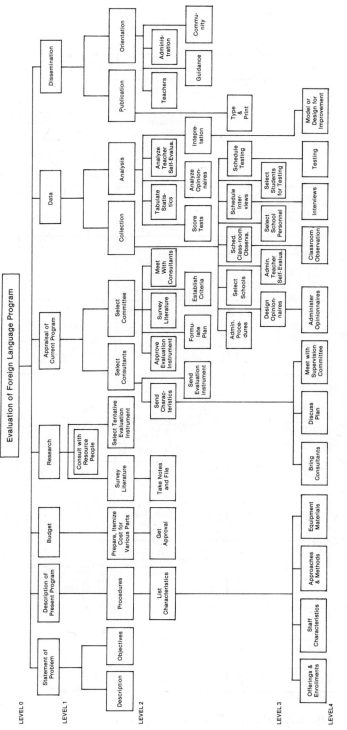

FIG. 6.2 Subdivision of Work Units in a Work Breakdown Structure

93

O	Level 1	Level 2	Level 3	Level 4
Evaluation of Foreign Language Program	State-ment of Problem	Description Objectives		
	Descrip-tion of present program	Procedures	List characteristics of present program.	List offerings and en-rollments. List staff charac-teristics. List approaches and methods. List equipment and materials.
	Budget	Prepare budget. Item-ize cost for consultants, testing, materials, sup-plies, publication of re-sults.	Get budget approved.	
	Re-search	Survey literature on foreign language evalua-tions. Consult with resource persons. Select ten-tative evaluation instru-ment.	Take notes and file.	
	Apprais-al of current program	Select consultants.	Send characteristics. Send evaluation instru-ments and work of steering committee.	Bring consultants. Discuss plan. Meet with supervisor, committee of teachers, administrators and for-eign language teachers.
		Select committee of foreign language teach-ers-"steering committee."	Read pertinent articles on foreign language evalua-tions. Establish approach for self study and involve-ment of the whole foreign language teaching staff, ad-ministration. Design evalua-tion instruments. Formulate plan. Meet with con-sultants.	
	Data	Collection	Administrative proce-dures. Design opinionnaire. Select schools for visita-tion. Administer teacher self-evaluation instrument. Schedule classroom observation. Schedule inter-views. Select the students to test. Schedule test.	Administer question-naires. Classroom observa-tions. Interviews. Testing.
		Analysis	Score tests. Tabulate sta-tistics. Analyze opinion-naires. Analyze teacher self evaluations. Interpretation.	Design model for Im-provement (includes data analysis by super-visor, Director of Re-search, and Outside Consultants).
	Dissemi-nation	Publication	Type Print	
		Orientation	Teachers Guidance Administration Board of Education	

FIG. 6.3. Tabular Work Breakdown Structure for Foreign Language Program Evaluation

see "activity on the arrow" (6). Generally circles or bubbles are used to represent activities or events, but other symbols such as squares or rectangles would work as well.

It would be well to note here that it is not the purpose of this chapter to teach the PERT system. Although there are intricate details involved in the PERT-ing of a project, this tool has proved useful and productive for designing an evaluation in the Nashville-Metro Schools, and it offers ideas for systematic planning and structuring of other evaluations.

As one focuses on the charts of this model, it is obvious that the structuring of an evaluation demands much attention to the details of all aspects of the project. This model for structuring the evaluation of a foreign language program gives direction for other evaluative inquiry. PERT-ing is but one technique for delineating, obtaining, and providing useful information to judge decision alternatives; for further models, see the report of Phi Delta Kappa National Study Committee on Evaluation (25).

Evaluation Strategies

Evaluation is a multifaceted activity calling for different strategies and methodologies according to the purpose, scope, and conceptualization of the evaluative process. Multi-data collection approaches can be utilized to provide information about pupils, curriculum, staff, finance, facilities, and the community. Often evaluation efforts have failed to yield data adequate for diagnostic studies of instructional programs. In the Nasvhille Evaluation, a multi-faceted data collection approach was used. All the instruments and data from this evaluation are contained in a publication entitled *Evaluation: A Perspective for Change* (28), which may be obtained from the Foreign Language Department of the Nashville-Metro Public Schools. Data from a variety of information forms was collected, analyzed, and presented to the decision-makers for further scrutiny and interpretation.

Program and Staff Characteristics. The leadership team of foreign language teachers, working with the supervisor, sought to describe the current program in these ways: the number of students, and the percentage of the student body enrolled in foreign languages were identified; the foreign languages offered and their sequences were cataloged; the number of foreign language teachers, their background in the languages, including travel and study abroad, and the number of teachers who taught only one foreign language a day were charted; and texts, audio-visual materials, methods, and approaches were listed. Every school in which foreign language was offered was profiled. These profiles included the number of students enrolled in the school, the number of students enrolled in a foreign language, the number of students enrolled in different languages, and percentages for each category.

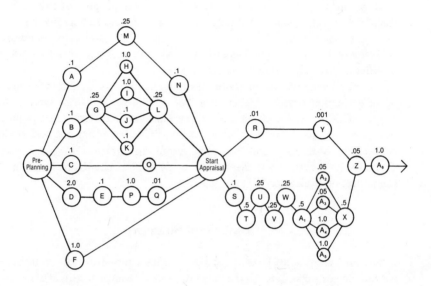

ACTIVITY IDENTIFICATION

A - State problem
B - Describe present problem (general)
C - Prepare budget
D - Survey literature
E - Select tentative evaluation instrument
F - Consult with resource persons
G - Work out procedures for specific descriptions of present program
H - List offerings and enrollments
I - List staff characteristics
J - List approaches and methods
K - List equipment and materials
L - Organize description
M - Describe the problem
N - State objectives
O - Get approval of budget
P - Take notes
Q - File
Dummy - Start appraisal
R - Select consultants
Y - Contact consultants
Z - Sent consultants characteristics of foreign language program
A⁶ - Feedback from outside consultants on approach, evaluation design

S - Select committee
T - Read literature on evaluation
U - Formulate plan or approach
V - Establish criteria
W - Design evaluation instruments
A¹ - Work out procedures for collection and analysis of data
A² - Select proficiency tests to administer
A³ - Draw up evaluator's schedule
A⁴ - Design student opinionnaires
A⁵ - Design personnel and community opinionnaires
X - Organize and write up work of committee
Dummy - Start collection of data
A⁷ - Selection of schools to visit
A⁸ - Schedule personnel and students for school observation and interviews'
A⁹ - Contact school principals, guidance counselors, and foreign language department chairmen
A¹⁰ - Select classes for testing
A¹¹ - Test
A¹² - Score
A¹³ - Convert into percentiles and stanines

FIG. 6.4 Summary Network for

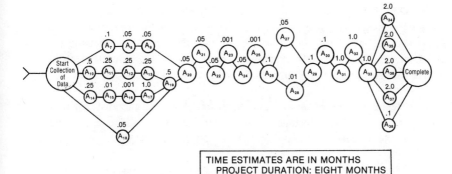

TIME ESTIMATES ARE IN MONTHS
PROJECT DURATION: EIGHT MONTHS

A¹⁴ - Select foreign language and non-foreign language classes to take opinionnaires

A¹⁵ - Administer

A¹⁶ - Receive back

A¹⁷ - Analyze data and draw conclusions

A¹⁸ - Teachers fill out self-evaluation forms

A¹⁹ - Compilation of all data

A²⁰ - Bring outside consultants (evaluators)

A²¹ - Review evaluative process with consultants

A²² - Joint meeting of steering committee of foreign language teachers and consultants

A²³ - Consultants approve, improve plan and review with foreign language supervisor

A²⁴ - Evaluators meet with central office administrators

A²⁵ - Evaluators assimilate data (tests, opinionnaires analysis, teacher self-evaluation forms, and information on each school's foreign language program)

A²⁶ - General meeting of evaluators with foreign language teachers

A²⁷ - Evaluators visit foreign language departments of schools, students, school personnel

A²⁸ - Evaluators write up report of findings each day

A²⁹ - Evaluators interpret data and observations

A³⁰ - Evaluators draw up tentative Evaluation Report

A³¹ - Design a model for improvement for the foreign language program

A³² - Type Report

A³³ - Publish results

A³⁴ - Disseminate results to foreign language teachers

A³⁵ - Disseminate results to guidance counselors

A³⁶ - Disseminate results to community leaders

A³⁷ - Disseminate results to administration

A³⁸ - Disseminate results to Board of Education

Foreign Language Program Evaluation

Teacher Self-Evaluation Instruments. The leadership team devised an evaluation instrument based on the self-evaluation instrument included in *Evaluative Criteria* (*24*), and adapted for specific use by the Nashville foreign language teachers. It was not felt that a change would take place in the foreign language teachers because they used this instrument to self-evaluate, but it was used to provide additional information to the evaluators concerning how the teaching staff viewed themselves.

Opinionnaires. Two opinionnaires were designed with the help of the Director of Research. One was administered to both foreign language students and non-foreign language students to determine attitudes toward foreign language study. The other was designed to compare the attitudes of administrative personnel, guidance personnel, foreign language teachers, and community leaders toward the foreign language program and the value of foreign language study.

Proficiency Tests. The *Pimsleur Proficiency Tests* (*26*) were administered to a random sampling of French, Spanish, and German language students to provide an index of student achievement, and teacher effectiveness.

Classroom Observation. Three leaders in the foreign language field were asked to make classroom visitations in 11 schools chosen at random out of 37. They were to observe a designated language teacher in each school, have a conference with the teacher, and speak with students about their foreign language experience. These experts were given wide latitude in critiquing teacher effectiveness. Some might quibble over the reliability of data gleaned from short visits to teachers' classrooms. Yet, even if teacher Jones directs the best learning situation possible, what he or she does or does not do is revealing. Interviews with students, guidance personnel, foreign language teachers, and principals may be included along with classroom observation to get a picture of the environment of the schools' programs.

Reports and Recommendations. As has been stated the goal of evaluation is educational improvement, The report of the visiting team of evaluators can provide the decision team with appropriate information and recommendations for making decisions regarding educational improvement. A written report by this team might be put in outline form:

An Overview of the Foreign Language Program

I. Major Findings
   A. Outstanding features
   B. Worthy innovations
   C. Weaknesses

II. Suggestions for improvement
    A. Guiding principles for the future development of the foreign language program
       1. Consideration given to hiring practices
       2. Consideration given to staff development
       3. Consideration given to needed curriculum changes
    B. Promising practices that should be further developed
    C. New practices suggested for consideration of the school system
    D. Present practices that should be discontinued.

Because of the wide range of activities to be accomplished in planning and implementing an evaluation of a foreign language program, a wide range of professionals needs to be involved. We have stated a need for three teams (a leadership, an evaluator, and a decision making team) whose roles interface as they initiate and implement a program evaluation.

SUMMARY

In this chapter, accountability and program evaluation have been defined. For accountability to be effective and purposeful, program evaluation must be initiated and implemented.

Educational evaluation was defined as the process of delineating, obtaining, and providing useful information for judging decision alternatives, and each of the eight key terms was analyzed. The decision-making process is a complex one, and is at the crux of any evaluation. In order to handle decision information effectively and responsibly, it was suggested that three teams be set up to assist and facilitate the evaluative process: a leadership team plans and executes the process of evaluation; an outside evaluator team interprets evaluative input and data and gives expert, unbiased insight into it; and a decision making team assesses the information that has been gathered and recommends improvements and changes.

PERT (Program Evaluation and Review Technique) was used as a process for modeling an evaluation. This multi-faceted data collection approach was presented along with the data systems in which the information was categorized and described.

CONCLUSION

The implementation of a program evaluation must be planned carefully: the evaluation must be budgeted for; units must be established in which personnel can participate; models for evaluation designs must be developed; and a climate must be created in which evaluation is neither feared nor mistrusted. In effect, a program evaluation requires thought and action. Above all, however, there must be an awareness of the need for change. As a change process, evaluation is a part of a continuous recycling activity.

Such a complicated process as program evaluation reminds one of the line from Albee's play *The Zoo Story*: "going a long way out of the way to come back a short distance correctly." Often it appears to some as quixotic "chasing after windmills." Nevertheless, evaluation is the first step in moving from responsibility to accountability. It gives us a perspective on where we have been, where we are, and where we want to go.

BIBLIOGRAPHY

(1)   Barro, Stephen M. "An Approach to Developing Accountability Measures for the Public Schools." *Phi Delta Kappan* 52 (1970): 196-205.

(2)   Brodbelt, Samuel. "The Impact of Educational Accountability Upon Teachers and Supervisors." *The High School Journal* 52, ii (1972): 55-66.

(3)   Brown, Arthur. "What Could be Bad? Some Reflections on the Accountability Movement." *English Journal* 62 (1973): 461-63.

(4)   Brunner, Jerome S. *Toward a Theory of Instruction.* Cambridge, MA: The Belknap Press of Harvard University Press, 1966.

(5)   Combs, Arthur W. *Educational Accountability: Beyond Behavioral Objectives.* Washington, DC: Association for Supervision and Curriculum Development, 1972.

(6)   Cook, Desmond L. *Program Evaluation and Review Technique: Application in Education.* Monograph No. 17. Washington, DC: Bureau of Research, 1966.

(7)   Deck, L. Linton, Jr. *PERT and Educational Administration.* Unpublished PhD. dissertation, Harvard University, 1966.

(8)   Durstine, Richard M. "An Accountability Information System." *Phi Delta Kappan* 52 (1970): 236-40.

(9)   Dyer, Henry S. "Toward Objective Criteria of Professional Accountability in the Schools of New York." *Phi Delta Kappan* 52 (1970): 206-12.

(10) Glass, Gene V. "The Many Faces of Educational Accountability." *Phi Delta Kappan* 52 (1972): 636-39.

(11) Grittner, Frank M. *Teaching Foreign Languages.* New York: Harper and Row, 1966.

(12) Harmes, H.M. "Improvement in Education: Criteria for Change." *Educational Technology* 10, xi (1970): 46-50.

(13) Hatfield, William N. "Foreign Language Program Evaluation." In *The Britannica Review of Foreign Language Education, Volume 1*, edited by Emma M. Birkmaier, pp. 375-88. Chicago: Encyclopedia Britannica, 1968 [1969]. [Reprinted as *Foreign Language Education: An Overview*. Review of Foreign Language Education, vol. 1. Skokie, IL: National Textbook, 1972.]

(14) Havighurst, Robert J. "Joint Accountability: A Constructive Response to Consumer Demands." *Nation's Schools* 89, v (1972): 46-47.

(15) Henry, David D. "Accountability: To Whom, For What, By What Means." *Educational Record* 53, iv (1972): 287-92.

(16) Krystal, Sheilia, and Henrie, Samuel. *Educational Accountability and Evaluation Prep Report No. 35.* Washington, DC: U.S. Government Printing Office, 1972.

(17) Landers, Jacob. "Accountability and Progress by Nomenclature: Old Ideas in New Bottles." *Phi Delta Kappan* 54 (1973): 539-41.

(18) Lessinger, Leon. "Engineering Accountability for Results in Public Education." *Phi Delta Kappan* 52 (1970): 217-26.

(19) _____ . *Every Kid a Winner: Accountability in Education*. Palo Alto, CA: Science Research Associates, College Division, 1970.

(20) Lieberman, Myron. "An Overview of Accountability." *Phi Delta Kappan* 52 (1970): 194-96.

(21) Lopez, Feliz M. "Accountability in Education." *Phi Delta Kappan* 52 (1970): 231-36.

(22) Mallon, Maridoris. "Accountability: A Two-Way Street." *School and Community* 58, viii (1972): 30.

(23) Morrisett, Irving. "Accountability, Needs Assessment and Social Studies." *Social Education* 37 (1972): 271.

(24) National Study of Secondary School Evaluation. *Evaluative Criteria for the Evaluation of Secondary Schools*. 4th ed. Washington, DC: National Study of Secondary School Evaluation, 1969. [1785 Massachusetts Avenue, Washington, DC 20036.]

(25) Phi Delta Kappa National Study Committee on Evaluation. *Educational Evaluation and Decision Making*. Itasca, IL: F.E. Peacock Publishers, 1971. [Daniel L. Stufflebeam, Committee Chairman.]

(26) Pimsleur, Paul. *Pimsleur Proficiency Tests: French, German, Spanish, Forms A & C*. New York: Harcourt, Brace & World, 1967.

(27) Porter, John W. "Accountability: Challenger and Opportunity." *Business Education Forum* 27, vii (1972): 37-39.

(28) Reynolds, Meta Sue. *Evaluation: A Perspective for Change*. Nashville, TN: Metropolitan Public Schools, 1971. [2601 Bransford Avenue, Nashville, TN 37204.] Mimeographed.

(29) Robinson, Donald W. "Accountability for Whom? For What?" *Phi Delta Kappan* 52 (1970): 193.

(30) Rosenshine, Barak, and McGaw, Betty. "Issues in Assessing Teacher Accountability in Public Education." *Phi Delta Kappan* 53 (1972): 640-43.

(31) Selden, David. "Productivity, Yes. Accountability, No." *Nation's Schools* 89, v (1972), 50-56.

(32) Sension, Donald B., and Rabehl, George J. "Test Item Domains and Instructional Accountability." *Educational Technology* 14, iv (1974): 22.

(33) Serafino, Robert P., et al. "A Relevant Curriculum: An Instrument for Polling Student Opinion." In *Foreign Languages and the 'New' Student*, edited by Joseph A. Tursi, pp. 7-30. Reports of the Working Committees of the Northeast Conference on the Teaching of Foreign Languages. New York: Modern Language Association Materials Center, 1970.

(34) Sikula, John P. "Accountability: Some Teacher Misconceptions." *The High School Journal* 56, iii (1972): 154-57.

(35) Silberman, Charles E. "How the Public Schools Kill Dreams and Mutilate Minds." *The Atlantic Monthly* 232 (1970): 83-96.

(36) Stewig, John Warren. "Bandwagons Are For Riding: Accountability and Drama." *The Elementary School Journal* 74 (1974): 192-94.

(37) Thomson, Scott D. "How to Custom Cut Accountability to Fit Students and Parents." *Nation's Schools* 89, v (1972): 48-49.

(38) Wildavsky, Aaron. "A Program of Accountability for Elementary Schools." *Phi Delta Kappan* 52 (1970): 212-17.

Chapter Seven
Communication That Is Relevant, Enjoyable, and Live: Group Dynamics in the Language Classroom

Virginia Wilson
Beverly Wattenmaker

Effective communication in a foreign or second language can begin on the very first day of classes. Students learn quickly when the new language is the tool for meaningful communication about things that are important to them—who they are, what they like and don't like, what they do or hope to do. Techniques for such teaching can be developed from the studies and experiences of researchers in various fields, including psychology, linguistics, and education. The result is that teachers and students find more pleasure, challenge, and reward in the teaching and study of languages.

RELEVANT LANGUAGE LEARNING

How can learning a new language be made interesting and important for students? Consider which of the two following exercises would be more likely to succeed:

1)
Substitute the correct form of the verb *tener* in the following: Yo tengo un libro. (I have a book.)
El
Nosotros
Ella
Ustedes

2)
   "Que tienes que te hace sentir a gusto?" (What do you have that makes you feel good?)
   "Tengo una motocicleta."
   "Tengo mi perro (dog). Me siento contenta."
   "Tengo un perro tambien. L _____ y yo tenemos perros."

A very shy girl who always chose to sit in the corner pulled her chair into the circle and asked, "¿Como se dice 'baby sister'?" "Tengo mi hermanita."
"Tengo mi bolsa (purse). Me hace sentir cómoda."
"Tengo mi color," answered another girl as she looked down at her black hand. "Me siento . . ."
" ¿Orgullosa (proud)?" asked the teacher.
"Si, me siento orgullosa."
Students recall what each one has answered:
"B____, tienes tu motocicleta."
"M____, y L ____, ustedes tienen los perros."
"D____, tienes tu hermanita."
"A ____, tienes tu bolsa. Te sientes cómoda."
"C ____, tienes tu color. Te sientes orgullosa."

It is obvious that the second exercise would be more interesting; yet it may seem unrealistic to expect that it could happen in a classroom. Efforts at conversation in foreign language classes have usually been more in the nature of directed dialogs or lists of questions designed to elicit data about students' personal lives. For example:

"Demandez à Monique si elle est allée en France." (Ask Monique if she has gone to France.)
"Monique, répondez-lui que non, jamais." (Monique, answer no, never.)

" ¿Eres buen estudiante?" (Are you a good student?)
" ¿Eres muy rica?" (Are you very rich?)
" ¿Eres feliz?" (Are you happy?)
" ¿Eres alto o bajo?" (Are you tall or short?)
" ¿Es rubia tu madre?" (Is your mother blonde?)
" ¿Es grande tu cocina?" (Is your kitchen big?)

Responding to directed dialogs is useful as a linguistic exercise, but quite unlikely to trigger any free conversation. Personal questions, instead of stimulating students' interest, may offend them. A South American friend once objected indignantly to her English teacher's questions: "She asked me, 'Are you married?' 'What does your husband do?' " A popular workbook has questions such as " ¿Es inteligente tu padre?" (Is your father intelligent?) Teachers who are aware of, and who perhaps share, their students' discomfort in answering such personal questions may say, "Answer anything, just so you use the verb correctly. It doesn't have to be true." That may be conversation, but it is not communication.

Asking personal questions is not, in itself, enough to establish a willingness to communicate. Something has to happen to generate feelings of trust and confidence. Because interaction among members of the group is necessary to the development of these feelings, the physical arrangement of the class is important. If students sit in rows facing the teacher with their backs to each other, any sense of involvement with one another is lost, and little meaningful communication can take place among them. On the other hand, a flexible classroom permits movement from large to small groups, or to pairs. When students are sitting in small groups engaged in some activity such as interviewing one another, everyone becomes involved. If it is understood that the person being questioned may decline to answer and may ask the interviewer the same question, the necessary trust for open communication becomes a possibility. Teachers and students find it enjoyable and rewarding to engage in personal conversations using simple techniques that enable students to talk about themselves, their thoughts, and feelings while learning a new language.

Real Communication at Kenston High School

What can happen when teachers and students are involved in learning to accept each other and work together toward their goals of language mastery and personal development is demonstrated in a sound-slide report on the foreign language program of Kenston, a rural high school near Cleveland, Ohio (8). The school serves a consolidation of culturally different communities that include wealthy families living in suburban parks, families of second-generation European origin living in small farms, and black families living in a rural ghetto. The high school is small, with approximately 800 students. In 1965, there were fewer than 100 students studying two foreign languages. Now, in spite of the fact that there are no foreign language requirements for any student, nearly half the school's population studies French, Spanish, or Russian; and some students take all three. Furthermore, they are not simply amused by a novel program or planning to travel abroad; they are learning languages. Visitors observing the classes are impressed by the students' ability to understand, and astonished by their unselfconscious use of the language in conversations with one another. Students who have taken the Ohio Tests of Scholastic Achievement have ranked high. In 1975, six of the eight Kenston students who took the tests received honorable mention or higher (11). A second-year Spanish student achieved the highest score in competition with students from throughout the state.

At Kenston the four- to five-year programs in French, Spanish, and Russian use a curriculum based on both the audio-visual method originally developed for French by CREDIF (Centre de Recherches et d'Etudes pour la Diffusion du Français) at the Ecole Normale Supérieure de Saint Cloud (14), and what we call "Real Communication" exercises that enable students to generate personally meaningful language in the context of their own lives. A student's performance is not marked by letter grades; no failure is recorded. The levels, or years, of the program are defined by grammar and vocabulary objectives. Students either receive credit with a pass for each level, or nothing is recorded. If necessary, levels may be repeated without penalty.

Second-year Spanish and French students can choose between two programs: They may continue their studies in the normal one-hour-a-day classes; or they may study intensively two and a half hours a day to complete the second level in three months, followed by a three-week homestay in a French- or Spanish-speaking community. On returning to school after the homestay, most students possess both the skills and motivation to join third-level classes for the second semester. Their enthusiasm and cultural experiences add interest and life to the entire program.

Joshua Gordon, a free-lance reporter, photographed and recorded interviews with Kenston students and teachers who have been involved in homestays abroad (8). Excerpts from these unrehearsed conversations illustrate the deep involvement of the students and their good feelings toward the language programs.

REPORTER (interviewing first the head of the department): What is the essence of the program at Kenston that makes it unique?

B. WATTENMAKER: The actual method of teaching is a self-discovery one that involves the students and helps them to discover meaning for themselves. Then probably the most exciting part is using what they have learned in terms of helping them to communicate things that are important to them.

REPORTER: Basically, the unique concept behind the Kenston program is that foreign language is something to be used and learned as a communications tool and not as an abstract book exercise. The language is used to communicate things of direct importance to the students, and emotional growth is one of the program's most valuable side products.

Cindy P., a student in the intensive Spanish program, described the class experience to Mr. Gordon.

CINDY P.: It's two and a half hours long. Usually we start off the day, like a lot of times, with a filmstrip and we just repeat what it says. We'll get that over with in about half an hour, and then we will go to our workbooks and we will be using what we have just learned, like the verb tense. We don't have to repeat necessarily what's in the filmstrip. Maybe, after a while, we will have a discussion using what we have just learned. We will sit around in a circle and—but we always relate it to what we do in our lives. She doesn't ask us what did Pablo do in the film. She asks us things like, What did you like to do when you were a child? or What's an instance of what someone did for you that made you feel really wanted or really loved? She asks us things like this and we will just answer, going around in the circle. Then when you finish the worksheets and the workbook that goes along with that unit, then you'll take a test. It's using some of the questions we have learned, but we don't talk about other people. She asks us about ourselves and about things we have gone through in our lives, but using the verb tense that we just learned or whatever so that it's relevant all the time.

REPORTER: Could you explain the grading system?

CINDY P.: It's that everything you pass in, 80 percent of it has to be correct. If it's not, then you just do it over again. You keep doing it over until it's correct. And the teacher will help you with it! She's not going to just say, 'Go correct it!' She'll help you with it and show you what you have done wrong and then, when you are ready to take the test again, you take it over again. And you don't have a certain deadline to get it in, but you always want to keep up with yourself because you don't want to be ten tests behind, and then the last day of the semester have to get all those tests in.

REPORTER: Grades are not the motivation making the students work. The students must be self-motivated.

B. WATTENMAKER: Getting involved and really staying with it has been a tremendous help to the students to really get somewhere. With the extra time allotment, we are able to do a lot of things together, like going on trips. We got to kids' homes; we sit on the living room floor . . .

REPORTER: Paul L., a parent of a student who has been in the intensive language program, describes his reaction to having a foreign language class meet in his living room.

PAUL L.: I think we had about four meetings at our house. The one thing that struck me was that I couldn't understand a word that they were saying. From the moment they came into the house, it was total Spanish. When they broke for their lunch, it would continue.

REPORTER: For most students the high point of the intensive program is the trip abroad. In talking to the students, activities with the people abroad seemed to be a very meaningful experience.

CHERYL H. (a student from a small, segregated black community): I went to Mexico. My family [there] was pretty rich. We had a lot of problems at first, but finally I felt just like one of them also. I liked the food there, and a lot of the people there in Mexico. They were really nice.

TALLEY R.: I think one of the things I really liked about it was that your ear has to get so trained, and it's like you are just listening the whole time you are down there. You just listen so hard; it's such an effort to carry on a conversation. When you get back home, you are still doing the same thing. Before, you were missing so much, I found out.

REPORTER: How did you adapt to the different customs? Were any of them hard to reconcile?

TALLEY R.: It's something that's good to go through. You find that you can adapt to situations, which makes it better. I thought before I went that I wouldn't be able to stand the food at all, and I really liked it when I got down there. I thought . . . everybody told me that some of the living conditions were really bad. You know I had a fine time, and at the end nothing even bothers you, barely at all.

REPORTER: Was there any trouble with regard to people who had to adapt to a situation and couldn't?

CHERYL H.: I think so, in our town. One girl—normally here she lives in like a pretty good rich house, and there the house wasn't all that rich. The first night it caused sort of a problem because she didn't like those situations too good, but later on it did improve because she learned, you know, to respect the people more.

CONNIE L.: You learn a lot about yourself too. You learn everything about Mexicans that you possible can, but you learn your real feelings, how you can act in a different situation, how you can act to [sic] a different culture, and how you can relate to people that are completely different. You learn that you can be more emotional toward people; you just learn so much about yourself.

CHERYL H.: You learn how to accept people more, especially of a different culture. That carries on [sic], you know, like when you come back to the United States and face the real situation here.

REPORTER: The Russian classes at Kenston are not part of the intensive program. Russian instructor Bill O'Neil says that arranging a home-study experience is difficult in the Soviet Union, but he is hopeful for the future. Nonetheless, some of his students have made the trip to Russia.

MARK M.: We met a lot of Russian students at both Leningrad and Moscow. I talked with one of the Russian students at Leningrad for almost two hours. He was really interested in the United States.

BILL H.: The students were very friendly and interested in the United States and what we live like. One thing I noticed was that when you went out on the street, just walking around, it's just like any city—Cleveland, Ohio—there's a lot of people running around the sidewalks and nobody really cares if you are in the way. But then when we met with the students inside one of the schools, they were really friendly and interested.

Gordon interviewed other teachers, administrators, and a reporter from the local press. He found both approval and disapproval. The chairman of the English Department noted the good feelings of students involved in the intensive foreign language program: "I've noticed a tremendous difference in their behavior, their attitude toward each other, and I think it even helps their attitude toward school in general after they have had this experience." The superintendent of the school district believes that the foreign language program is an active and exciting part of the high school program, that it has added a new dimension to the school and the community, and that it is becoming generally accepted as criticism is sought and changes are made.

The first year that students went abroad for three weeks they had great difficulty making up work missed in other classes. In response to criticism from other teachers, the intensive class schedules were altered so that the homestay is now during the first three weeks in December. In January, students use the intensive class period to make up work missed in their other classes. Mike M., a reporter from the local newspaper, responded to Gordon: "I know that there have been times when the community has responded negatively to this program. You will find that the program has gained strength and greater acceptance as it has gone along. It has been accepted by such a diverse community, blacks and suburban whites and rural whites."

Home-study-experience coordinators from the Experiment for International Living (Brattleboro, VT 05301) have found Kenston students unusually well prepared to adapt to homestays. A student once explained this to visitors in a Kenston foreign language class: "I didn't realize it, but what most prepared me was learning to get along with people in our class. I could get along with people down there and accept their differences because we do it here in class."

GROUP DYNAMICS OF
TEACHING COMMUNICATION

Group dynamics, the interaction of physical, mental, and emotional forces of individual members, are likely to stimulate greater change and more productive activity than could be achieved by one member alone. This interaction implies that there is a greater potential for growth and learning within a group. The teachers at Kenston learned this after a year of trying to work in a completely individualized program where students moved ahead at their own pace. Progress was soon bogged down in boredom. Stimulation and joy were lacking. The dynamics that are operating now involve students in both the cognitive and affective domains.

Discovery Methods

It was in the cognitive domain that the first major changes were made at Kenston. In 1970, the audio-visual method developed by CREDIF (*14, 10*) was introduced, and the question-answer techniques for explaining dialog and grammar structure soon proved to be conducive to group participation, involvement, and interaction. The scope and simplicity of the learning that takes place using this process is astonishing. The simplicity of the questions belies their importance: "What is this?" "Who is this?" "What are they doing?" "Who or what are they doing it to?" "How?" "Why?" "Where?" Actually, these are the basis of a universal grammar; their meaning may underlie the deep structure of any language (*17*).

In a foreign or second language situation illustrated by pictures or filmstrips, students hear recorded dialog between native speakers. The teacher then re-plays the dialog, line by line, asking carefully planned questions designed to help students discover the structural components of each sentence and isolate the words or phrases which are meaningful in response to each question. The following example is from an Iñupiaq Eskimo text used in Barrow on the Arctic coast of Alaska (23). The teacher has the sentence recorded either on tape or on a language master card and plays it after asking each question.

Teacher's question	Recording	Student's response
Kiña una? (Who's this?)	Niksik minniqtaqtuq quviasukluni. (Niksik is jumping up and down because he is happy.)	Una Niksik.
Suva Niksik? (What is Niksik doing?)	"	Minniqtaqtuq.
Minniqpa naakka minniqtaqpa? (Did he jump once or is he jumping up and down?) Demonstrate with action.	"	Minniqtaqtuq.
Niksik quviasukpa naakka ipiqtusukpa? (Is he happy or sad?) Demonstrate with expression.	"	Quviasuktuq.
Summan Niksik minniqtaqpa? (Why is Niksik jumping up and down?)	"	Nisik minniqtaqtuq quviasukluni

The group process is worthy of note. Individuals within the group answer. When one cannot think of the answer, then someone else can; as a last resort, the teacher suggests, "Ask me!" The beauty of this, in practice, is that it is not always the same person who answers. For example, a student with a talent for linguistic analysis may not have the quick ear to identify new words in the sound stream of the recorded sentence. All the varied talents of the group are required to hear the sentence, separate it into meaningful segments, and determine the meaning. Questions are repeated several times to give three or four people the opportunity to answer, and to give everyone time to assimilate the new material. Those who give incorrect responses are always given an opportunity to correct themselves after hearing someone else's correct answer.

Niksik mingiqtaqtuq quviasuktuni.

FIG. 7.1

Part of the learning process is that students discover the value of making mistakes. They generalize on the grammatical structure from what cannot be said, as well as from what can be said. Valuing what they learn from mistakes, students become more willing to make them and, therefore, more willing to try to generate new, previously unheard sentences.

There are pitfalls in the use of the audio-visual method. An unskilled teacher might make such a "mish-mash" of the questions that students would have great difficulty formulating valid generalizations as to language structure. Furthermore, according to Stevick, the barrage of questions by a judgmental teacher could be threatening to some students. It is important for success of the method, then, that there be "an atmosphere of unconditioned personal acceptance by the teacher, group spirit among the students, opportunities for greater personal investment and a wider range of creativity" (*18*, p. 152).

Success Philosophy

The elimination of competitive grading is very important to building confidence among members of the group. It influences both their willingness to risk making mistakes and their readiness to help each other learn. A student's work is evaluated on the basis of his or her mastery of grammar and vocabulary. Because no one is marked with failure, it is what Glasser calls a "success" philosophy (*7*). Students receive credit only for successful mastery. Thus, standards of achievement can be kept high, and students are ready for each new level of study without being penalized by bad marks if they need extra time to achieve it. At the end of a scholastic year a student's report indicates "Pass" or "Incomplete." If students' work is incomplete, they may continue to study during the summer, take tests, and go on to the next level; or the teacher and student may decide that it is advisable to continue study at the same level. This is only partially repetitive because the communication activities of a new group are necessarily different to some extent. The greater success of the more experienced student is often stimulating to the other group members. Records do not indicate when the completion of a level has required more or less than the "normal" time. If students decide not to continue their studies to achieve the standard for a mark of "Pass," then the incomplete course is dropped from their records.

A happy result of this procedure is a greater freedom to learn. Under a conventional grading system, students who want "As" cannot risk making mistakes which might lower their marks. Their learning is circumscribed by what they know is right. When students can only achieve a mark of "Pass," and when they have the opportunity to try again, they are free to venture into the realm of the unknown and make their own discoveries. Teachers have noted with pleasure that students quickly begin to think in the new language and express themselves much like native speakers, both in speaking and in writing.

Non-judgmental Attitude

Under a success philosophy, the more open, less judgmental evaluation is helpful to teachers as they learn new attitudes which make them better facilitators of the group dynamics of trust and cooperation. Teachers have a dual role in the groups: They are leaders and models on the one hand, and participating members on the other. Teachers have the same opportunity to grow and the same responsibility as the other group members to warmly accept and appreciate others as individuals, express genuine feelings, be open to others and their worlds as *they* see them, and listen actively to others.

In the terminology of transactional analysis (*1*), this relationship between students and teacher would be, adult-adult, or child-child. The adult-adult relationship is between persons who ask questions regarding the matter at hand, make decisions, and act on them. The child-child relationship is one of creative—perhaps fanciful—thinking, enjoyment, and fun. The parent-child relationship is the more traditional one of the classroom, the parent being either nourishing or domineering, and the child either obedient or rebellious. This is the judgmental relationship which Stevick (*18*, p. 152) has found detrimental in some teachers' use of the CREDIF discovery method. Successful practitioners of this audio-visual method, however, maintain an adult-adult relationship. A long time master teacher for the Center of Curriculum Development, now part of Rand McNally & Company, seemed to us, his students, to play the role of a friend helping us to understand the strange voice on the tape.

Reflective Listening

Listening actively to others means showing that you really hear what they say and understand what they mean. This may be done effectively by paraphrasing what the other person has said and reflecting the emotional content (*9*). The results can be astonishing. A student in the first intensive class at Kenston came to Beverly Wattenmaker and said, "I can't go to Mexico. I have been to the doctor. I'm sick."

Bev paraphrased her statement, "You can't go because you're sick."

The student hastened to add, "Well, I'm not really sick, but that's a very scary thing."

Then Bev reflected back the feelings of fear that she had perceived. The student, ordinarily so self-confident that no one would have suspected the underlying fear, then admitted to her feelings, examined the problems, decided to make the trip, and found it a very rewarding experience.

Bev did not tell the student that she should not be afraid; she did not blame or ridicule her, nor even praise her usual poise and sense of security. She accepted the student's feelings, taking care to make no value judgments.

Practicing reflective listening helps a person become more accepting and less judgmental. However, teachers may still wonder if their role demands that they be judgmental. They sometimes ask if they shouldn't show disapproval of students' wrongdoing. According to Rogers (15), people become free to change when they are first accepted as they are. Reflective listening is a way to show acceptance of people and their feelings rather than their actions.

"Magic" Circles

Systematic sharing of personal experiences and feelings, combined with reflective listening, creates an atmosphere for growth in awareness of self and others. Bessell (2), a psychotherapist who believes that people can learn good mental health and not need therapy, has designed a structured classroom approach to human development. He suggests that teachers and students participate in groups of no more than 16, sitting in a circle and responding to a feeling question. This should be very simple at first, such as, "Look around the room. What do you see that makes you feel good?" When each person has answered, or chosen not to do so, then the leader and participants recall what each one said using reflective listening techniques: " ____ , you like ____ ; you feel ____ ."

Day by day, the conversation topics elicit deeper feelings of a wider range. The following sequence of topics is from the Spanish version of the Human Development Program (3). Although it was designed for first-grade children, experience has shown that the sequence is appropriate also for high school, university, or graduate students.

"Vamos a hablar de algo que nos hace sentir bien" (p. 9).
    (Let's talk about something that makes us feel good.)
"Sentimientos agradables y desagradables. Me senti bien y mal acerca de algo" (p. 13).
    (Good and bad feelings. I felt good and bad about something.)
"Algo que quiero hacer, pero no sé como" (p. 67).
    (Something I want to do, but don't know how.)
"Hice algo que agradó a alguien" (p. 83).
    (I did something that made someone feel good.)
"Alguien hizo algo que me agradó" (p. 85).
    (Someone did something that made me feel good.)
"El maestro hizo algo que no me agradó" (p. 96).
    (The teacher did something that made me feel bad.)
"Cada uno de nosotros hizo algo que no le agradó a otro" (p. 97).
    (Each one of us did something that made someone feel bad.)
"¿Qué puedo hacer por ti? " (p. 102).
    (What can I do for you?)

The teacher, or leader of the group, models the accepting attitude that permits people to share their real feelings. During each session, the participants recall what each one has said. The magic of these circles is that sharing little things with real meaning and being remembered makes people feel good, feel accepted, and helps them develop a sense of their own worth.

Bessell's (2) reply to people who worry that talking about feelings is somehow dangerous and out of place in the classroom is that emotions are no more pathological than arms and legs. The questions discussed are personal, but not intimate. Participants are free to share or not to share, and are completely in control of what they share.

Realizing that the language of these questions is simple while the human growth potential is great, we have planned a sequence of topics, all related to the progression of grammar and vocabulary objectives, that enables students to share experiences, thoughts, and feelings; in addition, they develop awareness and valuing of self and others, and promote group interaction. These topics exemplify such a progression for conversation circles from *Real Communication in German* (4):

Das Verb *sein* im Präsens (the verb *to be* in the present):
  „Wo bist du froh?" (p. 16).
  (Where are you happy?)
Das Präsens (the present tense):
  „Was machst du gut?" (p. 21).
  (What do you do well?)
Akkusativobjekte (direct object):
  „Was hast du, was schön ist?" (p. 2).
  (What do you have that is beautiful?)
Das Futur (the future):
  „Wie wirst du jemand anderem helfen?" (p. 28).
  (What will you do to help someone?)
Verben im Perfekt, Hilfsverb *haben* (verbs in compound past, with auxiliary *have*):
  „Was hat dir jemand gesagt, was dich glücklich gemacht hat?" (p. 33).
  (What has someone said to you that made you feel good?)
  „Was hast du jemandem gesagt, um ihn glücklich zu machen?" (p. 33).
  (What have you said to someone to make them feel good?)
Dativobjekte (indirect object):
  „Was für Leute gefallen dir gut?"
  (What kind of people appeal to you?)
Perfekt und Imperfekt (compound past and imperfect past):
  „Als du klein warst, was machtest du, um das zu bekommen, was du wolltest?" „Wann hast du das zum letzten Mal versucht?" (p. 50).
  (When you were small, what did you do to get what you wanted? When did you last try it?)

Students and teachers share their experiences, thoughts and feelings; they listen and recall the experiences and feelings of others. Accepting and being accepted, they learn to value themselves enough to believe that they have something to share, and value others enough to want to share with them. There is no longer only one teacher in the group; everyone is a teacher and everyone is a learner.

The "magic" circle is not a language-teaching device; it is a place to use language and learn about yourself and others. Therefore, it is important to make sure that necessary language structure is thoroughly understood before beginning the communication activity. Vocabulary, however, cannot be anticipated; therefore, new words must be supplied as needed. The quickest and most natural way is to use the teacher as a resource person, a role well-developed by Stevick in "Counseling-Learning." (18, pp. 126-33).

When learning languages in which there are few cognates, students need some way to associate new words with meaning. Using a technique of making picture books to illustrate conversation topics (22), teacher and students draw quick sketches to explain their answers to the question, and the teacher identifies the pictures with the new words. In 1975, Emily Wilson and Larry Kaplan, teachers of an Eskimo class at the University of Alaska in Fairbanks, ventured an experiment in making picture books in spite of their fear that university students would react negatively to a child-like activity. Emily asked the question, "Sullatuvich?" (What do you like to do?) Larry drew a rough sketch of himself sailing, which Emily identified, "Umiaqtullaturutin." (You like boating.) While the students were drawing, Emily interpreted their pictures: "Iqalliqillaturutin." (You like to go fishing.) "Kanaakkiullaturutin." (You like to dance.) "Qiniq-tuallaturutin uvlugianik." (You like to look at the stars.) Students wrote under their drawings: "Iqalliqillaturuna." "Kanaakkiullaturuna." "Quiniqtuallaturuna uvlugianik." (I like to. . . .) As the teacher moved on, students began asking each other, "Iqalliqillatuvich?" Or, "Sullatuvich?" The students felt successful using the language in a really meaningful way. The teachers also felt pleased and happy, especially when one young Eskimo spoke "Iñupiatun" for the first time. Previously she had seemed embarrassed to try to make the unusual sounds.

When the drawings are finished, teacher and students sit together in a circle and share their answers to the question, illustrating their meaning with their pictures. Afterwards they remember and recall what each one said. The drawings are collected and fastened into a booklet with the question written on the cover as a title.

The university students entered enthusiastically into the activity. They enjoyed being involved in the class and getting to know one another. When one of them subsequently dropped out of the university, he said, "If all my classes had been like the Iñupiaq class, I would not have left."

Interviews

Data from the personal lives and thoughts of group members and visitors are an inexhaustible source of relevant communication, and interviewing is a valuable technique for exploiting it. The teacher may interview the entire group; the group may interview one of its members or a visitor; or participants may interview each other. Ground rules, to insure rights of privacy, should be clearly established: The person interviewed may decline to answer any question. The person interviewed may ask the same question to the interviewer. The scope of the subject matter is limited only by the linguistic ability and the imagination of the participants. Inspiration to stimulate the imagination may be found in Simon's handbook of strategies for values of clarification (*16*, p. 139ff).

Brenckle, a professor of Russian at the University of Alaska, uses reading assignments to stimulate interviews between students. Each week he assigns a reading selection and asks students to write out five personal questions with their own answers. Although they use the topic and vocabulary of the text, these questions are not about the text; they are individualized and serve to stimulate conversation. For example, after reading a story of the crash landing of a plane in the Neva River (*13*), one student asked the following questions:

Вы любите летать самолётом?
(Do you like to fly in an airplane?)

Вы часто летаете?
(Do you fly often?)

Вы волнуетесь, когда вы летаете?
(Are you afraid, when you fly?)

Вы хотите ездить в Советский Союз?
(Do you want to go to the Soviet Union?)

Какие районы Советского Союза вы хотите смотреть?
(Which parts of the Soviet Union do you want to see?)

The questions are simple and the language basic; yet the answers reveal information interesting enough to stimulate more questions. The students like to talk in pairs, so they do not have to worry about an audience. The slower pace of their questions, as compared to the teacher's, gives them time to comprehend meaning, and think of their responses. Students feel good about beginning to know each other in a friendly and cooperative atmosphere. People are willing to risk making mistakes when they know that the worst result will be friendly laughter.

Advanced Spanish classes in Fairbanks High School frequently have Spanish-speaking visitors. The most charming was the five-year-old daughter of the German teacher. Christina, who speaks Spanish, German, and English, is a little reluctant to speak until she is sure that people will understand her. She soon lost her shyness when the students introduced themselves to her in Spanish, telling her about things they like. She had brought some storybooks to class. Following the pictures page by page, she told stories in Spanish to the delighted students. Another unusual interview was with Larry Kaplan, a young linguist who came to Alaska to help write an Eskimo grammar and dictionary. The students introduced themselves to him, and told what they liked about Alaska; then they interviewed him about his family and travels. When they asked about his work, he decided to explain the structure of the Eskimo language. There was much laughter as he walked to the board and gave a lecture on Eskimo linguistics, in Spanish.

A Swiss exchange student studying Spanish visited a beginning class. The students introduced themselves, and talked about places they liked. They then interviewed her, and she was amazed by their ability to communicate. Students like to have visitors who are also learning the language; the fluency of native speakers who do not understand the limitations of beginners can be frustrating and, sometimes, frightening. Through experience with interviews, students learn that they have a better chance of understanding a conversation if they are asking the questions. They then understand at least half the conversation and have some control over the remainder. Another interesting discovery is that students often talk about themselves more openly in a foreign language than in English—rather like writing a diary in code.

Thoughtfully planned interview questions take most language practice out of the textbook and into the reality of students' lives; however, interviewing requires a change in attitude for many teachers. An impatient teacher should not rush a student: "Say just anything; it does not matter as long as it is grammatically correct." It *does* matter to the students. Unless teachers care *what* students say, as well as *how* they say it, communication will be dead and, perhaps, language teaching along with it. Today's students will only commit themselves to what interests them, and language per se interests only a few. What interests them most is themselves and other people. Teachers who are open and honest invite students to be the same. They establish rapport and trust, and create an accepting, non-judgmental environment.

Interaction

With the non-judgmental attitude of the teacher as a model, students become more accepting of each other. They are able to experiment with new relationships in the group.

Simon, Howe, and Kirschenbaum (*16*) describe a great number of values clarification activities, many of which can be adapted to foreign or second language use. One strategy for breaking down barriers between people is a "trust walk." The following description of its use is from *Real Communication in French* (*19*, pp. 70-71):

"Comment communiquons-nous? Nous parlons—oui—mais nous communiquons par des gestes et des sens. Nous employons les yeux, les mains, la figure, les pieds, le corps—tout—pour nous aider.

"Maintenant, nous allons avoir une expérience de communication employant tous nos sens sauf la vue et la parole.

"Trouvez un partenaire. Vous allez vous promener ensemble. D'abord, un partenair va guider et l'autre va suivre avec les yeux fermés. Vous allez communiquer sans parler—et l'autre personne sans voir. La personne qui guide va essayer de rendre l'expérience très intéressante pour l'autre personne. Après 10 minutes, échangez de rôle. Ainsi, vous deux aurez l'occasion d'avoir chacun la même expérience—celle de guider et celle de suivre. Retournez au cercle après 20 minutes."

(How do we communicate? We talk, yes, but we also communicate with gestures and senses. We use our eyes, hands, face, feet, body—all of them to help us. Now we are going to have an experience of communicating using all our senses except sight and voice. Find a partner. You are going to take a walk together. First, one partner will guide and the other will follow with eyes closed. The person guiding will try to give interesting experiences to the other person. After 10 minutes, change roles. Thus, each of you will have the chance to experience both guiding and following. Return to the circle after 20 minutes.)

"Parlez avec votre partenaire.

—Qu'est-ce que tu as touché, goûté, entendu, senti? As-tu imaginé des couleurs? Lesquelles?

—Mettez en ordre d'importance ce qui est le plus important pour toi: les yeux, les mains, les oreilles, le nez, la bouche."

(Talk with your partner. What did you touch, taste, hear, smell? Did you imagine the colors? Which ones? Put in order of importance for you: your eyes, your hands, your ears, your nose, your mouth.)

"Trouvez un autre couple et vous 4 discutez les questions suivantes.

—Quelles réactions et quelles pensées avais-tu? Avais-tu peur: étais-tu inquiet, surpris?

—Préfères-tu suivre ou guider? "

(Find another couple and the four of you discuss these questions: What reactions and thoughts did you have? Were you afraid, uneasy, surprised? Did you prefer to lead or follow?)

"Retournez au grand groupe et complétez chacun une des phrases suivantes en faisant très vite le tour du cercle.

—Je me suls rendu compte de/que_____ .
J'ai remarqué _____ .
J'ai appris que _____ .
(Return to the large group and each one completes one of the following
     sentences, going quickly around the circle.
I became aware that _____ .
I noticed that _____ .
I learned that _____ .)

Correction and Evaluation

When to correct, and when to overlook mistakes, is a matter of some importance
when a teacher wants to maintain high standards of correct language usage and,
at the same time, encourage communication. When teaching new grammar
concepts, correction must be precise and prompt in order to help students
internalize accurate generalizations as to the structure of the language. For
example:

"¿De dónde eres?" (Where are you from?)
"Yo soy los Estados Unidos." (I'm the United States.)

Students laugh and the teacher, glad that they understand and can see the joke,
quickly helps the student who has made the error:

"¿Eres tú (=) los Estados Unidos, o eres tú de los Estados Unidos?"
"Soy de los Estados Unidos."

As language use becomes freer and more personal, an accepting, non-judgmental
attitude should prevail, and correction should be made only to clarify meaning.

The nature of evaluation has a great effect on group dynamics. Grading tends
to encourage competition rather than cooperation, generate resentment rather
than trust. Teachers and students of Kenston High School like working with a
success philosophy in which "Pass" is the only record. In the world of school
administration, registrars, and transcripts, however, most teachers find it
difficult to stop grading. Class meetings (7) provide an opportunity for students
to have input into alternative methods of grading which they might suggest. One
alternative that allows a great deal of student responsibility is to let students
contract for a grade of "A," "B," or "credit." All work would have to be up to
the agreed standard or done over; in this way students are competing only with
themselves, not against each other.

Honest feedback that enhances learning is the aim of correction and
evaluation. It can best be accomplished in a caring, non-judgmental environment.

Learning About Group Dynamics

Teachers who want to improve the group dynamics of their classes, who want to harness the energy for greater learning, both cognitive and affective, may need some help to begin. It is valuable for teachers to experience in a group the kind of communication and interaction that they want for students. Workshops in personal growth and interpersonal relationships help their members relate to one another, while workshops in communication skills in foreign language give teachers guidance, confidence, and the mental and emotional energy to answer the question, "What shall I do on Monday?"

Workshops are not the only way to learn. Some colleges and universities are now emphasizing the affective aspects of teaching in their methodology classes; among them are West Chester State College in West Chester, Pennsylvania, Temple University in Philadelphia, and Ohio State University in Columbus. There are many books with exercises that can be adapted to foreign or second language use, as well as some that are designed especially for language teachers. Our own series, *Real Communication in Foreign Language*, has editions in English by Wilson and Wattenmaker (*24*); in Spanish by Wilson (*21*); in French by Stoller, Lock, Wilson and Wattenmaker (*19*); and in German by Bruce, Wilson, and Wattenmaker (*4*). These can be accompanied by Wilson's workbook in basic Spanish (*20*), Lanys' exercises in Russian (*12*), and exercises in English designed for translation by Galyean (*6*). Disick and Barbanel (*5*) have carefully reviewed the literature on affective education and cite the work adapted for foreign language by David Wolfe and Stefano Morel. Teachers can read and learn and talk among themselves. They can plan communications exercises that complement the content of their lessons and create an atmosphere in their classes for growing and learning with their students.

Although learning to lead groups is not really difficult, it is wise to build your confidence by practicing with your most responsive students. A group of four to eight may be formed simply by asking those who have finished reading a story to join you in talking. Positive response and good feedback will reinforce your skills and inspire confidence that the group experiences will work. One of the greatest pleasures derived from such experiences is finding yourself valuing a person for whom you had felt little regard in the usual classroom situation.

It takes courage to try a different way of teaching; and, somehow, teaching in the affective domain has an aura of risk. Teachers think that perhaps they need some special counseling training, that they need to be psychologists. That is far from the case for, in actual use, these communications exercises bear no resemblance to therapy. However, because the subject matter is personal, teachers know their students well and may discover some need for therapy. In that case, teachers need to know how to help their students find skilled counseling help; the teacher's skill is knowing how to listen.

Wattenmaker got a startling response one day while conducting a "magic circle" in English. The task was to tell about something that made you feel good.

STUDENT: I have a sickle. I felt good one night when I cut down our neighbor's grain.

TEACHER: You felt good when you cut down his grain. It seems to me that you feel angry with him.

STUDENT: Yes, I do. He wouldn't pay me.

The teacher made no value judgment. She accepted the young man's emotions. He may have needed to share the burden of his vindictive deed, for he was, and is, a responsible member of the community. By reflective listening the teacher showed acceptance of the person, if not the act.

Successful Use of Group Dynamics

Teachers, students, and parents are proud of the program at Kenston High School; its success can be measured in terms of student involvement, human growth, class enrollment, and language ability.

Student involvement is evidenced by interaction and language use observed in the classroom. Baker, the Ohio State Foreign Language Supervisor, has commented often on his surprise and pleasure in finding first-year language students at Kenston using the language informally.

Human growth is apparent in the students' own statements of self-awareness and understanding of others, and in the teachers' professional development. In 1971, we were asked by the Center for Curriculum Development to write a workbook (20). As consultants, we have prepared materials and trained teachers in language methodology and communication techniques. Working with Joanne Lock, Gail Wise, Gary Smith, John Zachritz, and Phyllis Stoller, we have conducted workshops at national conferences of the American Council for Teachers of Foreign Languages and at state and regional conferences in schools and colleges throughout the continental United States, and in Hawaii, Alaska, Mexico and Canada. In 1974, Russian teacher William O'Neil was selected to teach English for three months in Moscow and Leningrad; and, in 1977, he was one of seven high school teachers and 27 college professors who spent a summer of intensive study in Russia.

Class enrollment steadily increases, while nationwide it may be dropping.

Language ability can be measured by a first place and five honorable mentions (11) in 1975 on the Ohio Tests of Scholastic Achievement, and by congratulatory letters from colleges on the achievements of some of our students.

Although we have worked harder than we ever anticipated, we actually find our classroom activities much easier. We are spending our energy in creating lesson plans, not in disciplining and "pulling answers" from uninvolved non-students. Our classes are alive. The class atmosphere has changed from one where the teacher does all the work to one where the students are working hard on their own and helping each other. When a group of Kenston students participated in a panel before a class of doctoral students at Ohio State University, one of them said, "Being in the foreign language classes has helped me to realize I do have an ability to learn and a talent to lead."

We feel good that we are helping students learn to cope in a society which has become desensitized. The word "love" is debased; there is no money in "good and beautiful." Cataclysms, murder, war, and violence are reported in terms of hundreds and thousands so that our senses are numbed. Our miraculous media, with its instant communication to the farthest corner of the earth, bombards us with real and make-believe horror to the point that we are insensitive to it. In order to awaken our sensibilities and become aware of ourselves and others, we need to share the good and the beautiful, and feel the horror and the fear on a scale that each of us can comprehend.

We are doing a little of that in language classes, and learning language as well. It seems worthwhile.

CONCLUSION

The purpose of this paper is not to describe methodology or explain the use of communication exercises, but rather to say, as convincingly as possible, that there are teaching methods which are stimulating for both teachers and students. The use of a new language in communications exercises is a way to establish open, affective, trusting relationships within a group learning the language. And freedom to learn is best achieved in a cooperative atmosphere.

BIBLIOGRAPHY

(1) Berne, Eric. *Games People Play: The Psychology of Human Relationships*. New York: Grove Press, 1964.
(2) Bessell, Harold, and Palomares, Uvaldo. *Methods in Human Development*. San Diego, CA: Human Development Training Institute, 1970.
(3) ———. *Metodos en desarrollo humano*. Chihuahua, Chihuahua, Mexico: Instituto Interamericano de Estudios Psicologicos y Sociales, 1973.
(4) Bruce, Douglas; Wilson, Virginia; and Wattenmaker, Beverly. *Real Communication in German*. Saratoga Springs, NY: National Humanistic Education Center, 1976. [110 Spring Street.]
(5) Disick, Renee S., and Barbanel, Laura. "Affective Education and Foreign Language Learning." In *The Challenge of Communication*, edited by Gilbert A. Jarvis, pp. 185-222, ACTFL Review of Foreign Language Education, vol. 6. Skokie, IL: National Textbook, 1974.
(6) Galyean, Beverly. *Language from Within: A Handbook of Teaching Strategies for Personal Growth and Self Reflection in the Language Class*. Santa Barbara, CA: Confluent Education Development and Research Center, 1976. [Box 30128, zip code 93105.]

(7)   Glasser, William. *Schools Without Failure*. New York: Harper and Row, 1969.

(8)   Gordon, Joshua. "Kenston High School and a Unique Approach to the Teaching of Foreign Language." An unpublished sound-slide report, 1976. [Transcript available from Beverly Wattenmaker, 4162 Giles Road, Chagrin Falls, OH 44022.]

(9)   Gordon, Thomas. *Parent Effectiveness Training*. New York: Peter H. Wyden, 1970.

(10) *Integrated Multimedia Foreign Language Programs: French, Spanish, German, Hebrew, Russian, Italian, Portuguese, and American-English*. Chicago: Rand McNally, n.d. [zip code 60680.]

(11) "Kenston Language Pupils Excel," *The Herald Sun*, May 29, 1975. [Chagrin Falls, OH.]

(12) Lanys, Birute. "The Role of Values Clarification in Developing Communicative Competence." In *Strategies for Teaching and Testing Communication Competence in Russian*, edited by Rasio Dunatov, pp. 58-93. Champaign-Urbana, IL: Russian and East European Center, University of Illinois, 1976.

(13) Nakhabina, M., and Tolstaia, R. *Russian for Everybody: Reader*. Moscow: Izdatel'stvo "Progress", n.d. [Москва Г-21, Зубовский Бульвар, 21 издательство «Прогресс».]

(14) Renard, Collette, and Heinle, Charles H. "Principles of Audio-Visual Language-Teaching." In *Implementing*, Voix et Images de France, Part I, pp. 3-101. *In American Schools and Colleges*. Philadelphia: Chilton, 1969.

(15) Rogers, Carl H. *Freedom to Learn*. Columbus, OH: Merrill, 1969.

(16) Simon, Sidney B.; Howe, Leland W.; and Kirschenbaum, Howard. *Values Clarification: A Handbook of Practical Strategies for Teachers and Students*. New York: Hart, 1972.

(17) Smith, Philip D. *Toward a Practical Theory of Second-Language Instruction*. Philadelphia: Center for Curriculum Development, 1971.

(18) Stevick, Earl W. *Memory, Meaning, and Method: Some Psychological Perspectives on Language Learning*. Rowley, MA: Newbury House, 1976.

(19) Stoller, Phyllis H.; Lock, Joanne T.; Wilson, Virginia; and Wattenmaker, Beverly. *Real Communication in French*. Saratoga Springs, NY: National Humanistic Education Center, 1975. [110 Spring Street.]

(20) Wilson, Virginia. *Entender, leer y escribir: A Workbook in Basic Spanish*. Chicago: Rand McNally, 1972.

(21) ———. *Real Communication in Spanish*. Saratoga Springs, NY: National Humanistic Education Center, 1973. [110 Spring Street.]

(22) ———. *Teaching Native Language as a Second Language*. Unpublished master's thesis, University of Alaska Library, 1976. [Also available in abridged version as *A Model of Teaching A Second Language: Inupiaq Eskimo*. Barrow, AL: Barrow School Inupiat Program, 1976.]

(23) ———, and McLean, Eileen. *Niksik Quviasuktuq*. Barrow, AL: Barrow School Iñupiat Program, 1975.

(24) ———, and Wattenmaker, Beverly. *Real Communication in Foreign Language*. Saratoga Springs, NY: National Humanistic Education Center, 1973. [110 Spring Street.]

Chapter Eight
Windmills and Dragons
Jermaine D. Arendt
Marcia Hallock

INTRODUCTION

... "Look there friend, Sancho Panza, where thirty or more monstrous giants present themselves, all of which I mean to engage in battle and slay, and with those spoils we shall begin to make our fortunes, for this is righteous warfare, and it is God's good service to sweep so evil a breed from off the face of the earth."

... "Look, your worship," said Sancho, "What we see there are not giants but windmills, and what seem to be their arms are but sails that turned by the wind make the millstone go." (1)

Twice in the twentieth century, between 1920 and 1950, and after 1970, foreign language teachers have found themselves engaged in a quixotic effort to battle a band of enemies apparently bent on destroying a curriculum area to which the teachers had devoted their lives.

Language enrollments began a long decline at the end of World War I. By 1949, enrollments in United States public schools hit their low point, with only 13.7 percent of the students learning a modern or classical language. That decline bottomed out in 1950, and began a slow recovery that climaxed in the heady years of 1960-70. That decade, stimulated by NDEA, gave a feeling of rediscovery; languages were once again not only an acceptable part of the curriculum, but an asset to the school program. NDEA disappeared with mind-boggling suddenness. Colleges dropped language requirements; general student enrollments began to fall; and public schools developed crippling budget shortages. The language teacher was bewildered, frightened, and often jobless.

For years, the high school language teacher has been trying to earn the praise of college departments by sending on students who have achieved advanced standing. For their part, the colleges supported the high school teacher by strongly recommending secondary school language learning, and often by requiring such study for college admission or graduation. Now, in some cases, college language requirements have been dropped or modified.

In the face of declining enrollments, one hears charges that teachers, students, parents, counselors, and/or administrators are at fault. Some say standards are too high, others that they are too low. Some charge that there is too much lockstep instruction, and others that there is too much individualization. One hears that students have changed somehow. They are said to be less willing to do homework, and more ready to drop out of language classes in favor of other offerings that strike their fancy. At a time when language teachers must attempt to serve up an offering of interest to students, the students seem to have become strangers, lost to the generation gap.

The loss of enrollments is real. The proposed solutions are often contradictory. There is a danger that we will mount quixotic offenses against imaginary enemies, bumble through attempts to deal with our problems, and eventually lie unhorsed like Cervantes' hero.

WHAT DOES THE STUDENT WANT?

In the Minneapolis Public School District, faced with the inevitability of falling language enrollments as the overall school population drops from 70,000 students in 1970 to an estimated 40,000 in 1980, we realized that we must increase what business calls "market share" if we were going to survive. Enrollments in languages in this large metropolitan area were also threatened by the inexorable change to a school system serving a growing number of minority and poor white students, who seemed less interested in language learning than affluent white youth had been.

We asked ourselves three basic questions: Why don't more students enroll in second language classes? Why do students drop? How do students feel about the experiences they have in language classes?

Two questionnaires were developed: The first was for students who had never enrolled in language classes. The second was for those who either had been, or who were enrolled in language classes in the junior or senior high school.

In part, the survey was designed to examine some generally accepted beliefs about language programs: If you have an enthusiastic, well-qualified teacher, enrollments will flourish and students will not drop out. Counselors are anti-language, and are responsible for low enrollments. Students take languages because of college and university requirements. Students drop because of schedule conflicts. Students drop because of poor teaching. Students drop because their friends do. Language teachers are only interested in the best students. Inner-city students do not take language classes. Teachers do not appeal to individual student interests and abilities.

The Minneapolis Foreign Language Program

Starting in the seventh grade, youth who attend the Minneapolis schools may enroll in one or more languages. Twenty-two percent of secondary school students were enrolled in language classes at the time of the study. Like students in most schools in the United States the dropout rate is large from year to year. Between 1970-75, 66 percent continued into the second year, 23 percent continued into the third year, 12 percent continued into the fourth year, and six percent continued into the fifth year.

Students in Minneapolis use mainly audio-lingual texts for at least the first two years of language learning. The method could more properly be termed "eclectic," or a "four skills approach," because teachers try to develop competencies in listening, speaking, reading, and writing as they develop vocabulary, grammar generalizations, and cultural awareness.

Although all schools have language laboratories or electronic classrooms, their use has fallen off in the last few years. Many teachers still use the taped programs of instruction that accompany basic learning programs; they also use a substantial library of films and slide/tape programs.

To encourage enrollments, in recent years the school system has offered exploratory language programs in the intermediate grades or in the junior high schools. In addition, the summer school has Spanish for grades four through six. Each year about 250 junior high youth attend a free two-week camp that features programs in French, German, Ojibwe, Norwegian, Spanish, and Russian. During the school year, the students participate in foreign food preparation, trips to museums and local restaurants, international days, heritage days, and career days. There are also two city-wide offerings, the foreign film festival, and spring trips to France, Germany, Mexico, and Spain.

Teacher teams spend part of each summer developing new curricula for classroom use, such as supplementary learning packets correlated to textbooks, and units for all levels from exploratory to third or fourth year.

The Population

Involved in this study were 6,800 senior high school students from six schools, and 4,500 junior high school students from five schools. The survey was conducted in schools ranging from those that represented low socio-economic areas to those that served upper middle class families. The percentage of students enrolled in language in the various schools ranged from 9 percent to 45 percent in the senior high schools, and from 2.8 percent to 64.6 percent in the junior high schools.

This paper reports on only six schools, three each from the junior and senior high levels. The schools chosen represent for each level a center city school with

Table 8.1

	Have not enrolled		Have enrolled		Dropped		Totals		TOTALS
	Junior High	Senior High	Junior High	Senior High	Junior High	Senior High	Junior High	Senior High	
Inner-City School	194	65	232	161	101	117	527	343	870
Transitional School	120	167	192	282	59	162	371	611	982
Fringe School	135	274	73	404	20	260	228	938	1166
TOTALS	449	506	497	847	180	539	1126	1892	3018
	955		1344		719				

a predominantly low socio-economic student body, a fringe area school with a heavily middle class population, and a school falling approximately midway between the two extremes. Table 8.1 gives a comprehensive picture of student enrollment.

Purpose of Study

The study was undertaken to develop insights that could help develop a program which would help meet student needs and interests. Many questions had to be answered in this regard: How do students in different socio-economic areas feel about modern language learning? Why do many students not enroll in modern language sequences? Why do students drop out of modern language sequences? How do students feel about their experiences as modern language learners?

Procedure

The questionnaire for this study used items from questionnaire forms previously developed by the modern language staff of the school system. We are indebted to them.

Language departments of the participating schools volunteered to collect information on their students. Data was collected through English classes, where the survey forms were distributed, completed, and collected. Information was processed by the Department of Research, Minneapolis Public Schools.

THE SURVEY

Students Who Have Not Enrolled

Students were asked to check one or more of a number of possible reasons why they have not enrolled in a second language class. Numbers indicate the percentage of students choosing a particular reason (see Table 8.2).

"A" represents an inner-city school; "B" is neither center city nor fringe; "C" schools are fringe schools.

Replies by this sizable group of young people (955 total) suggest directions for the profession if it is going to try to lure a larger percentage of school-age youth into foreign language classes.

Clearly, the major part of this group is uninterested in language learning. We need to know more about these students. What *are* their interests? Can we develop courses that appeal to those interests and yet offer worthwhile language courses? How can these students have their appetite whetted for language

Table 8.2. Total Students Responding to Survey
Who Have Not Enrolled in Modern Languages

	A Inner	B Transitional	C Fringe	TOTALS
Junior High	194	120	135	449
Senior High	65	167	274	506
TOTALS	259	287	409	955

Why Have You Never Taken a Foreign Language in School?

	Inner		Transitional		Fringe		TOTALS	
	Frequency	%	Frequency	%	Frequency	%	Frequency	%
1. Not Interested								
Junior High	103	(53%)	64	(53%)	81	(60%)	248	(55%)
Senior High	30	(46%)	95	(57%)	178	(65%)	303	(60%)
2. Schedule Wouldn't Allow It								
Junior High	29	(15%)	23	(19%)	42	(31%)	94	(21%)
Senior High	18	(28%)	37	(22%)	60	(22%)	115	(23%)
	47	(18%)	60	(21%)	102	(25%)	209	(22%)
3. Too Hard								
Junior High	35	(18%)	16	(13%)	19	(14%)	70	(16%)
Senior High	12	(18%)	35	(21%)	52	(19%)	99	(20%)
	47	(18%)	51	(18%)	71	(17%)	169	(18%)
4. Couldn't Get the Language You Wanted								
Junior High	37	(19%)	26	(22%)	14	(10%)	77	(17%)
Senior High	13	(20%)	22	(13%)	33	(12%)	68	(13%)
	50	(19%)	48	(17%)	47	(11%)	145	(15%)
5. Didn't Know Anyone Taking a Language								
Junior High	29	(15%)	0	(0%)	8	(6%)	37	(8%)
Senior High	3	(5%)	7	(4%)	14	(5%)	24	(5%)
	32	(12%)	7	(2%)	22	(5%)	61	(6%)
6. Didn't Like the Teacher								
Junior High	8	(4%)	4	(3%)	3	(2%)	15	(3%)
Senior High	2	(3%)	3	(2%)	19	(7%)	24	(5%)
	10		7		22		39	(4%)
7. Parents and Relatives Recommended Against								
Junior High	6	(3%)	1	(1%)	1	(1%)	8	(2%)
Senior High	0	(0%)	2	(1%)	11	(4%)	13	(3%)
	6	(2%)	3	(1%)	12	(3%)	21	(2%)
8. Counselor Recommended Against								
Junior High	2	(1%)	0	(0%)	1	(1%)	3	(1%)
Senior High	0	(0%)	2	(1%)	11	(4%)	13	(3%)
	2		2		12		16	(2%)

learning in the face of competition from other school electives and attractive out-of-school opportunities? Is their lack of interest a sign of ethnocentrism? If so, what can the language department do to try to make foreign languages and culture less "foreign"?

The fact that 18% of the students who have not enrolled in language classes think language learning is difficult indicates that their friends or relatives have encouraged this idea. Is the department ready to accept all comers and let them achieve to a degree which is comfortable for them? If it is, how does it get this message out to colleagues, parents, and students?

An impressive 22% of these students listed the schedule as a factor that kept them from enrolling in a language class. Has the department worked with the administration to avoid scheduling conflicts when possible? Has the department been willing to accept scheduling innovations which allow students more flexibility in scheduling courses? Have administrators been willing to develop schedules which make it easier for students to enroll in electives?

A surprising percentage of these students (15%) claimed they did not enroll because they could not get the language they wanted. One of the high schools, senior high school A, offers six languages, and three languages are offered in all of the other schools cited. Therefore, we can assume that students are really saying that they could not schedule the language that they wanted into their program.

Only a small number of students reported they avoided languages because of friends (6%), relatives (2%), counselors (2%), or the teacher (4%). These statistics fly in the face of claims that teenagers are governed by a herding tendency when they register for classes. The responses regarding parents and relatives do not tell us how parents feel about language learning. Nor is it clear whether students are reporting that they would not be influenced by parental recommendation. As we will see later, many parents apparently recommended that their sons and daughters learn a foreign language. Students in the survey tend to eliminate the old rumor that counselors are hurting the program. The counselor appears to have had little influence in the decision not to enroll. It is possible that the students feel that they made up their own minds. Finally, few students claimed that they did not enroll in the language classes because of the teacher. This response belies the oft-made claim that students are avoiding a language class because they do not like the teacher.

Students Who Have Enrolled in Languages

This group of students (see Table 8.3) includes all students who were enrolled in language at one time, although they may no longer have been enrolled when the survey was taken.

Many might argue that, if we could only retain the students who enroll in language classes, our enrollment problems would be over.

Table 8.3. Total Students Responding to Survey
Who Have Enrolled in Modern Languages

	A Inner	B Transitional	C Fringe	TOTALS
Junior High	232	192	73	497
Senior High	161	282	404	847
TOTALS	393	474	477	1344

Why Did You Enroll?

	Inner		Transitional		Fringe		TOTALS	
	Frequency	%	Frequency	%	Frequency	%	Frequency	%

1. Thought It Would Be Nice to Speak Another Language

Junior High	162	(70%)	136	(71%)	51	(70%)	349	(70%)
Senior High	105	(65%)	183	(65%)	271	(67%)	559	(66%)
	267	(68%)	319	(67%)	322	(67.5%)	908	(67.5%)

2. Thought It Would Be Enjoyable

Junior High	139	(60%)	117	(61%)	36	(49%)	292	(59%)
Senior High	101	(63%)	149	(53%)	218	(54%)	468	(55%)
	240	(61%)	266	(56%)	254	(53%)	760	(56.5%)

3. Thought It Would Be Challenging

Junior High	70	(30%)	73	(38%)	22	(30%)	165	(33%)
Senior High	60	(37%)	73	(26%)	117	(29%)	250	(30%)
	130	(33%)	146	(31%)	139	(29%)	415	(31%)

4. Wanted to Learn About a Foreign Culture

Junior High	67	(29%)	50	(26%)	14	(19%)	131	(26%)
Senior High	50	(31%)	59	(21%)	81	(20%)	190	(22%)
	117	(30%)	109	(23%)	95	(20%)	321	(24%)

5. Parents and Relatives Recommended in Favor

Junior High	46	(20%)	60	(31%)	23	(32%)	129	(26%)
Senior High	26	(16%)	79	(28%)	121	(30%)	226	(27%)
	72	(18%)	139	(29%)	144	(30%)	355	(26%)

6. Friends Enrolled

Junior High	46	(20%)	23	(12%)	15	(21%)	84	(17%)
Senior High	21	(13%)	28	(10%)	57	(14%)	106	(12%)
	67	(17%)	51	(11%)	72	(15%)	190	(14%)

7. Because of College Requirements

Junior High	12	(5%)	33	(17%)	25	(34%)	70	(14%)
Senior High	29	(18%)	118	(42%)	161	(40%)	308	(36%)
	41	(10%)	151	(32%)	186	(39%)	378	(28%)

8. Because of Foreign Language Trips

Junior High	14	(6%)	13	(7%)	9	(12%)	36	(7%)
Senior High	8	(5%)	20	(7%)	24	(6%)	52	(6%)
	22	(5.5%)	33	(7%)	33	(7%)	88	(6.5%)

9. Because of Job Interests

Junior High	5	(2%)	6	(3%)	9	(12%)	20	(4%)
Senior High	8	(5%)	20	(7%)	28	(7%)	56	(7%)
	13	(3%)	26	(5%)	37	(8%)	76	(6%)

10. Lived Once in a Foreign Country

Junior High	14	(6%)	12	(6%)	4	(5%)	30	(6%)
Senior High	8	(5%)	20	(7%)	20	(5%)	48	(6%)
	22	(6%)	32	(7%)	24	(5%)	78	(6%)

Table 8.3 (continued)

	Inner		Transitional		Fringe		TOTALS	
	Frequency	%	Frequency	%	Frequency	%	Frequency	%
11. Because of Teacher								
Junior High	9	(4%)	12	(6%)	1	(1%)	22	(4%)
Senior High	8	(5%)	6	(2%)	8	(2%)	22	(2.5%)
	17	(4%)	18	(4%)	9	(2%)	44	(3%)
12. Counselor Recommended in Favor								
Junior High	5	(2%)	6	(3%)	1	(1%)	12	(2%)
Senior High	11	(7%)	8	(3%)	12	(3%)	31	(4%)
	16	(4%)	14	(3%)	13	(3%)	43	(3%)

In this part of the survey, students were given an opportunity to tell why they enrolled. By examining these responses, teachers may be better able to plan recruitment efforts and course content to satisfy the student expectations.

A clear majority of the students polled—67.5 percent—stated that they wanted to learn to speak the language. Although this part of the survey does not show this desire is being satisfied, the next section indicates that it is not. At the same time, 31.5 percent of the students who enrolled indicated that speaking was not important to them. What skill or skills would they prefer to stress. Are their desires being met? Can learning occur in all four skills to the extent that all students will feel that they are achieving their goals?

A second major reason students gave for enrollment was that they expected it would be enjoyable; 56.5 percent gave this response. The expectation that language would be pleasurable places a great burden on the teacher. More needs to be known about student expectations in this regard. What do they find enjoyable: Hard work? Little work? The satisfaction of achievement? "Fun and games"? Competition? Cooperation? Or, a combination of these?

Far fewer students chose the remaining responses. Only 31 percent elected a language course because they thought it would be challenging. Thus, the majority of students do not enroll because they want to work hard. And only 24 percent of the enrollees wanted to learn about foreign cultures.

Although only 26 percent of the students enrolled because of parent urging, this percentage may be important. Furthermore, within the context of these three school types, χ^2 statistic applied to these data supports the conclusion that parental influence may be greater as socio-economic level rises. How can communication with parents, especially those in low socio-economic areas, be improved? How can existing parental support be further encouraged? What are parental expectations of the language program? Friends are almost as influential as parents in enrollment decisions in inner city schools, but considerably less important in other schools. In any case, peer pressure does not appear to have a consistently strong influence overall.

College requirements, imagined or real, have a varying effect on students; they influenced only 10 percent of inner city students, 32 percent of transition students, and 39 percent of fringe students in their decisions to elect a language. Furthermore, senior high students are more influenced—36 percent—than junior high students—14 percent. In Minnesota, where most of these students will attend college, only a few colleges require language for graduation, and none require it for entrance. Unless colleges begin to reinstate language requirements, fewer students will enroll for this reason.

Job plans play little part in determining whether or not students decide to learn a foreign language; only 6 percent list jobs as their objective. The replies can be interpreted in a number of ways: perhaps American secondary school students are not yet accustomed to thinking about careers; perhaps modern language teachers have failed to convince the public and the school population that foreign language skills can be useful for the worker.

The Minneapolis Public Schools have offered short, school-sponsored trips to France, Germany, Spain, or Mexico for language students. These trips have been seen as a valuable experience for youth, and as an inducement for enrollment. Apparently, the trips are not as great a lure as they were expected to be; only 6.5 percent gave them as a reason for enrollment. A smaller number—6 percent—gave previous residence in a foreign country as the reason they decided to learn a foreign language; perhaps this motive will become more important as more families travel or reside abroad.

For years, teachers have been blamed for low enrollments and lauded for high enrollments. And counselors have been thought to discourage students from enrolling in language classes. The Minneapolis student survey forces one to rethink this commonly accepted cause and effect. Only three percent of the students reported they enrolled because of the teacher, although later they generally gave their teachers and classes positive ratings. Only a small percentage of students—three percent—stated that counselors influenced their decision to enroll in language classes.

Students Who Dropped the Foreign Language

This section of the study asked previously enrolled students why they dropped a language course (see Table 8.4).

Earlier, it was seen that students enrolled primarily because they thought language learning would be enjoyable. Now, it is discouraging to find that 53 percent of those who dropped did so because classes were not interesting. Their replies raise the question, "What activities would be interesting to students?" The responses show a need for staff in-service to develop alternatives to current activities that appear to be driving students out of language classes.

In a previous section of the survey, students said they did not enroll in

Table 8.4. Total Students Responding to Survey
Who Have Dropped the Modern Language

	A Inner	B Transitional	C Fringe	TOTALS
Junior High	101	59	20	180
Senior High	117	162	260	539
TOTALS	218	221	280	719

Why Did You Drop?

	Inner		Transitional		Fringe		TOTALS	
	Frequency	%	Frequency	%	Frequency	%	Frequency	%
1. Not Interesting								
Junior High	52	(51%)	29	(49%)	9	(45%)	90	(50%)
Senior High	64	(55%)	75	(45%)	151	(58%)	290	(54%)
	116	(53%)	104	(47%)	160	(57%)	380	(53%)
2. Schedule Wouldn't Allow It								
Junior High	20	(20%)	19	(32%)	10	(50%)	49	(27%)
Senior High	49	(42%)	49	(30%)	81	(31%)	179	(36.5%)
	69	(32%)	68	(30.5%)	91	(32.5%)	228	(32%)
3. Did Not Like the Teacher								
Junior High	29	(29%)	10	(17%)	6	(30%)	45	(25%)
Senior High	26	(22%)	37	(23%)	96	(37%)	159	(29%)
	55	(25%)	47	(21%)	102	(36%)	204	(28%)
4. The Course Was Too Hard								
Junior High	19	(19%)	11	(19%)	1	(5%)	31	(17%)
Senior High	25	(21%)	45	(28%)	52	(20%)	122	(23%)
	44	(20%)	56	(25%)	53	(19%)	153	(21%)
5. Low Grades								
Junior High	11	(11%)	7	(12%)	4	(20%)	22	(12%)
Senior High	11	(10%)	41	(25%)	42	(16%)	94	(17%)
	22	(10%)	48	(22%)	46	(16%)	116	(16%)
6. Because Friends Dropped								
Junior High	1	(1%)	1	(2%)	1	(5%)	2	(2%)
Senior High	5	(4%)	3	(2%)	10	(4%)	18	(3%)
	6	(3%)	4	(2%)	11	(4%)	21	(3%)
7. Teacher Recommended Dropping								
Junior High	1	(1%)	2	(3%)	0	(0%)	3	(2%)
Senior High	1	(1%)	5	(3%)	8	(3%)	14	(2.5%)
	2	(1%)	7	(3%)	8	(3%)	17	(2.4%)
8. Parents and/or Relatives Recommended Dropping								
Junior High	5	(5%)	0	(0%)	0	(0%)	5	(3%)
Senior High	1	(1%)	3	(2%)	3	(1%)	7	(1%)
	6	(3%)	3	(1%)	3	(1%)	12	(1.6%)
9. Because of College Requirements								
Junior High	2	(2%)	0	(0%)	0	(0%)	2	(1%)
Senior High	5	(4%)	10	(6%)	8	(3%)	23	(4%)
	7	(3%)	10	(4%)	8	(3%)	25	(3%)
10. Counselor Recommended Dropping								
Junior High	2	(2%)	0	(0%)	0	(0%)	2	(1%)
Senior High	0	(0%)	0	(0%)	3	(1%)	3	(0.5%)
	2	(1%)	0	(0%)	3	(1%)	5	(0.6%)

language classes because of the scheduling problem. In this section, 32 percent say the schedule caused them to drop. There is strong evidence that the typical American school schedule makes it difficult for students to enroll in languages. Junior High School C, in which 50 percent of the students who dropped blamed the schedule, is a small school with an especially restrictive schedule.

A sizeable percentage of students—28 percent—blamed the teacher for the fact that they dropped. Presumably, many frustrations that students have had with language learning are turned against the teacher. If the class seems difficult, boring, or confusing, the teacher is held responsible. Here is a fertile field for further research and teacher education. What kind of teacher behavior has contributed to this negative image? What substitute behaviors are possible? Can the teacher image be improved through individualization, group work, or values clarification?

Course difficulty was given by 21 percent as a reason for dropping out. In a related item, 16 percent said that low grades contributed to their not continuing in language learning. Can courses be redesigned so that more students will be successful? Should teachers use diagnostic tests and surveys to identify the best learning style for each student? Poor grades seem to be more of a threat to transitional and fringe area students. Were they graded more harshly than their inner city counterparts? Or are they and their parents simply more concerned about grades?

Few students—three percent—say they were influenced to drop by their friends. Nor do sizeable numbers say that teachers, counselors, or parents—two percent, one percent, and two percent, respectively—caused them to drop. It is possible, of course, that peer pressure was subtle, and not recognized as a factor. Similarly, we only learn that teachers, counselors, and parents did not exert *overt* pressure. In any case, students themselves have identified far more important factors.

Another oft-heard claim is that students drop out of language sequence because they have to take another subject to meet special college requirements. Based on this report, the statement does not ring true; only one percent of the students reporting gave this reason.

It is possible that when students drop out, they do so primarily because another school-offering interests them more.

Grades in Other Subjects

The next section of the survey (see Table 8.5) sought to determine the grades foreign language students were accustomed to getting in school subjects, and the grades they earned in language classes. "Enrolled" indicates students who are still enrolled. "Dropped" indicates students who have dropped.

Table 8.5. General Grades

	A Inner		B Transitional		C Fringe	
	Junior High	Senior High	Junior High	Senior High	Junior High	Senior High
Mostly "A" and "B"						
Enrolled	75%	86%	84%	85%	84%	89%
Dropped	67%	63%	70%	77%	80%	82%
Mostly "C"						
Enrolled	21%	13%	14%	13%	14%	10%
Dropped	28%	27%	24%	22%	20%	18%
Mostly "D" and "F"						
Enrolled	4%	0%	2%	2%	2%	1%
Dropped	6%	0%	5%	4%	0%	0%

Table 8.6. Foreign Language Grades

	A Inner		B Transitional		C Fringe	
	Junior High	Senior High	Junior High	Senior High	Junior High	Senior High
Mostly "A" and "B"						
Enrolled	73%	79%	92%	81%	87%	85%
Dropped	65%	63%	72%	49%	50%	67%
Mostly "C"						
Enrolled	20%	14%	8%	15%	13%	13%
Dropped	24%	29%	23%	35%	35%	19%
Mostly "D" and "F"						
Enrolled	7%	7%	0%	5%	0%	2%
Dropped	12%	7%	5%	15%	15%	14%

Students who enrolled in language classes say they have received largely "A" or "B" grades in other school subjects. More "A" and "B" students continue in language classes than drop, whereas larger numbers of "C," "D," and "F" students drop than continue. However, a majority of those who drop out indicate that they were "A" and "B" students in other school subjects. Thus, a large number of students who were quite successful in school opt out of language after a trial.

Grades Received in Language Classes

Do students receive grades in language classes equal to those they receive in other curriculum areas? When compared with the previous table, Table 8.6 sheds light on that question.

These data show that students' foreign language grades are similar to those earned in other subjects. However, in Junior High School B, a much larger percentage of "A" and "B" was awarded; and in Senior High School B and Junior High School C, a comparatively larger share of lower grades was awarded to students who ultimately dropped. Earlier sections of the survey show that many students from Senior High School B cited the difficulty of the course and low grades as their reasons for dropping.

Additional Survey Data

These data include both students who have dropped out and those still enrolled. Overall, 21 to 47 percent of the students surveyed found their language classes unpleasant (see Table 8.7). However, at the junior high level, 70 to 79 percent of the students called their classes enjoyable or very enjoyable; and, at the senior high level, 53 to 70 percent of the students felt the same way.

At the junior high school level, 73 to 83 percent of the students reported satisfaction with the amount of language learned (see Table 8.8). Nearly half of the senior high school students—45.5 percent—reported dissatisfaction with the amount of language learned. Are student expectations unrealistic at the senior high school level? Have teachers at both levels failed to help document real achievement? Or have large numbers of senior high students failed to achieve?

The section of the survey shown in Table 8.9 attempted to pinpoint activities which are popular with students. Knowing what activities students like may lead to maximizing their use. It is important to note how activities were rated by junior high students as opposed to those in senior high, as well as between types of schools at a given level.

Classroom activities, as a whole, were viewed positively by less than 50 percent of those surveyed. This reaction indicates a need to look more closely at

Table 8.7. How Do You Rate Your Modern Language Class?

	A Inner		B Transitional		C Fringe	
	Junior High	Senior High	Junior High	Senior High	Junior High	Senior High
Very Enjoyable	24%	16%	34%	17%	9%	11%
Enjoyable	49%	46%	45%	53%	61%	41%
Somewhat Unpleasant	15%	29%	17%	23%	25%	35%
Very Unpleasant	12%	9%	4%	7%	5%	12%

Table 8.8. How Satisfied Are You With
Amount of Modern Language Learning?

	A Inner		B Transitional		C Fringe	
	Junior High	Senior High	Junior High	Senior High	Junior High	Senior High
Very Satisfied	26%	11%	36%	10%	21%	11%
Satisfied	47%	42%	46%	46%	60%	42%
Not Very Satisfied	26%	47%	18%	44%	19%	46%

Table 8.9. What Class Activities Did You Like?

	A Inner		B Transitional		C Fringe	
	Junior High	Senior High	Junior High	Senior High	Junior High	Senior High
Games						
Enrolled	64%	57%	74%	53%	66%	65%
Dropped	68%	51%	63%	42%	65%	55%
Conversations						
Enrolled	44%	64%	52%	55%	49%	51%
Dropped	38%	52%	39%	48%	35%	39%
Foreign Film						
Enrolled	34%	45%	40%	51%	38%	45%
Dropped	32%	37%	29%	31%	45%	35%
Learning About the Foreign Country						
Enrolled	40%	43%	44%	47%	43%	46%
Dropped	33%	36%	25%	38%	25%	24%
Classroom Activities						
Enrolled	47%	41%	47%	46%	45%	42%
Dropped	48%	32%	42%	35%	25%	39%
Learning About the People						
Enrolled	34%	48%	39%	46%	40%	41%
Dropped	27%	34%	24%	34%	20%	28%
Field Trips						
Enrolled	32%	34%	38%	32%	28%	18%
Dropped	27%	38%	27%	33%	30%	22%
Foreign Meals						
Enrolled	23%	52%	54%	56%	42%	51%
Dropped	21%	46%	32%	36%	20%	49%
Worksheets						
Enrolled	22%	18%	29%	16%	9%	23%
Dropped	28%	19%	19%	16%	10%	16%
Pop Songs						
Enrolled	6%	27%	26%	37%	21%	9%
Dropped	7%	14%	17%	18%	25%	10%
Folksongs						
Enrolled	3%	36%	13%	17%	17%	22%
Dropped	8%	21%	19%	11%	15%	17%
Textbook						
Enrolled	7%	18%	5%	14%	6%	14%
Dropped	8%	15%	10%	14%	5%	8%
Workbook						
Enrolled	7%	11%	5%	2%	2%	13%
Dropped	7%	7%	5%	6%	5%	8%
The Teacher						
Enrolled	35%	52%	72%	40%	40%	40%
Dropped	31%	36%	41%	34%	30%	27%

the range of classroom activities. What activities are viewed as especially popular? What activities are viewed as especially unpopular? How can these unpopular learning activities be replaced by effective and more interesting learning tasks?

Because students had earlier indicated a strong wish to learn to speak the language, it is not surprising that they give strong support to oral activities in the classroom. These activities are generally enjoyed more in senior high than in junior high and are chosen most often by those who continue in language classes. The typical chapter dialogue-related activities are seen as enjoyable learning vehicles by 44 to 64 percent of those who reenroll in language courses, and by 39 to 52 percent of those who drop out.

Each year the Minneapolis Modern Language Department sponsors a foreign film festival, inviting all language students. The activity is obviously more appealing to senior high—37 to 51 percent—than to junior high—29 to 45 percent—and to students who reenroll—34 to 51 percent—than to students who drop—29 to 45 percent.

Although earlier it was noted that only 20 to 31 percent enrolled to learn more about a foreign country, 40 to 47 percent of those who reenrolled signified they enjoyed learning about the country, and 24 to 38 percent of those who dropped also approved. Similar positive responses were recorded in the category "Learning About People"; 34 to 48 percent of the reenrollees approved, as opposed to 20 to 34 percent of those students who dropped.

Still another related category, "Foreign Meals," received positive comments from students—20 to 56 percent. For years, many classes have taken an annual outing to an ethnic restaurant. Lately, many classes have tried their hands at food preparation. Senior high school students—36 to 56 percent—were more positive about "Foreign Meals" than junior high school students—20 to 54 percent. And those who continued in language study—23 to 56 percent—were more positive than those who dropped—20 to 49 percent.

In rating the teachers, student responses varied considerably among schools. However, both students who dropped—30 to 41 percent—and those who reenrolled—35 to 72 percent—indicate rather strong support for language teachers. The replies are certainly no comfort to those who would have instruction turned over to teaching machines.

Field trips, in general, were approved by 18 to 38 percent of the students reporting. This item includes such activities as trips to restaurants, foreign feature films, art institutes, parks, and cemeteries.

Pop songs, with 6 to 37 percent of the students responding positively, received especially weak support in several schools. Folk-song support fell in the same range—3 to 36 percent. Center city schools were particularly negative toward songs from other cultures. It is interesting to note that, although songs are often introduced into class for their supposed motivational qualities, they actually rank below most class activities in the minds of students in this survey.

Particularly depressing is the negative student response to the regular classroom tools, textbooks, workbooks, and worksheets. Worksheets rank higher in student esteem, 9 to 29 percent, supporting to a degree special individual teacher and team efforts to develop special, interesting materials for the learner. The relatively weak support—5 to 18 percent—for adopted texts raises the question whether they are appropriate to our needs. In the junior high school, we would seem to be better off using almost anything else. Perhaps our way of using the texts is at fault. Should students be involved in textbook selection? Should students be surveyed regularly regarding various learning materials? Workbooks received only 2 to 13 percent approval from students. Long castigated as unimaginative, boring, busy work, workbooks are widely used by teachers in many subject matters. Student responses to this item imply that workbooks should be carefully scrutinized by teachers before using; flexible use might also be indicated.

SUMMARY OF SURVEY RESULTS

This survey reenforces the fact that students are individuals. They have different interests, motivations, and expectations. Had the survey asked other questions, it might have detected different learning styles, as well. Even in the case of workbooks, which were roundly condemned by the vast majority of students, from 2 to 13 percent of the students indicated that they liked the workbooks. The survey reminds us that there is no single panacea which is likely to start a stampede for language learning.

On the other hand, the study tends to refute some long-held opinions regarding factors which affect enrollment.

Teacher Factors

Student replies indicate that few students initially select a language class because of the teacher. If they drop out of the sequence, however, 17 to 37 percent of the students say the teacher was responsible for their leaving.

Counselors

According to students surveyed, the high school counselor has an undeserved reputation. Students report counselors had little impact on their decisions to enroll, reenroll, or drop out.

Parents

From 16 to 32 percent of the students who enrolled in language classes said parents played a relatively important part in their decision.

College Requirements

College requirements, imagined or real, are apparently a more powerful influence on enrollment in senior than in junior high schools, and in schools serving higher socioeconomic populations.

Schedules

Students claim that secondary school schedules that limit them to five or six classes do indeed deter them from enrolling in language classes. Among students who had not enrolled, 15 to 31 percent blamed scheduling problems; and 20 to 50 percent of those who had dropped cited the school schedule as the reason.

Student Factors

Friends
By and large, few students—from zero to 15 percent—who had never enrolled in languages admitted that they failed to enroll because their friends did not enroll. Among students who did enroll, a larger number—10 to 21 percent said they had registered to be with friends. Only a miniscule number who dropped—1 to 5 percent—gave friends as the reason.

Interest
Student interest was very important in affecting enrollment. Among students who had never enrolled, 46 to 65 percent indicated they were not interested. Students who did enroll felt it would be enjoyable—49 to 63 percent—or challenging—26-38 percent. Of those who dropped, 45 to 58 percent found language uninteresting, and 5 to 28 percent said it was difficult. Of all the language class activities, students liked games best; they also enjoyed conversations, cultural activities, foreign films, and food-related activities. Less well-liked were workbooks and foreign language textbooks.

Speaking and Language Learning
When students enrolled in modern language classes, a large majority—65 to 71 percent—wanted to speak the language. Among senior high students who had

taken or were taking a modern language, nearly one-half—44 to 47 percent—said they were not satisfied with the amount of foreign language learned.

Grades

It appears that above average students enroll in language classes, and there is a relationship between general grades and success in language courses. From 10 to 25 percent of those who dropped out of the language sequence gave low grades as the reason. The majority of those who dropped out of language classes—49 to 67 percent—claim they were "A" or "B" students in overall grade point average.

IMPLICATIONS FOR CHANGE

The Minneapolis survey suggests some changes in direction for recruitment and instruction of modern language students. It strongly indicates that our profession has been tilting with windmills or if you will, fighting dragons when we should have been dealing with the real problems that keep students out of language classes; for example, there is evidence that a cease-fire should be declared with counseling departments.

Parents

The survey describes parents as a positive force, and therefore, one that teachers might cultivate to stabilize enrollments. Were modern language teachers to become involved with such groups as parent advisory committees and parent-teacher associations, parents might channel their support of the modern language program. The survey results suggest continued efforts are justified to keep parents informed about the program through school and other newspapers, and through occasional letters, memoranda, or newsletters.

Schedules

Presently, the Minneapolis senior high schools are organized on a trimester system. Under this system, the students enroll three times per year, selecting from a broad array of classes in each department. Under the trimester program, fewer students than formerly continue in language throughout the year. The high schools schedule classes in a standard six-period day. Approximately one-half of the periods are taken up with required subjects such as English, social studies, physical education, mathematics, or science. Because most subjects are offered five days per week, students usually enroll in five or fewer subjects at a time. Although a host of offerings is available, the limited number of hours in the school day restricts the number of electives that a student can take. Often singleton classes compete with other singleton classes in the same time block, French III and choir, for example. The survey shows that students have been confronted with scheduling problems and languages have lost students as a result.

If schedules were more flexible, languages would probably benefit. More flexibility would result if students did not have to attend classes in a given subject five days per week. Could not a student attend English three days per week and German two days in a single hour slot?

Scheduling changes mean changing the entire establishment. Less difficult for the teacher to engineer is the revision of the ebb and flow of classroom activities. The trimester program seems to demand a language class that is self-contained within the twelve weeks, one that permits students to enroll even though they missed the trimester or two which preceded it. Further, the trimester schedule demands a time for summing up, for evaluation, as well as a time for a very important task, promoting interest in the next trimester.

Students

A number of students who have never enrolled in language classes indicate simple lack of interest. Yet, approximately 50 percent of those students expect to travel abroad at a future date. We need to know more about these students to find out whether their interests and goals can be met in language classes. Perhaps they only need to know more about the process of language learning. By providing exploratory modern language experiences, schools may better help them determine whether such learning can be rewarding.

The sizeable dropout from language sequences has always been discouraging. The survey provides considerable information for teachers who want to reduce the numbers of dropouts who lose interest. Conversation activities hold first priority in a curriculum that includes a variety of learning materials and methods, and considerable use of games and community resources. The typical language text and workbook might be used as a guide, but should not dominate the course; and workbook-like texts are particularly undesirable.

Student dissatisfaction with the amount of language learning involved in modern language study is a danger signal. Apparently students have unreal expectations about the amount of language they will learn in class. It appears that they need a greater feeling of success. Clear indication of the goals for units of work, encouragement from the teacher, cooperative learning which provides peer reinforcement, and support for individual learning styles appear to offer promise of building student satisfaction.

BIBLIOGRAPHY

(1)   Cervantes, Miguel de. *The History of Don Quixote de la Mancha* in Robert Manhard, Great Books of the Western World, vol. 29. Translated by John Ormsby. Chicago: Encyclopedia Britannica, Inc., 1952.

Chapter Nine
Individualizing and Sequencing Training for Inter-cultural Communication
H. Ned Seelye

INTRODUCTION

The effectiveness of intercultural training can be increased by basing teaching strategies on a closer identification of the trainee skills needed to adjust to another culture. Skills required differ somewhat from individual to individual. Intercultural training skills are affected by situational variables, such as the role of the trainee in the host society, and the point at which the trainee finds himself in relation to his entrance to or exit from the host country, and also by personality variables, such as special avocational interests. This paper argues the need for perceiving cross-cultural training to be both continuous and responsive to the particular trainee needs at the time of training. The paper makes two largely untested assumptions: 1) the ability of a person to function in another culture can be improved through training; and 2) this training will be more effective when it addresses the trainee's problems within a time frame that approximates his "need to know."

For those who venture abroad, there are many things to learn and skills to develop. Some ideas for classroom teachers relating to six problem areas relevant to second-culture adjustment have been published elsewhere: strengthening self-identity (*11*), developing skill in evaluating statements about another culture, learning the expected response in conventional settings, understanding cultural assumptions underlying behavioral patterns and cultural connotations accompanying their expression, and understanding the functionality of a behavioral pattern (*12*). This paper focuses on one complex of adjustmental concerns—those that commonly arise during the first six months of residence abroad. It suggests some approaches for alleviating the anxiety and disorientation associated with the initial immersion in a different culture. The discussion of these approaches concentrates on two separate constituencies: persons from a foreign cultural background who are in an Anglophone school setting, and Anglophones who are preparing to go or who already are abroad.

Ideally, the instruction that any student gets in school is an outgrowth of teacher probes to discover what the student already knows in relation to what he *can* know by the end of the course, or what he *needs* to know to function more effectively. This needs-assessment suggests the content of instruction; it is the teachers' job to determine how best to present the content so that their particular students will benefit from it.

A teacher can begin this needs-assessment by using past observations of cultural problems that have asserted themselves either in the school setting (*1*), or in foreign travel (*5*). Bilingual and monocultural teachers can jointly draw up a "case study" in intercultural communication, with a view toward identifying anticipated problems that can be dealt with humanely. Most such case studies will describe culture problems in a number of areas. Some concern adults; others involve children. In some, people of one or another ethnic background are involved in different ways. Some problems call for skill development of one kind or another; others require affective treatment. The identification of specific problems clarifies what the problems are and who has them, and facilitates the development of an appropriate response to each of the many uncertainties that arise when different cultures come into contact. Only when this has been clarified can steps be taken to solve the problem.

The term "culture problems" projects as many images as a kaleidoscope in the hands of a leaping Don Cossack. In one sense, virtually all that man learns to do is culturally conditioned. In the sense that most bilingual teachers use the term, "culture" refers to first-language heritage, second-culture adjustment, and self-identity—all of which are generally seen as interrelated concerns. These concerns are usually dealt with in bilingual programs during social studies periods or in "culture" classes; occasionally they become a part of "language arts" classes in English or the native language. "Culture," from the perspective of the foreign language teacher, is associated with those extra-linguistic concepts and skills that enable a foreign language learner to communicate more effectively in the target language in the larger societal context that is present in speech with a native speaker.

For convenience, cross-cultural training is discussed in five different phases: the first concerns training priority to entry in the target culture; the second deals with the first twenty-four hours of residency abroad; the third phase deals with preparation for the initial month of immersion after the first twenty-four hours; the fourth is concerned with needs that arise during the period that corresponds to the second through the fourth months abroad; and the fifth phase covers the transition period that occurs at about the fifth month of residency abroad. These phases are meant to be suggestive of a learning sequence based on a student's "need to know." The phases, and especially the time designations for them, are only illustrative.

TRAINING PROGRAM

Phase I: Pre-entry Training

The goal of the pre-entry training phase is usually described as one of sensitizing the trainee to the nature of intercultural communication, and of preparing him psychologically for the inevitability of culture fatigue.

Pfeiffer (*10*), Seelye (*12*), and Weeks, Pedersen, and Brislin (*17*) are three sources of techniques appropriate for classroom or workshop use that immediately come to mind. These techniques vary widely in scope, duration, and the materials necessary for their execution. To illustrate the possibilities, brief descriptions of five techniques follow: two different types of values clarification exercises, a cross-cultural simulation, a programmed reading approach to deciphering critical incidents, and a combined background reading and film viewing approach to understanding cultural differences.

Judgments are a function of personality and cultural condition, so it is not surprising that different people reach different judgments after weighing the same information. Students generally enjoy spending five or ten minutes discovering what their perspective is toward a given scenario, and then bringing to consciousness some of the factors that contributed to the perspective. Values clarification exercises, as they are called, generally ask the student to make a judgment, either individually or as part of a small group. The instructor leads a review of the information contained in the scenario, being careful to have respondents distinguish objective statements from subjective impressions. Finally, students are invited to explain why they judged as they did. A theoretical description of this technique is available in Simon, Howe, and Kirschenbaum (*15*). Cross-cultural scenarios are easy to generate from news fragments, or common or imagined situations. The following example is taken from Kearney (*6*).

DEMOCRACY IN AMERICA

You are part of a seminar on the American Political Process. One of your colleagues, a young black woman, has just presented her paper which she has titled NEGRO POLITICS AND NEGRO POLITICIANS; her concluding paragraph, which she says sums up her attitude toward the subject, is a quote from the noted black sociologist Andrew Billingsley which reads:

Negroes should control the conditions which affect their own lives and should organize to express their will and to use their ethnicity as a positive force in this direction as is done by other ethnic groups. In order to facilitate such political realignment, all branches of government must make a maximum commitment to political democracy. As a first step all white liberals who represent Negro communities should resign and campaign for their black replacements selected by the Black community. All Southern Whites who represent Negro communities should be expelled by the Congress or the courts for they are clearly in violation of the constitution and thirdly, the doctrine of one man one vote should be extended to all levels of government and enforced with open and explicit rather than devious recognition given to ethnicity. It is only upon these premises that the Negro will truly find political solidarity in White American Politics.

You are white as is most of the class. Most of your life has been spent in a homogeneous suburb in a large metropolitan area to which your family moved when you were very young. The neighborhood from which they moved was once the port of entry into the region for your ethnic group of European origin. That neighborhood is now the center of a larger part of the city which is virtually entirely occupied by Negroes.

You are under considerable pressure on the part of the instructor to respond to your colleague's paper. You know that you have to do so honestly and intelligently. What will your response be?

Decision Sheet:
1. Your response to your colleague's paper (and to Billingsley's argument) will be:

_____
_____

2. The reason why you choose this rather than some other approach is:

_____
_____

Discussion Starters
1. To what does Billingsley want all branches and levels of government to make a commitment?
2. According to Billingsley, what should white liberals who represent Negro communities in Congress do?
3. Again according to Billingsley, what should happen to Southern Whites who represent Negro communities?
4. Is Billingsley's definition of *democracy* the same as the one you learned in your grammar school civics class?
5. Why should Northern liberal Congressmen be treated differently than Southern Whites?
6. What does Billingsley mean by Black *community*?
7. Do you think most Black people agree with Billingsley? Why?
8. Which social pattern do you feel would come closest to accomplishment of Billingsley's end, segregation? or integration? Why?
9. Do you feel that only Blacks can represent Negroes? only whites? represent whites? Why?

A different approach to value clarification can be made through a commercially available video-tape presentation of people interacting quite normally in U.S. school settings (7) or in a foreign setting (8). The adult participant attempts to identify inductively by a process of hypothesis refinement the mainstream U.S. culturally conditioned value that underlies the behavior of the Americans as viewed in each of the 14 to 22 different sequences of the video-tape. Each sequence is composed of four or so brief episodes showing different roles interacting. All of the episodes in a given sequence share a common mainstream American value. Some of these values are: each person is a distinct entity, and ought to assert and achieve independence from others; all human beings are equal in their intrinsic worth; everyone should be action-oriented; interpersonal encounters should be perceived primarily in terms of their immediate utility, and their social significance should be downgraded; oneself and others should be defined in terms of work and achievements; the collective wisdom of the group is superior to that of any individual; the process of decision making requires evaluation of the consequences of alternative courses of action, and selection of the one that, on balance, seems most advantageous; competition is a good way of motivating people; there is usually a best way of doing something, which should be determined and then followed; knowledge gained through observation is superior to knowledge gained in other ways; experience needs to be quantified; a higher value should be placed on utilitarian aspects of experience than on aesthetic ones; there are "problems" in the world, and in one's existence in it, for which one must find "solutions"; thoughts cannot directly influence events; and reasoning must be in terms of probability.

Over the course of the sixteen-hour workshop, participants learn to identify symptoms of intercultural misunderstanding and to recognize *in themselves*, rather than in other people, the U.S. value conditionings that lead to confused communication. Participants are not expected to alter their values in a cross-cultural encounter, but they do develop the skill to analyze the cultural underpinnings of much of their own behavior. As a consequence of this workshop, the participant may begin to make fewer unconscious assumptions in intercultural encounters. The following brief scenario, taken from Kraemer, illustrates the behavioral manifestations of the common American tendency to define and describe people primarily in terms of their work and achievements. On the videotapes, this is, of course, illustrated visually and verbally.

EXCERPT 2

(Teacher 1: Mrs. Jones. Teacher 2: Mrs Ramirez)

TEACHER 2: Yes, I'm sorry I couldn't come to the party. Did you enjoy it?

TEACHER 1: Oh, yes. I met so many interesting people there. There was one woman, Marlena, who used to be an English teacher, but now she is high up in the Office of Education. And, oh, there was another man who works for IBM as a computer engineer, and has just been assigned to the Paris office.

TEACHER 2: Mmm?

TEACHER 1: And, let's see, I talked for a long time with another gentleman who would never tell me what he was doing. I called him the mystery man.

TEACHER 2: Why did you call him that? (7, pp. v-vi)

Some of the demands that cue anxieties associated with culture fatigue have been artfully simulated in a game that takes about two and one-half hours to play (*14*). Bafá Bafá, or Rafá Rafá as a later edition is named, generally is successful with adults or secondary school students. It can be described in four stages: First, the class or workshop is divided into two groups of about a dozen each. Each group is assigned to an Alfa or Beta culture, and given instructions for ten minutes concerning how people from their culture behave. The two cultures have highly contrastive norms. Second, people in each culture begin interacting among themselves to reinforce norms. Third, each participant gets to be a tourist for a few minutes in the other culture, and then to explain that culture to peers upon return. When all have been tourists, the game ends and the fourth stage begins. It is in this stage, the debriefing, that the "lights go on" in the heads of participants. Alfa culture is asked to describe Beta, then vice-versa, followed by each culture describing itself. Participants reflect on the relative usefulness of descriptive vs. interpretive statements. They are asked to relate what they felt about the other culture. This simulation builds up a surprising amount of feeling in the participants; many gain strong insights into what it is like to interact with another culture.

Critical incidents that commonly lead to intercultural misunderstandings in secondary school settings where Latino students interact with mainstream U.S. teachers have been studied by Albert (*1*). She has produced a programmed text for mainstream teachers, and a bilingual English-speaking version for Latino students, that present a series of episodes centering around culturally produced misunderstandings. The reader is presented with four possible explanations for the described behavior and is asked to choose the most accurate explanation. The reader is then directed to another page where he is provided feedback for his choice. The following is a typical episode taken from the teachers' text:

Jesus had recently arrived in the U.S. He was walking to his class one day and was stopped in the hall by the principal. The principal told him that he was ten minutes late and said that this was not the first time this had happened. The principal then told Jesus that he wanted to see his mother the next day so that they could talk about his being late for class.

HOW DID JESUS REALLY FEEL ABOUT BEING LATE?

Jesus Really Felt:

Choose the best one:
1. Scared because his mother would scold him.
   Go to page   of your workbook.
2. Surprised because he did not understand why it was such a problem.
   Go to page   of your workbook.
3. That he was not doing something wrong.
   Go to page   of your workbook.
4. Ashamed about being late.
   Go to page   of your workbook.

Workbook
Page   :   You have chosen number 1 which says:
          Scared because his mother would scold him.

Although this answer is very plausible from the Latin-American point of view, it is not the answer chosen most often by Latino students.

Try again.

Page   :   You have chosen number 2 which says:
          Surprised because he did not understand why it was such a problem.

This answer was chosen by most Anglo-American teachers, but not by many Latino children.

Try again.

Page   :   You have chosen number 3 which says:
          That he was not doing something wrong.

This is not what Latinos think. Try again.

Page   :   You have chosen number 4 which says:
          Ashamed about being late.

This is the answer given by most Latino students. It is interesting that very few Anglo-American teachers chose it. Jesus knew he had to be on time because this is just as important in Latin-American schools as it is here in the U.S. Consequently, he felt shame, a common reaction among Latino children when they do something wrong.

It is true that the Latino conception of time differs from the American one and thus it would be natural for you to suppose that this applied also to arriving late for school. However, this is not really so. Arriving to school on time is a very important value in Latin American countries. In many other situations, Latinos do tend to be less concerned about time limits than Americans. The primary reason for this is that interpersonal relations are more important for Latinos than sticking to a pre-arranged time schedule. For this reason one will always talk to a friend when one runs into him or her even if one has an appointment or another important obligation. It is not that time is not important, but rather, that interpersonal relations take precedence over time schedules. (*1*, in press)

The final example of a technique that may be appropriate at this consciousness raising phase involves the use of print and film media. Marquardt and others (*9*, Appendix, pp. 137-141. 157) have noted that successful literature with a cross-cultural setting, both factual and fictitious, enables the reader to vicariously experience a sense of what it is like to live in another society and/or to experience intercultural conflict. Reading lists likely to be regarded as relevant by the trainees can be prepared by the instructor for out-of-class reading, followed perhaps by in-class discussion. A recent, mostly annotated bibliography (*13*) contains a wide range of potential titles relevant to an understanding of intercultural communication.

An initial paradox of intercultural training is that the more a trainee is made aware of the realistic range of obstacles that may await him abroad, obstacles that are going to interfere with effective cross-cultural communications, the more his potential for anxiety increases. Excessive anxiety can be expected to inhibit maximum adjustment to a second culture. Someone who is going abroad, or who is already abroad, does not want his anxiety increased by simply being told of the thousand and one problems that he is going to have. The goal of cross-cultural training is to *intelligently* reduce this anxiety.

Phase II: The First 24 Hours

People who are eager to go abroad often feel that general cultural training lacks the immediacy of culturally specific training. They sit in cross-cultural training programs worrying whether somebody is going to be waiting for them when they arrive at Kennedy, Heathrow, or Teheran. Will they have to stay temporarily in a hotel while other arrangements are made? Will they be living with a family? Will they have a house by themselves? What will they eat? In what schools will they place their children? The more immediate the prospect of going abroad, the less attentive a student may be to the abstract intellectualizations of intercultural communication.

There are at least two ways to assess the timelines of the content of a program in intercultural communication: ask the person who is about to go abroad what he wants to know; and review the experience of others. Gorden (4), a sociologist from Antioch College, analyzed the problems that Americans experienced adjusting to the first month in Columbia. He highlights such mundane items as their need to know whether shots or visas are necessary, and whether reservations are required for the airline tickets. Gorden suggests trainers concern themselves with what one observes the first day in another country, such as getting through customs and tipping at the airport. The sequence of topics is simply ordered on the basis of the chronological probability of coming into contact with the topic in the target culture. If there is a need for the traveler to call from the airport to announce his arrival, the trainer needs to be culturally specific: Are tokens needed for the phone? Where are the phones? How are they used? Where is money exchanged? Should enough currency be bought through a local bank before going abroad to handle the airport scene and the cab ride into town?

The taxi trip from the airport is often a harrowing one, and Anglophones often suspect they have been cheated by the drivers. Guests are frequently terrified by host traffic patterns. What does the traveller see on the ride from the airport to his destination? When most of the roads go from the airport into the center of town and then disperse, the cross-cultural trainer can take pictures of what will be seen. After viewing the pictures, students are asked to reflect on whether they saw factories or suburbs, and on the mixtures of cultures and social classes that were in evidence. Riding from the airport, visitors inevitably look out the car window and form strong impressions. What is the physical lay-out of homes and neighborhoods? What is the weather pattern?

Students need to be prepared psychologically for the relative cost of common items in the target culture. A good source of information of this type has been compiled by Pan American World Airways (16).

What are local language conventions? What does one say when answering the telephone? Specific, subcultural, dialectical varieties of the language that are going to be heard frequently in conventional situations should be explained ahead of time.

Even the most sophisticated trainees are not going to go very many days without using the bathroom facilities. And often they are going to use them a lot more than they anticipated! Gorden's extensive and quite remarkable three-year study of communication difficulties of U.S. Peace Corps personnel and university students adjusting to life in Columbian homes indicates that use of the bathroom provoked more cross-cultural misunderstanding than the use of any other room in the host homes (5).

What are the daily and weekly traffic schedules? To avoid traffic, when must one take the autobus? When do people work and when do they return home? What is this new rhythm? How does one handle menus, foods, times, conventions? Is "military" time or the metric system commonly used? If one wants to make a ham sandwich, how much meat does one request in a butcher shop? What is the trainee's role perceived to be when he meets a stranger? What is the role of the immediate people he is going to meet during his first 24 hours, and what are the proper ways to address these people so as not to the appear overly familiar or overly formal? What is the host naming system? What are common names? How are telephone directories used? What is the composition of a household unit? What is the daily schedule of each member of the household? On what occasions does the whole family get together? What are some of the unfamiliar behaviors that trainees may emphasize unless they are prepared in advance to see these "strange" customs in perspective; for example, police may be armed with machine guns, or kitchen refrigerator doors may be locked.

Language training can focus on the skills needed to handle these situations, which might constitute the topics addressed in a cross-cultural program for this second phase of training.

Phase III: The First Month

The third phase of cultural training is a logical extension of the second: Its goals are to further reduce anxiety, increase self-confidence, and resolve simple problems relating to home management, food consumption, security systems, health care, transportation, telecommunications, and recreation. It continues to teach culturally appropriate ways to relate to peers, such as counterparts at work, and to subordinate relationships, such as maids. And it furthers the acquisition of rudimentary skill in the target language as it is needed in these specific situational contexts.

Phase IV: The Second through the Fourth Months

After one settles into a daily routine in another country, at least three areas assume heightened importance: One begins to notice messages emanating from the mass media; one again rekindles interest in recreational activities; and one is faced with establishing longer term rapport with host nationals.

Language training is especially helpful during this training phase. It prepares the student to comprehend billboards, newspapers, magazines, movies, and radio programs—especially music and sports events—with a degree of ease. Enjoyment of life in the host country is enhanced when one learns the "wheres and hows" of going to cultural events. Unfamiliar athletic events, such as sumo or bullfighting, often become interesting to sports fans once the game is understood.

Intercultural rapport is served by delving into local history, customs, songs, and jokes. These areas provide many of the symbols that can be shared advantageously with people in the host country. Sharing national symbols is taken as evidence of interest in, and appreciation of, host culture and history.

Phase V: The Fifth Month

The fifth phase of training is aimed at helping the student with problems he typically has encountered after about five months of residency in the host country. Its goal is to increase the quantity and quality of inter-personal relations through the initiation of friendships resulting from involvement in host institutional life. Here is when training focuses on getting the trainee into the institutional structure of the country so that lifelong friendships can be made. Schools, businesses, churches, governmental agencies, the judicial system, and volunteer services such as the fire department can help a trainee become institutionally involved with the country and its people.

CONCLUSIONS

Training needs are principally a function of the type of difficulties trainees will be, or are already, encountering. Because the press of these difficulties changes over time, cross-cultural training focused on these specific needs should be made available to acculturating individuals at strategic points during their sojourn abroad. Much of this training should be both culture-specific, role-specific, and personality-specific.

The hundreds of thousands of people who have been residing in the United States or Britain for less than three of four years will profit from the opportunity to receive special help in overcoming the hurdles to an effective cultural adjustment. Many of these individuals already are enrolled in bilingual or English-as-a-second-language programs, which increase understanding of the cultural context within which communication occurs. These existing courses can be administratively and structurally broadened to accomplish the points argued in this paper. The thousands of English-speaking students who travel to other cultures will also benefit from training in intercultural communication.

BIBLIOGRAPHY

(1)   Albert, Rosita. *Encuentros culturales para el bilingüe*. Manuscript.
(2)   Casteel, J. Doyle, and Hallman, Clemens. *Cross-cultural Inquiry: Value Clarification Exercises*. Gainsville: University of Florida, Center for Latin American Studies, 1974.
(3)   Fiedler, Fred E.; Mitchell, Terence; and Triandis, Harry C. "The Culture Assimilator: An Approach to Cross-cultural Training." *Journal of Applied Psychology* 55 (1971): 95-102.
(4)   Gorden, Raymond L. *Initial Immersion in the Foreign Culture*. Yellow Springs, OH: Antioch College, 1968.
(5)   _____. *Living in Latin America: A Case Study in Cross-cultural Communication*. Skokie, IL: National Textbook, 1974.
(6)   Kearney, John. *Five Exercises in Value Clarification*. Arlington Heights, IL: Bilingual Education Service Center, in press [599 South Dwyer Avenue, Arlington Heights, IL 60005.]
(7)   Kraemer, Albert J. *Teacher Training Workshop in Intercultural Communication: Instructor's Guide*. Alexandria, VA: Human Resources Research Organization, 1976. [300 North Washington Street, Alexandria, VA.]
(8)   _____. *Workshop in Intercultural Communication: Handbook for Instructors*. Alexandria, Va: Human Resources Research Organization, 1974. [300 North Washington Street, Alexandria, VA.]
(9)   Marquardt, William F. "Creating Empathy Through Literature Between the Members of the Mainstream Culture and the Disadvantaged Learners of the Minority Cultures." *Florida FL Reporter* 7, i (1969): 133-41. [Special anthology issue entitled *Linguistic-Cultural Differences and American Education*, edited by Alfred C. Aarons, Barbara Y. Gordon, and William A. Stewart.]
(10) Pfeiffer, J.; Jones, W.; and Jones, J.E., eds. *A Handbook of Structured Experiences for Human Relations Training*. Vols. I–V. Iowa City: University Associates Press, 1969-1975.

(11) Seelye, H. Ned. "Self Identity and the Bicultural Classroom." In *Perspectives in Bilingual Education*, edited by Hernan La Fontaine, Barry Persky, and Leonard Golubchick. New York: Kendall/Hunt, in press.

(12) _____. *Teaching Culture: Strategies for Foreign Language Educators.* Skokie, IL: National Textbook, 1974.

(13) _____, and Lynn Tyler, V., eds., *Intercultural Communicator Resources.* Provo, UT: Brigham Young University, Language and Intercultural Research Center, 1977.

(14) Shirts, Gary P. *Bafá Bafá: A Cross Culture Simulation.* La Jolla, CA: Simile II, 1973. [P.O. Box 1028, La Jolla, CA 92037.]

(15) Simon, Sidney; Howe, Leland; and Kirschenbaum, Howard. *Values Clarification: A Handbook of Practical Strategies for Teachers and Students.* New York: Hart, 1972.

(16) Stewart, Malcolm, ed. *Pan Am's World Guide: An Encyclopedia of Travel.* New York: Random House, 1976.

(17) Weeks, H. William; Pedersen, Paul B.; and Brislin, Richard W., eds. *A Manual of Structured Experiences for Cross-Cultural Learning.* Pittsburgh: University of Pittsburgh, Society for Intercultural Education, Training and Research, 1977.

Chapter Ten
Alternatives in Education
Wayne B. Jennings

One of the most exciting recent developments in education is the rapid growth of alternative schools. These schools follow a rich tradition of experimental schools and practices that have been little known to most educators. Alternative schools offer a real chance for lasting educational change because they can shortcut the resistance to change by educators and parents. Those who like schools as they are continue with conventional programs. Those who want changes choose the alternatives and avoid the usual confrontations that occur when all must accept a new program.

Most schools that have attempted to introduce a new program or new practices have had difficult handicaps to overcome. A school that decides to introduce significant change by building a climate of favorable opinion among parents, students, and staff faces a stiff five- to ten-year period of development; attitudes change slowly. On the other hand, alternative schools provide opportunities for instant change without having to overcome the flak and complaints that accompany a new program in a conventional school. Because enrollment in alternative schools is optional or voluntary, it tends to attract a clientele that favors the program.

Most public alternative schools owe a debt of gratitude to the private alternative programs that sprang up during the 1960s when many students were disaffected with school. The private alternative schools demonstrated that there were indeed students who needed the schools and parents who would support them. However, education is an expensive business; parents soon agitated for public alternative schools with per-pupil funding comparable to conventional public schools.

One category of alternative schools departs very little from accepted school practices, following the conventional curriculum and teaching the basic subject matter that is emphasized in most schools. The departure from conventional practices tends to be in the direction of a more humane environment that individualizes programs so students may work at their own pace, and provides enrichment such as dance, drama, and art. Some of these alternative schools pursue the conventional school program with even greater rigor than regular schools. Such schools might be called basic skills schools, academies, or fundamentalist schools. Indeed, there are customers for such programs.

The other category of alternative schools attempts to develop competencies needed for life in a complex, changing, and unknown world. The goals in these schools tend to be broader and more philosophical. Although the basic skills and some of the other academic areas of conventional education are taught, the stress is on preparing students to become lifelong learners. They should be inquisitive, enjoy learning, see themselves as worthwhile persons, work well and competently with many different kinds of persons, develop concern and the willingness to take risks, become involved and accountable, develop a sense of initiative and responsibility, and become active citizens in bringing forth a better world.

On the surface, these aims do not differ from the general statement of philosophy set forth by most school districts. However, to accomplish these goals, alternative schools utilize unusual practices and methods that tend to startle or disturb visitors. Not that these practices are new. They have existed for many years, if not for many centuries, in the literature. And the methods are compatible with what we know about psychology of learning; their aspect of newness springs from the fact that they are little used in most schools.

The balance of this chapter is devoted to a description of the practices and methods used in progressive alternative schools.

PROJECT LEARNING

A good deal is being written these days about "action" learning, or "problem-solving" learning. Students should be involved in projects of real significance to them, projects that cause students to interact with other people in the community or with various elements of the school itself. As a result, some improvement should be made in the lives of the students, the school, or the community.

This is not a new idea in education. Older curriculum textbooks referred to it as the fusion or correlation of subjects. The core curriculum, which in many schools consisted merely of English and social studies, was actually designed as a problem-solving approach; students selected areas of study that were of personal interest or that presented a persistent societal problem. Any subject matter or skill area was appropriate if it helped in the solution of the project or shed light on the topic.

In English primary schools (3), this method is referred to as the "integrated day approach"—integrated, because it brings many subjects into a specific problem that children are interested in solving. This thematic method of teaching and learning involves students in reading, writing, computational skills, art, science, and other subjects. Each area contributes to the solution of a real problem. Studies in England and the United States indicate that students who learn in this fashion are at least as successful—and often more successful—in conventional subject areas as students who follow a more departmentalized or separate-subjects approach.

Problem-solving teaching can involve small projects and need not depart far from a conventional classroom. For example, Spanish teachers sometimes have their students build models of the Aztec temples. In the process, students read and research, design, compute, measure, draw to scale, construct, and appraise the results. All of the skills involved in such a project are typical school-type skills that are generally taught in isolation in specific classes. When students learn such skills as part of a larger-scale project, the learning is thought to have more meaning and impact. Students remember the material longer, and they learn it more thoroughly.

Other students have worked on creating a Mexico City outdoor market. In this type of project, they examine books, pictures, and films that describe fruit and vegetable selling areas; they talk with people from the region, either natives or visitors; they seek ways to construct things safely from inexpensive materials; and they submit designs to a jury of their peers for final decisions. They then proceed with the actual construction, which may involve soliciting donations of materials, funds, or labor to assist them in areas that they cannot complete themselves. The end result is a project that has students involved with each other and with their community. And members of the community can be invited to give their reactions to the project.

Some students repainted a language room and became involved in the design, the environmental impact of colors, the calculations for materials, and the use of resource people.

Another group of students, whose school was subjected to the stench of industrial pollution from surrounding factories, met with representatives from the various industries involved and eventually went to court to enforce state pollution laws. The end result was the installation of complicated and sophisticated pollution equipment at a cost of more than one million dollars. As a side benefit, the students won the gratitude of the residents in the area (2).

COMMUNITY-BASED LEARNING

There is much interest these days in having students get into the "real world." Too much of school tends to be verbal or descriptive of that world, and students are left to learn about it in a vicarious manner. The world has become complex and shut away from easy viewing. For most students, there is no longer a Main Street with its many different kinds of businesses and friendly local businessmen. Students must choose careers on the basis of descriptive material; often they have not met a person who does that work, nor have they had a chance to try it out for themselves.

Students participating in community-based learning are concerned with how the transportation system works, what people do, where they do it, where resources are, and what agencies exist in the community. This leads to a sense of well-being and a knowledge of what the community is and how it can be utilized to accomplish goals. This approach does not call for a study of the community as such, but rather a direct use of resources in the community. Students use the telephone book to find resource people and materials.

Students report that projects in the community, travel experiences, and service are among the most beneficial of all of their school work. Apparently such activities answer real needs and give the students a better understanding of the real world in which they live.

Community-based learning can involve experiences in distant points of the country, or even out of the country. One group, aged 10 to 18, spent four weeks living with families in a town in Mexico. They then exchanged places, and their Mexican brothers and sisters came to live with them. This provided a very different experience from a typical Mexican travel tour. When students visited the families, most of whom did not speak English, they became immersed in the culture and traditions of the country. Students had to cope with the money system and the tradition of bargaining over the price of an item. Girls were confronted with an enormously different standard of male-female relationships and the role of women. The students encountered class sizes of between 70 and 100 students, learned how different the school libraries were, and discovered that they were expected to obey and not question. They became a part of much ritual and ceremony, going home from school at midday for several hours rest before returning for a late afternoon session. They smelled, tasted, bumped, and struggled in a society they could scarcely manage, but one in which the Mexican people moved naturally. Some students were so moved by the experience that they wrangled further trips and encouraged their parents to visit; some returned on their own for further study or post-high-school work. Many wrote letters. Many of them developed a year or more in language growth during the month.

For many years, students have had work experience or on-the-job training; but these have often been limited to very specific problems, perhaps allowing students to get out of school one hour early in the afternoon. Why not have students out at anytime during the day when businesses might need them? An important community-based experience involves internships or unpaid service to public, private, and commercial agencies and enterprises. This can take the form of extended field trips, shadow study, or simply work experiences in which students become involved in the activities of the world, finding out what adults do, what they talk about, and how they feel about their work.

These activities lead to self-discovery. Students are able to try out their abilities in job situations, in making travel arrangements, and in solving problems. Oftentimes, students learn something of their talents and abilities, and this can lead to a better selection of a career. Certainly it leads to a wider examination of various career possibilities.

Community-based learning and project learning are closely related. Together, they tend to make school exciting, dynamic, real, and highly effective for the growth and development of young people.

In order to facilitate use of the community, schools should have a van or bus available whenever a group wishes to schedule it. A restricted field trip budget covering one or two field trips per student per year is totally inadequate.

RESOURCE PEOPLE

Alternative schools are increasingly making use of personnel other than teachers and paraprofessionals in the instructional program. In a number of schools, there is a person in charge of locating, recruiting, and training resource people. This coordinator of resource personnel also trains the staff in the use of resource people, helps individuals with problems, and provides some evaluation. If all of these activities were assigned to the teaching staff, the use of resource people would fall off drastically because most teachers have little time for other duties.

Some schools also have a person working with resource people in the community to amass a large file listing individuals who have special interests or talents that the school can use. If a class or an activity needs help with the details of purchasing a home, learning magic, painting eggs in the Ukranian manner, or myriad other activities, a perusal of the file can generally locate someone with those talents.

There are a great many people in the community who are interested in working with young people—parents of students, ethnic groups, foreign students, businessmen, public and private agencies, and the elderly. Many are burning with information that they would like to share. The older citizens of a community are an extremely important resource. Many of these have time on their hands and would enjoy sharing the fruits of a lifetime. Some have valuable collections, exciting materials, or specialized knowledge not available otherwise; some are immigrants and recall the "old country" and their problems in adapting to America.

Not to be overlooked are the students themselves. Often students with a special hobby or ability can act as teachers or advisors. A student fluent in German taught a German class in one school that had no German teacher. However, this is not a one-way street; the students who do the teaching or tutoring gain a great deal in terms of organizing their thoughts, presenting their ideas, and developing their self-concepts.

CURRICULUM REDEFINITION

The preceding sections add up to considerable change in how we look at the school curriculum. Generally a school curriculum is considered to be those activities under the control of the school. In the past, the school curriculum was divided into the standard curriculum and extracurricular or co-curricular activities. This is an outmoded concept in alternative programs and modern educational thought.

If the outside activities or experiences that young people have are not considered as part of the curriculum, there will be duplication for some students. Students watch a great deal of television, and both their knowledge of the world and their vocabulary are expanded by the media. Today's students will travel widely and be bombarded by an enormous amount of information from various sources. It is no longer necessary to spend as much time in school, pounding away at the traditional facts. Many students have important contacts in the world to help them learn—parents, friends, jobs, clubs, and other activities. If these are not taken into account as a part of the school curriculum, the school will either overlook valuable resources or duplicate areas.

The curriculum must encompass all of the experiences of youth, irrespective of where they take place. Such a redefinition of the curriculum results in students looking upon learning as something that occurs continually, whether school is in session or not. One alternative school routinely catalogs summer experiences of its K through 12 students; these become part of a student's file. In this school, the sum total of experiences for all 500 of the students amounts to an incredible list of travel, work, courses, hobbies, volunteerism, reading, and businesses. These respresent school resources that can be shared. Thus summers, vacation times, weekends, and evenings represent a continuation of the learning process in the students' minds; school is simply one important feature in their growth and development. These students do not look cynically at school as an interruption of their education, or of their life. School is not seen as something to get out of—like prison—so they can get on with living and learning.

James Coleman stated the case splendidly in an article entitled, "The Children Have Outgrown The Schools." (4) His thesis is that, at the turn of the century, the situation for children was a world that was responsibility-rich and information-poor. Mass media did not exist; it was up to the schools to provide the information. At the same time, students had many responsibilities in the family. The situation has reversed in today's world. Students have few responsibilities because most homes are automatic, and, in a sense, young people are in the way; meanwhile, information has exploded. However, educators tend to go on acting as though it is still the early 1900s, when schools provided information, and a sense of responsibility was acquired in the world. Roles should be reversed, he argues, so that students learn to handle responsibility in school and receive information from the general society.

The expanded definition of the cirriculum is necessary. Most schools tend to be barren and sterile places, lacking richness in terms of people, use of the community, or learning beyond the narrow confines of a textbook. No one really wants it to be that way; but that's the way it actually is, and that's the way students see it.

PROVIDING FOR A VARIETY OF LEARNING STYLES AND LEARNING OUTCOMES

Schools tend to emphasize literary and academic skills. The students who are good at reading and writing will generally be highly rewarded in school. Actually, reading, writing, and academic skills are broadly distributed along a normal curve. This means that only about 15 percent of students are going to feel comfortable and successful in school. The others may obtain certain satisfactions from sports, extra-curricular activities, socializing, and, perhaps, a subject or two; but, in general, school will be a difficult and not very happy situation.

Alternative schools attempt to provide for an extremely wide range of learning styles and a variety of learning outcomes. The student who is good at speaking, at leadership, and at communication with his peers should be provided many opportunities to exercise these talents. Social leaders, communicators, people who are good at persuasion and conciliation in the handling of conflict are desperately needed in our society. Some students are gifted at design and have the ability to conceptualize, plan, or create in the mechanical and social fields. Schools must provide for them. The list of talents needed in this world is endless.

Schools must enhance students' strengths rather than accentuate their weaknesses in the areas of reading and writing. Students who are proficient at reading and writing deserve rewards, but not at the expense of those who have other talents.

There are also enormous differences in the learning styles of students. Probably very few of us would choose to divide our day into the tiny, fractionalized, departmentalized segments so prevalent in schools. If given a choice, most students would prefer to work for some length at a given task or area of interest.

Usually students with high verbal and literary skills are the only ones encouraged or expected to succeed in a second language. This ignores the fact that virtually all people living in areas where several languages are spoken become fluent. A 30- or 60-minute daily language lesson is far less successful than a foreign language camp or a foreign trip where one is immersed in all aspects of the culture. In such experiences, students can pursue many kinds of activities in the new culture (1, 6).

The interests and ideas that students bring to school are virtually kaleido-scopic. Schools need to provide opportunities for students to follow up in areas where they would like more information. The amazing thing in alternative schools is that, when student interests become the total curriculum, students end up learning the traditional subjects plus a great deal more. Furthermore, learning is more effective, efficient, and joyful for the students.

PLAY AS LEARNING

This section may be difficult for those in education who consider fun or joy the antithesis of learning, who say that unless learning is hard work it's not real learning.

It is said that play is a child's work. Consider, for example, a child under 5: without instruction, without remediation, that child has learned to speak the language and has learned its structure and grammar in an intuitive way. This is only a small part of the learning that occurs before formal schooling begins. Most of it is learned in the context of play, where the child's own experimentation creates meaning out of the world.

Some think that schooling ought to be an extension of this process—a place that is rich and stimulating, that offers many suggestions and exciting ideas, that is warm and supportive, that is accepting and appreciating, and that opens toward the world. In this setting, children would be allowed to play, roam, explore, and would probably learn a great deal.

What is play? And what is work? Consider the following:

- Students invent situations such as playing school, playing house, receiving a foreign guest in the home, playing doctor and nurse and make up their own scripts to suit the situations.
- Children devise dramatic situations that include role playing, brief skits, make-believe, commercials, confrontation experiences, short plays, full-length dramatic situations, and enactments of an international incident.
- Students use magical props and apparatus, visit a magic store, read books on magic, study the magic of the fakirs of India, put on a magic show for their friends or a neighborhood library, write a magic magazine, operate a magic store, attend a convention of professional magicians, and attend lectures by foreign magicians.
- Seven and eight year olds form a small club to study cats, dogs, horses, and other animals. They collect pictures of animals found on other continents, read for information, hold meetings, elect officers, and plan a bulletin board.
- Children have a fort room, a rugged play area with materials that can be rearranged to enact dramas they have watched on TV.
- Children use wood, bricks, timbers, and tires of a playground to build and

rebuild castles, ships, the Great Wall of China, and housing in Africa.

Most observers would consider these examples to be play. Yet might not the same potent learning be occurring that occurred before age 5? A good friend tells about his building of the Aswan Dam in elementary school. He is now an architect and remembers virtually nothing else about elementary school except the excitement of building that model. For him it was play, but, as it turned out, it was one of the most potent learning experiences of his schooling. It led to an interest in architecture and design in all parts of the world. Where does play end and education begin in activities that involve reading, writing, planning, weighing alternatives, using speaking skills, formulating presentations, determining budgets, calculating mark-ups, making borscht, interacting with adults, asking questions, or manipulating video equipment?

Are not all of these play-like situations potent learning experiences? If, indeed, we think of school as a place for stimulating learning and exploration rather than as a place for teaching, we will give more serious attention to such notions as learning through play. More than any other activity, play automatically provides for readiness. Students engage in play activities to the degree that they are able; sophistication comes later, and the play becomes more serious from an adult's point of view. In play, there is a greater attention to learning styles and a variety of learning outcomes, as students take on the role of players to the degree that they have skills, or are ready to learn certain skills.

TRUST

Most alternative schools give students a great deal of leeway in devising their own program of studies. This ultimate trust placed in a student has some surprising outcomes. Contrary to what most people think, students rise to assume a great degree of responsibility, accountability, honesty, and accurate self-appraisal when they are trusted. In some alternative schools, students choose their entire program; there are no required subjects or courses. Teachers help students to list goals and encourage them to talk of their hopes and dreams. Students then build their programs from the rich variety of activities that such schools have available. Periodically, there are conferences to discuss how the program is going, whether it is appropriate, and what changes ought to be made. The conferences include parents, students, and school personnel. Together they discuss the wisest course of action for the student's education. The student takes perhaps the most active role in the conference; after all, it is the student's welfare that is being discussed.

Increasingly, students are able to articulate their goals, list a variety of ways to attain those goals, select experiences that help attain the goals, and appraise their own progress. They become self-directed, fully functioning individuals who realize that the school provides many resources to help them accomplish their ends. For example: one student spent three months helping refugees in Bangladesh; another accompanied an exchange teacher to England for a year; another took university courses in several languages; and another took part in a sailing expedition to the Baffin Islands.

People often comment on the maturity, courtesy, and helpfulness of students in alternative schools. This is contrary to the popular stereotype that alternative schools are wild, permissive places with disrespectful students. They are indeed lively, noisy, and full of curious learners.

The above features prevail in many progressive alternative schools. All are aspects of widely accepted notions on the psychology of learning. According to Goodlad (5), most conventional schools and teachers do not follow sound, accepted principles of learning or the methods books of their own preservice training. Although many people can recite the principles of learning, few have taken the application step of stating specifically what is to be done to implement a given learning principle. The following is suggested as a simple formula for such implementation of a learning principle.

Learning principle:
The self-concept can be enhanced by effective learning.
Therefore, the following practices are to be abolished or diminished:
    competitive grading,
    the heavy emphasis on tests,
    negative and disparaging remarks.

The following practices are to be begun or increased:
    situations for successful experiences,
    rewards or recognition for many learning outcomes or skills,
    opportunities for students to work together on important projects.

Of course, according to the students' ages, many more items can be added under each principle.

In this chapter, alternative schools have been presented as a way to make substantial and quick changes in education. The more progressive programs make extensive use of action-learning projects, the world, and resource people; they provide for a variety of learning styles, recognize the value of play, trust students with important decisions, and have redefined the curriculum as all the experiences of youth.

Alternative schools are also pursuing widely accepted goals for American education and are among the few schools following modern principles of learning.

BIBLIOGRAPHY

(1) Aiken, Wilford. *The Story of the Eight Year Study*. New York: Harper and Bros., 1942.

(2) Cawelti, Gordon. *Vitalizing the High School: A Curriculum Critique—Major Reform Proposals*. Washington, D.C.: Association for Supervision and Curriculum Development, 1974.

(3) Central Advisory Council for Education. *Children and Their Primary Schools* 2 vols. London: Her Majesty's Stationery Office, 1967. [Referred to as the "Plowden Report."]

(4) Coleman, James. "The Children Have Outgrown the Schools." *Psychology Today* 5, 9 (February 1972): 72-75, 82.

(5) Goodlad, John. *Behind the Classroom Door*. Belmont, CA: Wadsworth, 1970.

(6) Willis, Margaret. *Guinea Pigs After 20 Years*. Columbus: Ohio State University Press, 1961.

Chapter Eleven
Suggestions for the Continuing Development of Pre- and In-Service Programs for Teachers of Second Languages
Dale L. Lange

Institutions of higher education in the United States that prepare teachers of second languages at both pre- and in-service levels have a unique opportunity at the end of this decade to reexamine their programs, ıd to plan for meeting the needs of language teaching and learning in the ten years to come. The massive demand for second-language teachers in the late 1950s, 1960s and the early 1970s finally having been met, the profession can now turn its efforts toward improving the quality of teaching and learning. Although the need for teachers kept the profession from examining its future and carefully assessing its growth, development did take place. During the period mentioned above, second-language teaching and learning evolved from grammar-translation and the behaviorist dogma of audio-lingualism to include a renewed interest in cognition, an emphasis on individual learning, an awareness of individual values, and a desire to use another language for human interaction in the context of the culture of which that language is part. In a word, the profession *grew*, although in a somewhat haphazard manner.

Such rapid evolution, however has essentially *boulversé* a profession which thought in relatively simplistic terms about language teaching and learning, as well as about the nature of language itself. There was almost no time in which to catch up with itself as it moved from one aspect of the evolution to another. The intent of this chapter is to discuss several principles of second-language teacher education that allow the profession to renew its concern for the quality of instruction. Some of these principles may not be new, but they offer a starting place for the discussion of related issues. They also remind us that these issues are of continuing importance. What may be new is the discussion of the implications for both pre- and in-service teacher education programs. At the outset, these principles can be considered applicable not only to teachers of the common second languages of French, German, and Spanish, but also to teachers of native languages, teachers in bilingual programs, and teachers of English as a second language.

The principles to be discussed are listed below; each will be discussed in turn:

1. Teacher self-selection and teacher selection are ongoing processes.
2. Teachers are cognitively and experientially aware of the intellectual, scientific, and artistic history of their world.
3. Teachers are proficient in the language, and are experienced in the cultural environments of the languages which they teach.
4. Teachers are knowledgeable about processes that help students develop their own experiences with the cultural environments of the language(s) they are learning.
5. Teachers examine developments in second-language teaching and learning through experience in order to understand both cognitively and affectively the implications of those developments for students.
6. Teachers and students contribute to a growing understanding of language teaching and language learning.
7. The student-teacher relationship allows for both student and teacher to understand each other's needs and goals in developing a program of second-language study.

TEACHER SELF-SELECTION AND TEACHER SELECTION ARE ON-GOING PROCESSES

There is probably no more difficult question to address than who should enter the profession and who should remain in it. The question is equally difficult for an individual, either teacher or teacher educator, or for the profession as a whole to answer. The situation, however, can be described. The current criteria for entrance are almost non-existent, yet the following items are used as criteria: an average GPA in both overall course work and course work in the language, perhaps an intelligence test, an expressed interest in teaching language, an internship experience, and the completion of courses in teacher education that include some work in learning psychology, language teaching methods, classroom management, and interpersonal and group interaction techniques. The last five courses are experiences which prove useful to teachers. However, their use as specific criteria has never been carefully established.

Current criteria for continuance in either pre-service or professional service are not clear. In pre-service programs, for example, the painful discussions, based on largely unstated criteria, with the teacher candidate about his or her poor performance in student teaching indicate an insufficiency of criteria to judge the student-teacher's performance. Although competency-based teacher education programs attempt to deal with this issue, they fail because they do not seem to be able to isolate teacher behaviors which can be validated. Once in the profession, criteria for continuance relate to largely political issues: functioning in the technical aspects of the job, exhibiting appropriate professional behavior in the classroom, and meeting in-service education requirements in order to keep a teaching license. In actuality, however, the proof of moral turpitude continues to be the only *real* grounds for dismissal from the profession. As the apparent single criterion for selection out of the profession, it exemplifies the lack of useful criteria needed to judge the continuing development of the professional competence of teachers. The selection and self-selection of persons, either into or out of preservice programs or of the profession itself, present problems for which there are no easy solutions. We have tried to find solutions, but perhaps we have not gone far enough in the quest; maybe we have allowed the status quo to operate instead of continually, or at least periodically, examining the situation. Therefore, what can self-selection and selection of teachers as on-going processes mean?

Pre-service

Teacher self-selection can be simply defined as the determination of an individual to opt for or against a career in teaching, in this case, a second language. As far as initial entry into the profession is concerned, often only two basic elements relate to self-selection: economics and attitude. The economic aspect relates to the question, "When I am finished will I find employment in a market where there seems to be a teacher oversupply?" The attitudinal aspect comes from an assertion by the applicant that teaching has been a lifelong desire. The individual, intent on fulfilling this desire, is therefore willing to risk the economic situation in spite of what may be its real or imagined difficulties.

A teacher self-selection process, however, should be based on more than questions of economics and statements of attitude. There should be information available concerning the personal, physical, intellectual, and emotional qualities of language teachers, their second-language proficiency, their second-culture awareness, and their range of knowledge about children and how they interact with learning materials and individuals. The expectations of the program with regard to time to be spent, effort to be given, and rewards to be gained should also be available to the potential applicant. College faculty should explore individual applicant needs and questions before the individual attends to the matter of choice. Such a process would include not only the questions of economics and attitude, but also detailed information and counseling prior to the applicant's decision. Teacher self-selection for pre-service second-language teacher education would thus be a process that drew together information about the individual, the program, and the profession; and this information could be used by the individual to determine his or her potential success, both in the program and in the profession.

Once the applicant made the decision and was initially accepted into a program, the process of teacher selection would begin. Selection of teachers suggests a defined or evolving set of criteria against which teachers can be measured. Because education is not a science, or at least not yet, there is no set of variables that one can plug into a regression equation and predict, with 99%

accuracy, the successful entry-level teacher of second languages. The fact that education is not yet a science, however, does not prevent a careful study of variables as potential criteria for selection. GPA related to both general course work and major language course work, general intelligence, and measures of language proficiency should remain important considerations in selecting language teachers. These three areas have been used with some success in predicting the achievement of teachers. To those points must be added indicators of personality such as flexibility, openness to new ideas, desire to self-generate, empathy, sensitivity to others, positive self-concept, positive feelings toward other peoples and cultures, a more specific statement of interest in working with students, a measure of second-language or general teaching aptitude, and evidence of ability to work with children. In addition, two other statements of potential criteria could be added: Evaluation of knowledge of, and proficiency in, the language, and knowledge of the processes for interacting with another culture could also be examined. These criteria could be developed in a specially designed study and travel period abroad. Knowledge of, and proficiency in, teaching would be reviewed in a structured yet flexible statement carried out in an experientially oriented program of second-language teacher education, where theory and practice would be united in micro-teaching, student teaching, and a carefully observed internship program. There appears to be no one single set of criteria that will suggest success or failure, but rather an interaction of criteria. The term interaction suggests the consideration of all of the gathered information in an evaluation process, which would of necessity have to include the initiate as well as the initiated.

A preprofessional counseling session by members of a committee representing general education, language, culture, and pedagogy would amass the necessary data, review the criteria and the data with the candidate, examine weaknesses and strengths, and arrive at a mutual agreement as to the candidate's readiness for licensure. A cumbersome process is surely indicated; practical and efficient it is not. However, it has the potential for ensuring a more global evaluation of a prospective teacher by using data which are both quantitative and qualitative; and it includes the candidate in the review of the data, and in the final decision-making process. Together, the continued careful study of the empirical data from currently available or to be designed instrumentation, and the description of the functioning of teacher candidates in different languages, cultures, and teaching environments could be important in the continuing derivation of criteria for teacher selection. A permanent set of criteria may never be found because criteria for teacher selection must evidence a changing process over time, situations, functions, roles, and needs. In seeking to find those criteria, attention must be given to the concern for quality in the initial selection of persons into the profession.

In-Service

The continuing selection of professional teachers is as difficult as pre-service teacher selection because all of the pre-service criteria continue to apply. It is even more difficult to discuss when such political variables as longevity, tenure, contract terms, and continued licensing are added. One or all of these factors may be used in the continued selection of teachers, regardless of the situation or discipline. The vagaries of these terms, or the sometimes nonaction-oriented discussions concerning the negative characteristics of the terms need not be discussed here. Such issues as longevity, tenure, contract terms, and continued licensing would essentially be tangential to the intent of this chapter. The process of continuing teacher selection is considered political, and thus will not be discussed here.

Another variable, however, can be added to these general considerations: the individual teacher should be responsible for his or her own professional development. It is the one basic aspect of professionalism which carries increasing weight as the teacher progresses from the pre- to the in-service stage. For the second-language teacher, its meaning is contained in a set of questions to be used as criteria in self-selection for those who wish to continue as professionals. Examples of such questions might be: Is my use of the second language current? Is my experience with the culture current? Am I aware of and will I carefully consider, as meaningful for my classroom, developments in the understanding of language learning, curriculum development, learning evaluation, and the nature of the individual? If not, am I willing to change my attitude so that I can explore such developments?

If the questions can be answered honestly and affirmatively, this resolution should allow the teacher to continue teaching with confidence, responsibility having been met until the next time the teacher poses the questions. That next time could be the end of the year. This self-evaluation could determine whether the teacher is ready for another year of commitment. If the questions are answered negatively, then a responsible choice should be made: a plan to correct the deficiencies should be formulated, or the teacher should resolve to leave the profession.

In the case of self-selection for professionals, the responsibility for quality must be accepted individually and collectively by members of the profession. As a member of the profession, the individual teacher must recognize and act on the question of continued and continual preparation, and the ultimate decision of the quality of instruction.

Teacher self-selection and teacher selection are processes which are applicable to both pre- and in-service teachers. Although somewhat different in distribution within these two levels, both respond to the ultimate goal, quality of instruction, in the continuing need for qualified teachers.

TEACHERS ARE COGNITIVELY AND EXPERIENTIALLY AWARE OF THE INTELLECTUAL, SCIENTIFIC, AND ARTISTIC HISTORY OF THEIR WORLD

One of the major components of any teacher education program is that aspect which is often labeled "general" or "liberal" education. For pre-service teachers, general education is designed to provide a broadly based appreciation of the intellectual, scientific, and artistic history of their world. For the teacher of a second language, however, that statement may require special interpretation. In order to even begin to understand another language and its cultures, the prospective teacher must understand the intellectual, scientific, and artistic contributions of individuals to their world across time, as well as the processes used to make those contributions. In addition to a broad awareness of human achievement in general, the same kind of study needs to be made of a specific world—in this case, the intellectual, scientific, and artistic contributions, including processes used, in the development of the culture of the United States.

What is important to consider, in this regard, is a broad range of courses and experiences which deal with the assumptions and processes used within the various disciplines to study the contributions of individuals to their world. Although information about the activity of men and women in a particular environment or era is important, the assumptions that are made about action and the means whereby these assumptions have been turned into action are certainly as important; the two aspects are complementary. All teachers may need a more direct use of both information and process together, but awareness of the complementary nature of information and process is probably more important for teachers of second languages because their responsibility in the classroom is different from that of a teacher in another discipline. The second-language teacher needs not only an awareness of the general world and a relatively specific understanding of his own culture, but also, and more specific to his or her professional task, an ability to relate to yet another world, that of the second language and its cultures. Consideration at the outset that information alone will not suffice is, therefore, necessary. Courses and experiences in the history of intellectual thought, scientific endeavor, or artistic tradition in the Western, Eastern, Middle Eastern, African, South American, and Australian worlds should deal with ideas, and should focus on the naming of and exploration of ideas toward processes which will allow pre-service second-language teachers an opportunity to experience that history, those endeavors, and that tradition. These courses and experiences give them the necessary tools to use in understanding their own culture, as well as a second language and culture. In using information and process together, second-language teachers will become aware of the intellectual, scientific, and artistic history of their world and be able to apply it.

Pre-service

Teacher general education programs are currently prescribed in terms of categories of course work such as Communication, Language, and Symbolic Systems, Physical and Biological Sciences, Man and Society, and Artistic Expression.

These categories encompass the concept of general education and should, therefore, probably remain as categories. However, the content of the categories should be more designated, and the content of some of the courses within the categories should be reoriented. The designation and reorientation is not intended to suggest rigidity. For example, within the category of Man and Society, designated courses and experiences dealing with the cultural development of Western civilization and a contrasting society should be mediated by a course through which the processes for the examination of cultural development could be applied in the examination of a relatively unknown society for the student, namely the United States. Specifically, the development and role of religion in Western civilization could be compared with that of an Eastern religion. The process for such examination could then be used to resolve any question as it applies to the analysis of the development of the United States. This is only an example, and is not intended to give a complete programmatic schema. The reader's imagination can supply the complete details. The example, however, could also relate to the other categories of the general education concept, but naturally the process would have to adapt itself to the content of the category.

In-Service

An in-service teacher education program in second languages could allow a teacher to choose a particular area of general education in which he or she was particularly interested, with the objective of exploring it in some depth in terms of knowledge, experience, and process. For example, if the person were interested in music, a survey of Western music from the 17th to the 20th century, specifically related to the target culture and U.S. culture, could be explored. This would lead to an understanding and recognition of different musical styles within the context or era, and would simultaneously examine the process of the creation of music within that context or era. Such courses or experiences perhaps do not currently exist, but ways of facilitating such experiences do exist through individual contracts or independent study programs. The in-service teacher who is responsible for the learning of students must certainly be considered capable and responsible for his or her own learning.

As a result of such efforts, both pre- and in-service teachers of second languages and cultures may perceive the relationship of information and experience to the learning of process and vice versa. Recognizing such a relationship could also make both aware of the need to understand information and experience by means of process in the ongoing nature of the world. The relationship points out the need for teachers of second languages and cultures to have contact with information, experience, and process prior to their specialization. These same elements are necessary beyond the professional entrance level as a means for teachers to deal with the changing nature of their specialty and the world in general.

TEACHERS ARE PROFICIENT IN THE LANGUAGE AND ARE EXPERIENCED IN THE CULTURAL ENVIRONMENTS OF LANGUAGES WHICH THEY TEACH

Probably no aspect of second-language teacher education receives greater theoretical support from teacher educators than the need for language proficiency and experience with the second culture. That all persons who are to teach the language should be proficient in the four language modalities, and that they should have lived for some time in the culture is taken for granted. The problem seems to be that teacher education programs at either the pre- or in-service level have not affirmed these needs by means of programmatic elements, such as courses or programs abroad, or evaluative devices. In other words, second-language teacher education programs tend to ignore or assume that language proficiency and cultural experiences have been attained and obtained prior to entrance into the profession, or that such proficiency and experiences continue to develop on their own. Another assumption is that language proficiency and cultural experiences are achieved through college or university courses. Because it is difficult, if not almost impossible to reduce the development of language proficiency at any level to a set formula of weeks or hours of instruction, and because cultural experience must of necessity require more than cerebral manipulation of cultural concepts, suggestions are in order for pre- and in-service second-language teacher education programs that can build more certainty for language proficiency and cultural experience into their programs.

Pre-service

Students preparing to teach must be given a thorough background in the language and its cultures in formal course work. Courses in the four modalities could prepare students in the phonology, morphology, syntax, and lexicon of the language. In addition, the use of language in realistic cultural situations would make the student cognizant of the range of language use in each modality.

For example, written and oral communication could express needs, ideas, feelings, and give information; listening and reading would entail the hearing and decoding of needs, ideas, feelings, information, and the understanding of the manner in which such meaning is expressed. However, such courses are clearly only preparatory.

This discussion is heading toward what seems to be the only reasonable and the most honest solution to the need for language proficiency and cultural experience among second-language pre-service teachers—a travel and study stay in a country where their language of study is dominant. Although a suggestion as to the length of stay is impossible because that factor depends on the needs of the individual student, it is possible to discuss a principle upon which such a stay might be organized. As far as the development of language proficiency and the offering of cultural experiences are concerned, that which cannot be done in a U.S. college or university, might best be done in the target culture. In a program based on this idea, formal instruction in language and culture could be drastically reduced in favor of the study of problems concerning both language and culture which the students themselves would have predetermined from their formal course work. Such problems would require the gathering of data from a wide variety of sources and experiences and would require students to deal with both language and culture together. For example, as a result of studying the economic system in France in an on-campus course, students might find the continued existence of small villages problematic. In a program abroad based on the stated principle, students would explore village existence, including government, resources, politics, and institutions by living in the village, by interview, and by examination of records. Students would also ask themselves what further questions their resolution would generate and how they might be resolved. Although no program can guarantee the student automatic language proficiency and a wide variety of cultural experience, results of such an effort would contribute markedly to the quality of the pre-service teacher. Such an experience should be required by all second-language teacher education programs. One could even go so far as to suggest that the evaluation of second-language teacher education programs by regional accrediting associations should include study-travel experience for pre-service teachers as one evaluative criterion.

In-Service

Study-travel experience is more difficult for in-service teachers who are faced with the realities of life, such as raising families, modest incomes, and the need for rest and relaxation. Yet in-service teachers also need to maintain and develop language proficiency and cultural experience. Summer programs of relatively short duration in a country where their language is dominant appear to be the best means of handling this necessity. Because teachers are very aware of what they need, the same principle should be used in the development of in-service programs abroad as was suggested for pre-service programs: That which cannot be done in a U.S. college or university, might best be done in the target culture. Professional teachers, however, require even more flexibility than pre-service teachers. Programs related to their needs could help them develop materials for their courses, practice cultural analysis, improve language skills, attack stereotypes, and work on personal attitudes toward the culture and the people. Such a program, using a contract system, could handle the needs of professional teachers; this has been evidenced by a program offered through the University of Minnesota in cooperation with l'Université de Franche-Comté in Besançon, France (6).

One way of assuring continued language development and culture experience would be to require that any language teacher who aspires to a Master of Education or Master of Arts degree in Education would be required, as part of that program, to participate in an experience of the kind described above. In order to avoid duplication of effort, to assure a measure of quality for such a program, and to ensure participants, several institutes of higher education with second-language teacher education programs could offer and administer joint programs in several environments, such as France, Germany, and Spain.

Continued language development and cultural experience would also be assured if the licensing agency included in its criteria for relicensing a statement requiring teachers of second languages to give evidence of foreign experience as a condition for relicensing. This latter suggestion puts the burden on the individual teacher, who should be able to choose from a variety of programs. The requirement would regularize the necessity for in-service professionals to seek continued language development and cultural experience.

TEACHERS ARE KNOWLEDGEABLE ABOUT PROCESSES TO HELP STUDENTS DEVELOP THEIR OWN EXPERIENCE WITH THE CULTURAL ENVIRONMENTS OF THE LANGUAGE(S) THEY ARE LEARNING

Most of the literature concerning the teaching of culture in the second-language classroom either analyzes culture or disseminates cultural facts and information. Seelye (10) is probably most clear about the need to deal with process in addition to information. His chapter in this book exemplifies a program which relies heavily on process as a means for training students to approach, cope with, and understand another culture as they meet it face to face. What we need to discuss here is how we can help the student develop awareness and experience with another culture.

To assume that teachers can be the repository for all information and knowledge of the culture whose language they teach is clearly unwarranted, untenable, and unrealistic. No amount of telling students about the culture could ever be complete. Even the assumption that one learns about another culture by hearing or reading about it must be called into question. Experience also counts. How can students experience the culture(s) whose language they are learning?

The response to this question does not relate to the pre-service—in-service dichotomy. It is the concern of all teachers of second languages. The concern centers not only on facts, experience, and information, but also on process. In the process of critically examining problems posed by the culture(s), students develop their own experience with those environments. What is important in this regard is not just a process, but the use of that process. Once it has been learned it can be applied to many different kinds of questions. For example, although in the context of this chapter process is related to the objective of understanding the target culture, it can also be used to deal with the broader goals of cross-cultural understanding because it fits not only the target culture, but also the native culture. In fact, it can be applied to the development of an awareness and understanding of any set of subcultures. The process, a problem-posing one (4, 5), is described as having ten steps.

1. *Identification of the Problem:*
Can the student identify a question related to the target culture? The question identifies a problem concerning the culture from within the student.
2. *Problem Statement:*
The problem statement is a straight-forward, honest statement about the experience with, and feelings about, the target culture that the student possesses, even though vague and impressionistic, from such sources as print and nonprint media, discussions, general information, and general experience.
3. *Observation:*
The student actively uses personal contacts, print and nonprint, and any other experience or source to make observations related to the problem. These observations are then gathered together without any attempt on the part of the student to be selective or judgmental.
4. *Description:*
Once the observations have been made and collected, a description of their content is written or recorded. This technique provides an overview of the nature of the observations, where they came from, and what they contain. A description of the observations generates questions as to how the student perceives the culture and the problem.
5. *Analysis:*
The analysis step attempts to answer these questions. The student looks for patterns that are similar in nature, that contrast with one another, and that mediate between opposite points of view. Patterns or phenomena which are

not classified easily into any scheme will stand by themselves. At this stage, an analysis of the sources indicates their particular point of view and bias.

6. *Conjecture:*

Speculation on the reasons for the existence of simple phenomena, or the existence of patterns or relationships is part of natural curiosity. This natural curiosity can be useful in seeking tentative explanations for the existence of the phenomena or patterns. Although this step is one of speculation, plausible explanations may be indicated in the observations themselves. Such explanations could possibly lead to the designation of other problems with the particular culture.

7. *Comparison:*

The patterns discovered in the analysis step are brought into focus as they are compared with the original problem statement. The result of this comparison is a realization that the original problem statement is accurate, and thus will stand as originally stated, or the original problem statement is not accurate and requires modification.

8. *Restatement of the Problem:*

The original problem statement is either rewritten to include modifications as they are needed, or the original statement is reaffirmed. In most cases, modification of the original problem statement will be necessary.

9. *Integration:*

The problem statement, either reaffirmed or modified, is examined in relation to how it fits into the totality of the culture. This consideration brings the statement to a broader question, but allows the process to continue in the same manner as the more precise original question and resulting problem statement. If the original problem statement is modified, it may be treated in two ways simultaneously. First, the original questions would need to be reexamined as a means for the student to understand the new problems that the modified statement has created. At this point, the process would be on the same plane as the original problem. The process would continue on this level. Second, while recognition of new problems is taking place, questions on the integration of the modified statement into the broader picture arise. Thus, while the modified statement is examined on one plane for its accuracy of perception, it is being reexamined on another plane in order to recognize the place of the pattern or phenomenon within the totality of that culture at that particular moment.

10. *Reentry:*

The questions of integration having been posed with either the affirmed original problem statement or a modified one, the process of observation and the steps following begin again with reentry.

Because of the momentary authenticity of the nature of cultural patterns and behavior, as well as the perceptions related to them, the process is a never-ending one. Continued searching is related to continued growth, obviously the very nature of education.

The process as stated can be used in either pre- or in-service second-language teacher education. It can be used by teachers in the development of materials to supplement printed language learning materials, or by students in the creation of their own language and cultural learning materials. It is a creative process that can be used by teacher educators in programs as they seem appropriate, no matter what the level or question.

TEACHERS EXAMINE DEVELOPMENTS IN SECOND-LANGUAGE TEACHING AND LEARNING THROUGH EXPERIENCE IN ORDER TO UNDERSTAND BOTH COGNITIVELY AND AFFECTIVELY THE IMPLICATIONS OF THOSE DEVELOPMENTS FOR STUDENTS

Clearly a wealth and a variety of developments have taken place in language teaching over the past 25 years. Because no well-developed theory or comprehensive set of carefully defined strategies of second-language teaching and learning is available, teachers have had to rely on what they know works for them or what they experienced in their own learning of a language. In addition, they pick and choose suggestions for classroom experimentation from what they hear at conferences and what they read. As a result, an essentially eclectic approach to the teaching/learning of a second language has developed. Eclecticism is a useful concept when the practitioner does not wish to choose among alternative theories, but finds something from each which functions in the classroom. A base of information and experience on language teaching and learning in an undergraduate, pre-service program is later modified by the continued examination of language teaching and learning developments in an in-service program. Both programs draw heavily on the role of the teacher as learner; developments should be experienced in second-language teaching and learning in addition to understanding of their implications. Understanding of both the cognitive and affective implications of developments in second language teaching and learning relates to the quality of instruction. Without a planned experience base in second-language teacher education, including micro-teaching and student teaching, both pre- and in-service teachers might have difficulty understanding the reactions of students to different language teaching and learning strategies.

Pre-service

Courses in second-language pedagogy, such as methodology and student teaching, require that the teacher serve in the capacity of student as well as teacher to amass a base of information and experience with a broad range of language teaching and learning strategies. Serving as both teacher and student in a course in second-language methodology, the pre-service teacher would sit as a student in peer-group micro-teaching (2). Here, he or she would not only experience learning language with various strategies, but would also serve as teacher-critic, reacting to those strategies being practiced or demonstrated in the learning situation so the "teacher" could appreciate the results of his or her planning. When feasible, this concept could also be carried into student teaching. Student teachers could rotate schools on a weekly basis to observe and critique each other (1). They would serve as observers in this situation, but could react sympathetically because they might have experienced a similar situation, or have had similar feelings, in their own classrooms.

Although the profession is unable to agree on a comprehensive theory of second-language teaching and learning, a practical framework is offered that could be applied to most classroom language teaching and learning activity. The classroom activities, classified into categories, serve as the basis for courses in second-language methodology and student teaching, two aspects of a second-language teacher education program that are inseparable. Observation of student teaching by cooperating teachers, a college or university supervisor, and other student teachers is facilitated by actual experience with the concepts developed through the methods course. By using such a framework, everyone is talking the same language (7).

The framework also allows alternative teaching and learning techniques of generally equal importance to exist in the same category. As the result of a methods course and student teaching, the pre-service teacher would have used such techniques with students in both simulated and regular classroom conditions. Hopefully such a framework would provoke careful thought about the application of such strategies to a particular classroom situation. In the practice of critically reviewing what, how, and why chosen strategies are used or needed, pre-service teachers would be equipped to use information, knowledge, experience, and intuition in a situation rather than rely solely on what they may have experienced in their own language learning. Using such a base, in-service teachers can examine further developments in the profession.

The framework mentioned above is defined in the following five categories, which may be considered applicable across language modalities. The first category is largely teacher- or materials-oriented. The last four could be directed by teachers, by materials, by students, or by any combination of the three.

1. *Presentation:*

The language to be learned is presented to the students either by the teacher, by the text, or by both. The presentation can be made in various ways, such as in dialog form, in narrative form, or in basic sentence form. A variety of techniques of presentation should be included as a means of adapting to different students in differing situations; objects, pictures, actions, films, and textbooks can be used.

2. *Familiarization:*

The student establishes meaning in relation to the sound system, sound symbol association, structure, syntax, and vocabulary through comparisons of the target and native languages. Comparisons are also made within the target language in sound, sound-letter correspondences, structure, syntax, and vocabulary study, including such strategies as derivation, word and experience study, and familiarity with shapes and sounds. This category deals with strategies that are primarily related to cognition.

3. *Practice:*

A variety of practice modes is applicable here. Small-group, large-group, and individual practice form a matrix in the production of both written and oral language. Strategies for practice include simple repetition, memorization, use of detailed questions with specific text-based responses, and drills of various kinds—contextual, substitution, transformation, translation.

4. *Variation:*

The student gains the experience needed to move away from strict practice to the application of concepts learned through practice. Strategies for implementation include directed dialog, guided conversation, dialog exploitation with oral production and restatement, expansion, contraction, and controlled description by means of objects or visuals in written production.

5. *Communication:*

This category may be the most important in the framework. Here, the student puts what he has learned into situations that use the language. Examples of situations in which the student is able to participate in any of the activities in the two-way matrix of the function and content of communication (*9*) are as follows:

Function of Communication (See Table 11.1.)
1. To express, to exchange
2. To describe, to explain
3. To argue, to persuade
4. To denote, to authenticate
5. To recall, to narrate (past)
6. To ask for, to order
7. To express beauty, to amuse
8. To translate, to interpret

Content of Communication (See Table 11.1.)
1. Information, inquiry: Comment on a neutral message.
2. Feelings, emotions: Comment on the affective state of being.
3. Attitude, behavior: Comment on the manner of being, reacting, or moral or physical conduct.
4. Idea, opinion: Comment on what is thought or believed.
5. Action, fact: Comment on events of present, past, or future.
6. Contact, account: comment on the maintenance or interruption of social contacts.
7. Animate, inanimate: Communication with persons, animals, or things.

Table 11.1. Content of Communication

	1	2	3	4	5	6	7
1							
2							
3							
4							
5							
6							
7							
8							

(Function of Communication — row labels)

The importance of the framework is that the pre-service teacher experiences it by observation, by participation, and by critical analysis in micro-teaching and in student teaching. To participate in all strategies in the five categories in a methods course would be impossible, but, if organized, the major strategies in all categories could be offered. Student teaching would then provide, as an extension of micro-teaching, an opportunity to experience a broad range of strategies through participation in teaching and observation of the cooperating teacher and/or other student teachers. With experience in the five categories, a pre-service teacher would be prepared to enter the profession.

In-Service

In-service teachers who participated in an experience-oriented methods micro-teaching/student-teaching program are prepared to meet the challenge of their continuing education. With this base of information and years of experience in the classroom, any development in teaching and learning can be examined.

An in-service course or program for second-language teachers should include the opportunity for any added development to be experienced in terms of 1) its contribution to a theory of second-language teaching and learning, 2) its place in the framework, 3) its potential for use in the classroom, as experienced in micro-teaching or some other simulated classroom situation, 4) its transfer to the classroom, and 5) its usefulness for a particular learning situation. Any such course or program, whether offered by an institute of higher education or a local school district, should consider these five points.

Teachers need to examine the theoretical contribution of any development in second-language teaching and learning beyond the base level of information and experience gained from a pre-service program. Teachers need to continue to develop competence not only in language and culture, but in teaching and learning strategies as well. Because language is a basic human quality, and because research in the nature of language and second-language teaching is so extensive, the examination of second-language teaching and learning developments must be considered in the totality of the teacher's current knowledge.

In general, second-language teachers are reluctant to examine the research in their field. Perhaps they feel that research in second-language teaching and learning is too complicated, or that the extant research is unapplicable to the classroom. Because teachers have such a fund of knowledge directly related to second-language classroom teaching and learning, their opinions should be sought in the initial process of preparing research projects in their field. In that way, teachers would be included in the ongoing research in second-language teaching and learning. When they know that their opinions are welcome, teachers' attitudes and behavior toward research could change.

How does a particular development in second-language teaching and learning fit into the framework of strategies? What does it have to offer for the classroom? First, we need to examine any development in relation to the categories of the framework to determine the category to which it belongs. Because the framework is not fixed, the examination of the development in relation to any category of the framework suggests that if it does not fit, the categories may be incomplete and require modification. Dealing with development in this way helps determine the usefulness of the framework categories. In addition, teachers gain an understanding of the development and its place in second-language teaching and learning. In any case, the teacher wants not only to understand the development cognitively, but also affectively. How does it feel to use it? What are student reactions to the development as used in the classroom? Micro-teaching with peers would give teachers an opportunity to explore the forms of the development best suited for the classroom; with such information, the teacher could modify its use prior to applying it to students, who should then be asked to give their reactions. Finally, the teacher could make a judgment as to the continued use of the development in the particular teaching and learning situation.

Considering both the political and financial situations of public schools, colleges, and universities today, as well as the political nature of teacher licensing, it is difficult to suggest a concrete form which this in-service task could take in order to be recognized as valuable and supported financially. The task is an ongoing one that requires peer-colleagues and students to study problems posed by recent developments, and to experience, evaluate, modify, and use them until the situation is no longer right for their use. A college or university might offer an ongoing seminar for in-service teachers in a teacher center, for example, where such an idea could be tried with teachers coming and going according to their needs or interests. Perhaps a group of teachers in a large school district, or teachers across a number of school districts could meet on a regular basis to experience such an idea. A state department of education might even recognize a teacher's participation in these activities as relating to recertification.

Both pre- and in-service teachers need the opportunity to experience developments in language teaching and learning; pre-service teachers need to understand the bases for language teaching and learning, and in-service teachers need to understand and evaluate developments. Experience with the base information is perhaps the most crucial aspect of any training program for pre-service teachers. A more problem-posing program for in-service teachers would enable them to connect their experience with the theory and applicability of those developments.

TEACHERS AND STUDENTS CONTRIBUTE TO A GROWING UNDERSTANDING OF LANGUAGE TEACHING AND LANGUAGE LEARNING

This principle is related to the process for examining developments in language teaching and learning. The suggestion that teachers seek students' reactions to language teaching and learning developments is taken one step further here. Teachers and students together contribute to an understanding of second-language teaching and learning. Through continuing evaluation, teachers and students arrive at an assessment of second-language teaching and learning strategies.

If student reactions to developments in language teaching and learning were actively sought by teachers, a monumental step would be taken toward improving the quality of second-language teaching and learning. Such a relationship could have been helpful over the past 20 years. Had teachers and teacher educators listened to the words of students, some of the second-language teaching and learning activities might have been modified to satisfy justifiable student criticism and concern. For example, the excesses of the so-called audio-lingual approach to second-language teaching and learning could possibly have been corrected had the profession listened carefully to student reactions. Students did not like rote memorization in either large or small groups; they preferred the printed word to executing dialogs in front of the class; they were bored by endless pattern drills. In fact, because they told us what we did not want to hear, we ignored them.

In the early experimentation with programmed instruction (PI) in second-language teaching and learning, investigators found that grammatical structure and the manipulation of that structure were generally understood, but students were not satisfied. They missed the teacher contact they felt they deserved. They may have lacked confidence and, therefore, may have needed support from their teachers. Some adjustments were made in PI, but the predicted success of the strategy was never achieved. If we had listened to students, the use of PI in second-language teaching and learning might have been modified into a more productive strategy. Other aspects of individualized instruction could have been treated in like manner.

While the collection of student reactions to classroom phenomena by means of questionnaire and other evaluation devices is appropriate (8), it may be important to supplement it. Systematic and empathic observation of students, as well as discussions with them about a particular strategy, may provide a more complete picture of the function and success of that strategy. Using evaluative devices in the observation and discussion of problems related to a particular strategy combined with the teacher's knowledge, feelings, and intuition will produce a complete picture of the productivity of a strategy in a particular situation.

One of the current trends in second-language teaching and learning is the drive toward the development of communicative competence in students. This term is a broad one that has not been very carefully defined. It includes strategies from humanistic education and values clarification, terms which in themselves are not carefully defined. One cannot argue against the development of communicative competence, humanistic education, or values clarification. Rather, the concern is with the effect of such strategies on students, and on their perception of second-language learning. Student and teacher dialog which attends to the use of strategies and their modification for the second-language classroom gives credibility to student reactions in a total assessment of a teaching and learning strategy.

If classroom teaching and learning strategies are examined with communicative competence and shared with others for their reaction and discussion, teachers and students will contribute to a growing understanding of second-language teaching and learning. That sharing can take place in the particular school or school district, at conferences, state and regional language teachers meetings, and meetings of professional associations, as well as in the professional journals of the field.

This process of student and teacher dialog is equally applicable to the educational program of either pre- or in-service teachers of second languages. Its use is perhaps more risky for pre-service teachers if they lack a positive self-image. In-service teachers can help pre-service teachers initiate a dialog with students. It is essentially a process which includes the teacher and student as co-learners in the learning process.

THE STUDENT-TEACHER RELATIONSHIP ALLOWS FOR BOTH STUDENT AND TEACHER TO UNDERSTAND EACH OTHER'S NEEDS AND GOALS IN DEVELOPING A PROGRAM OF SECOND-LANGUAGE STUDY

Language is the most personal expression of the self, and at the same time, it is a means of communication that allows for personal distance. In the classroom, it is the vehicle which expresses the relationships among students and teacher. Therefore, much of the climate of the second-language classroom is set by the manner in which language is used. If the relationship between students and their teacher is to be one of equality, it will respect the most personal expression of the self and the need for personal distance. This respect will allow students and teacher to share with each other and, by so doing, understand each other's needs.

In the model of education currently used, the industrial or product model, the teacher is the supervisor who is expected to know his or her own needs, as well as those of the students. Teachers need to mold students' lives, to think that they are responsible for student learning through their choice of appropriate materials, teaching strategies, and tests. These needs are applied to the student as a way of generating the desired product, the second-language student who listens, speaks, reads, and writes the language fluently. Teachers are supposed to produce such a product because parents and the general public require it. This set of needs and requirements, however, is out of proportion. Teachers are using the situation for fulfillment of their own personal egos; the parents force the issue. Accountability is an important issue, but the question needs to be asked: Is it accountability for learning facts and information, or for being able to deal with facts and information as indications of problems that need resolution?

The above statement is intended to be general and probably reveals bias. Certainly there are those teachers who are able to share their expertise with students; but there are also many who are ego-involved, and who fall into the trap of using others to fulfill their own needs.

Where do students fit in all of this? They are essentially silent partners who are not aware that their education is being decided by others. Their needs are not voiced because they feel that they are not supposed to have any. Their needs are imposed upon them by those who know. Although this is also a generalization, it contains more than a modicum of truth.

A resolution to the problem of teacher dominance over students is possible, but certainly not simple. Teachers must become students, understanding that they are on an equal level with their students, and then listen to them express their needs. In the ensuing and continuing dialog among equals, both student and teacher can begin to understand each other and each other's needs. Teachers recognize that their involvement can be a giving one that provides opportunities, resources, positive support, encouragement, and expertise, and so reduces their control and domination over learning. Students recognize their involvement as a giving one also. The resolution to the problems they have posed for themselves, when shared with others, provide an opportunity for individuals to critically dialog with each other about the problem posed and the suggested resolution. This critical approach provides the opportunity for students to become involved in the problems of the particular subject. It allows the teacher to participate, using his expertise and resources, in the problems which students have posed for themselves. In this way, the teacher teaches as well as learns from the students, who teach the teacher as well as each other.

Using this educational model, the goals of a second-language program would be determined in a dialog among students and teacher. Goals might not necessarily be recognizable in relationship to currently stated goals, and would of necessity not be the same with each class. The goals would actually relate to the problems posed by both the culture and its most important means of expression, language. The understanding of problems posed concerning the culture suggests that cultural problems would constitute a major content emphasis. Here language, the vehicle to learn about the problems, becomes a functional tool. The goal of understanding another culture through language may thus become the major purpose for the second-language program (3).

These ideas can be expressed in both pre- and in-service teacher education programs. Their expression is limited here because all of the implications of a dialogical approach in second-language teacher education have not been worked through to completion. This statement is not intended to be apologetic, but rather to indicate need for development of an emerging idea.

Pre-service and In-Service Implications

The old adage in teacher education, "One teaches as one has been taught," can directly be applied in a positive manner to teacher education in this case. It is difficult to teach humans in general how to grow into mature adults who have a positive outlook on life, who have faith and hope in humanity and in their fellow man. It is equally difficult to teach similar concepts in a course on the methods of teaching and learning second languages if the major concept to be taught is a process of dialoging with students about problems posed in the development of classroom learning of language and culture.

These are some of the questions in a second-language methods course that can generate problems are: What kinds of culture learning and language development methods have been used in schools over the past 100 years? What was their contribution in relation to the educational climate and goals for culture learning and for second-language development at that time? What could their contribution be within the current educational climate and goals for culture learning and second-language development in schools today? What current strategies are there? What do they contribute? What is their function? How do students react to them? How have and how will teachers react to them?

The process for responding to these questions is similar to the process applied to cultural learning.

1. *Identification of the Problem:*
What is the question the student is pursuing in relation to different methodologies or strategies for the teaching and learning of culture and language in the classroom?

2. *Problem Statement:*
The problem statement indicates the student's understanding of, knowledge of, and attitude toward a particular problem with a methodological question.

3. *Observation:*
Observation of the problem is gathered from books, professional journals, films, recordings, and interviews where appropriate. These observations are gathered without comment; the student makes no attempt to select or judge these observations.

4. *Description:*
The content of the problem observations found in different sources is described, giving an overview of the observations and generating questions as to how the strategy and the general problem are perceived.

5. *Analysis:*
The questions of perception are answered as the student examines the observations for similar, contrasting, and mediating patterns, as well as for phenomena which cannot be classified. Sources are also analyzed for point of view and bias.

6. *Comparison:*
The analysis-step patterns are compared with the original problem statement to make students aware of the breadth of the problem, and to allow them to realize the incompleteness or completeness of the original statement.

Discussion of their awareness and realization would be helpful for members of their group or class.

7. *Conjecture:*

At this point, the student examines the findings of the observation, description, analysis, and comparison steps to project a resolution to the originally stated problem.

8. *Suggested Resolution(s):*

There may be more than one possible resolution to the problem originally posed. Different resolutions are prepared for demonstration and dialog with other groups in a peer-group micro-teaching format.

9. *Further Problems:*

The discussion of the potential resolutions and the example of suggested resolutions realizes the potential for further problems with any of the resolutions. At this point, the process could begin again with the examination of any of these problems.

This process is essentially the same when used with pre- or in-service teachers. However, extensive experience with the process gives pre-service teachers, especially, an opportunity to have practical knowledge of an alternative learning model to that which is normally offered in college or university courses. Once pre-service teachers have experienced the model, they can take it into the classroom for use in student teaching. However, the model's full implications may not be felt there because of the need to adapt it to the teaching mode of the cooperating teacher. Nevertheless, an attempt at modification should be made. From active use and modification, the model can then be carried into a professional position. This alternative model is the larger framework into which the discussion of specific and current developments in second-language and cultural learning fit.

In-service teachers bring a depth of experience to the use of this model in the exploration of any question related to developing language in a functional way with culture learning. They are more aware of the problems and are more capable of interpreting the experiences of others from their own experience. Using his or her experience and the experiences of others, an in-service teacher can dialog extensively with other teachers and with students concerning his or her own problems; this dialog can result in a numerous set of potential resolutions.

Through the process of dialog, pre- and in-service teachers and their professors mutually realize needs and goals for the teaching and learning of culture and the second language. This practical knowledge and practical training enables teachers to take the alternative model into the classroom and teach as they have been taught.

FINAL STATEMENT

This article has suggested several principles for continuing development of both pre- and in-service teacher education programs in second languages and cultures education. These principles are intended to encourage the reader to think, and to dialog with others about the problems which the principles generate for each particular situation. It is hoped that every article in this book will generate professional dialog that will be relevant to the continuing development of second-language teacher education.

BIBLIOGRAPHY

(1) Brütsch, Susanna, and Heerema, Angelika Scheffer. "Discussions About the German System for the Training of Elementary School Teachers." March 1978.

(2) Clifford, Ray T.; Jorstad, Helen L.; and Lange, Dale L. "Student Evaluation of Peer-Group Microteaching as Preparation for Student-Teaching." *Modern Language Journal* 61 (1977): 229-36.

(3) Crawford, Linda M. "Paulo Freire's Philosophy: Derivation of Curricular Principles and Their Application to Second Language Curriculum Design." Ph.D. dissertation, 1978, University of Minnesota.

(4) Freire, Paulo. *Education for Critical Consciousness*. Translated by Myra Bergman Ramos, Introduction by Denis Goulet. New York: The Seabury Press, 1973.

(5) ———— . *Pedagogy of the Oppressed*. Translated by Myra Bergman Ramos, Foreword by Richard Schaull. New York: The Seabury Press, 1970.

(6) Lange, Dale L., and Jorstad, Helen L. "A Unique Experience in French Culture: A Cultural Materials Work-In in Besançon." *The French Review* 51 (1978): 391-97.

(7) Mackey, William F. *Language Teaching Analysis*. London: Longmans, 1965.

(8) Myers, Pamela J. "Student Factors as Indicators of Continuation in Secondary School Study of French/German/Spanish as a Second Language." Unpublished Ph.D. dissertation, University of Minnesota, 1978.

(9) Richterich, René. "Définition des besoins langagiers et types d'adultes." In *Systèmes d'apprentissage des langages vivantes par les adultes: Un système européen d'unités capitalisables*, pp. 33-94. Strasbourg: Le Counseil d'Europe, 1973.

(10) Seelye, H. Ned. *Teaching Culture: Strategies for Foreign Language Educators*. Skokie, IL: National Textbook, 1976.

Index

Tenses, 44
Tests, 28, 36, 63, 98
Textbooks, 29, 35, 120, 141
    sexism, 7
Toffler, Alvin, 1, 2, 3, 4
Tomb, J.W., 72
Transfer (learning), 51
Travel abroad, 133, 176-78
    See also Homestay program
Trevarthen, Colwyn, 70-71, 76

Valette, Rebecca J., 25

Values, 9-11
    clarification, 149-150
Vocabulary, 37, 72
    clustered, 30

Walden Two, 4-5
Warriner, Helen P., 10
Watergate hearings, 5
Wattenmaker, Beverly, 105, 106, 112,
    120-21
White, Burton L., 71-72
Wilson, Emily, 115
Workbooks, 141

About the Contributors

JERMAINE D. ARENDT (Ph.D., University of Minnesota), with the exception of two years when he was Foreign Language Consultant for the State of Minnesota from 1960-1962, has served the Minneapolis Public Schools since 1953. Currently he is Coordinator of Modern Languages, including Bilingual Education. In 1973, Dr. Arendt served as president of the American Council on the Teaching of Foreign Languages (ACTFL). He has also served on the Executive Committee of the American Association of Teachers of German.

DALE L. LANGE (Ph.D., University of Minnesota) is Professor of Second Languages and Cultures Education and Director of Graduate Studies for the Department of Curriculum and Instruction at the University of Minnesota, Minneapolis Campus. Professor Lange edited the *ACTFL Annual Bibliography of Books and Articles on Pedagogy in Foreign Languages* from 1968-73; he also edited volumes two and three and co-edited volume four of the ACTFL *Foreign Language Education Series*. Currently he is president-elect of ACTFL for 1980.

PAMELA J. MEYERS (Ph.D., University of Minnesota) has taught French, English, and Latin at the secondary and college levels and methods of teaching second languages and cultures at the University of Minnesota. She is currently completing an administrative intership as Assistant to the Superintendent of Schools, Columbia Heights, Minnesota Public Schools. Dr. Myers holds memberships in AERA, ACTFL, MCTFL, and AATF.

THEODORE ANDERSSON (Ph.D., Yale University) is currently Professor of Spanish and Education at the University of Texas at Austin. He was Director of the Bilingual Planning and Evaluation Project in Austin and served for over two years as Chairman to the National Advisory Committee on the Education of Bilingual Children.

The late MARGARET BROWN (M.A.T.S., University of New Mexico) was co-author of the Houghton Mifflin Series *Spanish for Communication*. She worked extensively on the development of the psychology of teaching a foreign language with the Peace Corps, San Diego School District, and developed an exemplary foreign language program at the UCLA Laboratory School.

The late PERCY FEARING was Coordinator of Foreign Language Education for the State of Minnesota; he had taught German, and English as a second language, at the junior and senior high levels in the Minneapolis Public Schools for many years. He had also served as director of the Honors Program in Germany for German high school students in connection with a program conducted at Indiana University in Bloomington; spent two years as an exchange teacher at the Max Planck Gymnasium in Trier/Mosel, West Germany; and taught at the University High School summer school program for the University of Minnesota. In 1962 the Modern Language Association named him one of 36 outstanding foreign language teachers in the United States; and in 1966 he served as president of the National Council of State Supervisors of Foreign Languages.

FRANK M. GRITTNER (Ph.D., University of Wisconsin-Madison) is the Foreign Language Specialist for the Department of Public Instruction in Madison, Wisconsin. He taught German, Spanish, and English at the high school level for eight years and taught graduate courses in foreign language methodology in 1970 and 1972 at the University of Wisconsin. He served as President of the American Council on the Teaching of Foreign Languages (ACTFL) in 1975 and is editor of and contributor to the 1980 Yearbook on Second Language Learning published by the National Society for the Study of Education (NSSE).

MARCIA S. HALLOCK (M.A., University of Minnesota) has taught elementary through high school levels of Spanish and French where she established a number of introductory programs. Ms. Hallock has co-authored a chapter in the 1972 publication from the Center for Curriculum Development, written numerous teaching and resource materials for the Minneapolis Public Schools, and published a copy-out in the *American Foreign Language Teacher*.

MADELINE HUNTER (Ed.D., UCLA) is an international lecturer and author of numerous books and articles dealing with the psychology of human learning, individualized instruction, bilingual and foreign language programs, school organization and teacher education. Currently, she is Academic Administrator, School of Education, UCLA, where she teaches classes and administers the laboratory school.

WAYNE B. JENNINGS (Ph.D., University of Minnesota) is Principal of Battle Creek Junior High School, St. Paul, Minnesota. He has served as president of the National Association for Core Curriculum, the Mounds View School Board, and Minnesota Core Teachers. He was also director of St. Paul Open School and is currently a member of PDK, AASA, and ASCD.

HELEN L. JORSTAD is an Associate Professor of Second Languages and Cultures Education at the University of Minnesota.

SAMUEL LIEBERMAN (Ph.D., Columbia University) is Professor of Classical Languages and Chairman of the Department of Classical and Oriental Languages at Queens College (CUNY), Flushing, N.Y. He is an active member and occasional officer of such professional organizations as the American Philological Association, the American Classical League, and the American Council on the Teaching of Foreign Languages.

META SUE REYNOLDS (M.A.T., Vanderbilt University) received a grant from the West German Republic in 1972 for the Goethe Institute in Passau, Germany and appeared in *Outstanding Young Women of America* in 1967. From 1972 to 1974, she served as president of Tennessee Foreign Language Teaching Association and was a member of the Board of Directors of the Southern Conference (SCOLT) and Central States Conference on Teaching from 1972 to 1976.

H. NED SEELYE is Chairman of the Board of International Resources Development, Inc. in Chicago, Ill.

VIRGINIA WILSON (M.A., University of Alaska) and BEVERLY WATTENMAKER (M.A., Case Western Reserve University) are language teachers who have been involved for many years with training foreign language teachers in methodology and the dynamics of classroom groups. Beverly Wattenmaker is the supervisor of foreign languages at Kenston Schools east of Cleveland, Ohio, and Virginia Wilson is at present teaching English to speakers of other languages. At Kenston High School they developed a foreign language program which is cited in a U.S. Office of Education study as one of the most innovative in the country; both are members of the Values Clarification Trainers Network and national consultants for the National Humanistic Education Center.